T0330434

Agriculture, Trade and the Environment

The Impact of Liberalization on Sustainable Development

Edited by

John M. Antle

Professor, Department of Agricultural Economics and Economics, Montana State University and University Fellow, Resources for the Future, USA

Joseph N. Lekakis

Associate Professor, Department of Economics, University of Crete, Greece

George P. Zanias

Associate Professor, Department of International and European Economic Studies, Athens University of Economics and Business, Greece

Edward Elgar

Cheltenham, UK • Northampton, MA, USA

Published by
Edward Elgar Publishing Limited
Glensanda House
Montpellier Parade
Cheltenham
Glos GL50 1UA
UK

Edward Elgar Publishing, Inc.
6 Market Street
Northampton
Massachusetts 01060
USA

A catalogue record for this book is available from the British Library

Library of Congress Cataloguing in Publication Data
Agriculture, trade, and the environment: the impact of liberalisation
on sustainable development/edited by John M. Antle, Joseph N.
Lekakis, George P. Zanias.
    Revised papers selected from the international conference
"European agriculture at the crossroads: competition and
sustainability" hosted by the Dept. of Economics of the University
of Crete, in Rethimno, 1996.
    Includes bibliographical references (p.).
    1. Agriculture and state—Europe. 2. Agriculture—Economic
aspects—Europe. 3. Sustainable agriculture—Europe. 4. Free
trade—Europe. I. Antle, John M. II. Lekakis, J. N. III. Zanias,
George P., 1955–
HD1917.A384   1998
338.1'84—dc21   98–13466
                                                                   CIP

ISBN 1 85898 783 0

Printed and bound in Great Britain by Bookcraft (Bath) Ltd.

Contents

List of figures   vii
List of tables   ix
List of contributors   xi
Preface   xiii

Introduction   Free trade, agriculture and the environment with a
                view to the European Union   1

PART I

1   Comparative statics on a two-country, one-commodity,
    two-factor agricultural trade model with process-generated
    pollution   13
    Panos Fousekis

2   Quantifying agriculture–environment tradeoffs to assess
    environmental impacts of domestic and trade policies   25
    John M. Antle and Susan M. Capalbo

3   Decomposing the effects of trade on the environment   52
    David G. Abler and James S. Shortle

PART II

4   Effects of CAP reform on the environment in the European
    Union   73
    Floor Brouwer and Siemen van Berkum

5   Consistency between environmental and competitiveness
    objectives of agricultural policies: economics of price support,
    set-aside, direct payments and other Common Agricultural
    Policy instruments   89
    Alain Carpentier, Hervé Guyomard and Chantal Le Mouël

6   EU agriculture and the economics of vertically-related markets   112
    Steve McCorriston and Ian M. Sheldon

PART III

7   Are support measures and external effects of agriculture linked together? Conceptual notes and empirical evidence from the Austrian agricultural sector   135
Franz Sinabell

8   Principles for the provision of public goods from agriculture: modelling moorland conservation in Scotland   154
Nick Hanley, Hilary Kirkpatrick, David Oglethorpe and Ian Simpson

9   The impact of the Uruguay Round on the agro-food sector and the rural environment in Italy   170
Margaret Loseby

10   The Common Agricultural Policy and the environment: conceptual framework and empirical evidence in the Spanish agriculture   185
Consuelo Varela-Ortega

11   The productivity of agrochemicals in Greece   208
Joseph N. Lekakis

PART IV

12   Agriculture and the environment in transition: a case study of Estonia   223
Tim T. Phipps and Paavo Eliste

13   European agriculture and the CAP: retrospect and prospect   240
George P. Zanias

Index   249

List of figures

2.1 A static spatial model of land use and crop management decision-making 27
2.2 Output–environment tradeoffs associated with alternative technologies 30
2.3 An integrated simulation model for tradeoff analysis 32
2.4 Output–leaching tradeoff in an Ecuadorian study 37
2.5 Carbofuran leaching–output tradeoffs for agroecological zones in an Andean study 38
2.6 USLE vs net returns for Northeast MT 42
2.7 SSFN vs net returns for Northeast MT 42
2.8 USLE vs net returns for the Southern Triangle of MT 44
2.9 SSFN vs net returns for the Southern Triangle of MT 44

3.1 Scale and mix effects in production 57
3.2 Scale and mix effects in consumption 58
3.3 Scale and mix environmental effects (agriculture less polluting at the margin) 60
3.4 Scale and mix environmental effects (agriculture more polluting at the margin) 60
3.5 Externality effects and the production possibilities frontier 62

5.1 Land allocation mechanism on a class by class basis: the case of an interior solution 97
5.2 Characterization of private and social optima for a given land quality 106

6.1 Retailer's own-label trends in Europe – % share of the retail market 119
6.2 Proportion of UK production shipped by foreign-owned firms 122

7.1 Subsidy equivalent and consumer tax equivalent in a partial equilibrium 139
7.2 Liberalizing a market in presence of production-related negative external effects 140
7.3 Regional shares of the aggregates of total willingness to pay (tWTP), regional transfers to the agricultural sector (tRTI) and the payments under the Austrian Programme for Environment and Agriculture (APEA 96) 147

10.1   Income trend: W1, 2 farms, scenarios P2 and P4, PHI = 1   197
10.2   Income trend: W2, 2 farms, scenarios P2 and P4, PHI = 1   198
10.3   Techniques and nitrate pollution: humid year, CAP reform
       scenario   199
10.4   Techniques and nitrate pollution: dry year, CAP reform scenario 199
10.5   Cropping pattern: CAP reform scenario   200
10.6   Cropping pattern: non-CAP reform scenario   200
10.7   Cropping pattern: CAP reform scenario, humid year   201
10.8   Income trend: farm 1, W1 (risk aversion comparisons)   202
10.9   Relationship between agricultural environmental and water
       policies   204

11.1   Natural logarithms of crop output, fertilizers and chemicals
       in Greek agriculture   217

List of tables

4.1 Main features of the 1992 CAP reform 76
4.2 Management rules on chemical use of set-aside land in Denmark, France, Germany and the United Kingdom 79
4.3 Structure and livestock density on farms with fattening bulls and suckler cows 82
4.4 Characteristics of programme budget of Council Regulation (EEC) 2078/92 by Member State 85

5.1 Comparative static results at the intensive and extensive margins of production 98

6.1 Industrial sectors in the EU (1994) 115
6.2 World trade in food/agricultural products, 1972–90 115
6.3 Four-firm seller concentration ratios, European food processing industries 116
6.4 Market shares of leading 2–3 firms in the UK food processing sector 117
6.5 Market shares in the UK food retailing sector, 1994 117
6.6 Own-brand market share in the UK, 1993 120
6.7 Acquisitions of majority holdings (including mergers), European Community food and drink sector 121
6.8 Foreign-direct investment in the EU food sector 121
6.9 Welfare effects of policy reform with successive oligopoly 125
6.10 Price incidence following EU banana market reforms 126

7.1 Effects of policy intervention in the presence of external effects of production 142
A7.1 Estimated parameters of nitrate pollution of groundwater (regression results for regions with more than 400 mm precipitation between October and March) 150

8.1 LP calibration results 163
8.2 Necessary reductions in sheep numbers and associated minimum payments to farmers 164
8.3 Changes in the mean minimum payment required (calculated at the mean stocking rate restriction) as support prices change 165

9.1   The ratio between market support and value of output for the
      most strongly supported sectors   172
9.2   Ratio between agricultural production subsidies and Regional
      value added   173
9.3   Some of the main items in agro-food exports, 1994   174
9.4   Agro-food exports – principal exporting Regions, 1994   175
9.5   Number of farms and total area by size of total farm area
      (area in ha)   176
9.6   The development of supermarkets between 1982 and 1995   176
9.7   Household purchase of food by type of retail outlet, 1994   177
9:8   Area and livestock units foreseen in zonal plans and those
      actually engaged in 1994 as compared with total utilized
      agricultural area and livestock units   180

10.1 Description of the representative farms   ·   190
10.2 Simulated results for farm 1 (PHI = 0, water scenario = 1,
      policy scenario = 2)   194
10.3 Simulated results for farm 1 (PHI = 0, water scenario = 1,
      policy scenario = 4)   195
10.4 Simulated results for farm 1 (PHI = 1, water scenario = 1,
      policy scenario = 2)   196

11.1 Coefficient estimates and Allen elasticities of substitution 214
11.2 Rate of cost diminution   215
11.3 Productivity indexes for fertilizers and chemicals   215
11.4 Annual average rates of productivity growth   216
11.5 Parameter estimates of Koyck functions   217

12.1 Gross Agricultural Output (GAO) index, 1986–96   232
12.2 Contribution of various farming categories to agricultural
      production in 1995   233
12.3 Benefits of Estonian wetlands by their geographical extent   235

List of contributors

David G. Abler,
Department of Agricultural
   Economics and Rural Sociology,
Pennsylvania State University,
USA

John M. Antle,
Department of Agricultural
   Economics and Economics,
Montana State University,
USA

Siemen van Berkum,
Agricultural Economics Research
   Institute (LEI-DLO),
The Hague,
Netherlands

Floor Brouwer,
Agricultural Economics Research
   Institute (LEI-DLO),
The Hague,
Netherlands

Susan M. Capalbo,
Department of Agricultural
   Economics,
Montana State University,
USA

Alain Carpentier,
Department of Economics,
INRA,
France

Paavo Eliste,
Department of Agricultural and
   Resource Economics,
West Virginia University,
USA

Panos Fousekis,
Institute for Mountainous
   Agriculture,
Karpenisi,
Greece

Hervé Guyomard,
Department of Economics,
INRA, ESR,
France

Nick Hanley,
Institute of Ecology and Resource
   Management,
University of Edinburgh,
UK

Hilary Kirkpatrick,
Department of Environmental
   Science,
University of Stirling,
UK

Joseph N. Lekakis,
Department of Economics,
University of Crete,
Greece

Chantal Le Mouël,
Department of Economics,
INRA, ESR,
France

Margaret Loseby,
Department of Economics and Rural
    Environment,
University of Tuscia,
Italy

Steve McCorriston,
Agricultural Economics Unit,
University of Exeter,
UK

David Oglethorpe,
Scottish Agricultural College,
Edinburgh,
UK

Tim T. Phipps,
Department of Agricultural and
    Resource Economics,
West Virginia University,
USA

Ian M. Sheldon,
Department of Agricultural
    Economics,
Ohio State University,
USA

James S. Shortle,
Department of Agricultural
    Economics and Rural Sociology,
Pennsylvania State University,
USA

Ian Simpson,
Department of Environmental
    Science,
University of Stirling,
UK

Franz Sinabell,
Department of Economics, Politics
    and Law,
University of Resource Sciences,
Vienna,
Austria

Consuelo Varela-Ortega,
Department of Agricultural
    Economics,
Polytechnical University of Madrid,
Spain

George P. Zanias,
Department of International and
    European Economic Studies,
Athens University of Economics and
    Business,
Greece

Preface

Agriculture, Trade and the Environment: The Impact of Liberalization on Sustainable Development addresses the sustainability and policy aspects of trade liberalization with a focus on European agriculture. The efforts of many individuals were pooled together in making this book. In 1995, in the light of the recent World Trade Organization (WTO) agreement and the need for sustainable development, we initiated an informal network on 'agriculture, trade, and environment' with an aim to organize a major European–North American gathering to discuss the future of European Union (EU) agriculture. In 1996 the Department of Economics of the University of Crete in Rethimno hosted an international conference, 'European Agriculture at the Crossroads: Competition and Sustainability'. The conference was sponsored by the European Commission, DG XII for Science, Research and Development (contract no ENV4-CT-96-6514), the Global Environmental Change Programme (contract no L320263049) of the British Economic and Social Research Council (ESRC), the Hellenic Ministries for Agriculture and for Environment, and the University of Crete.

Selected papers were subsequently revised on the basis of comments from conference panel leaders, delegates and individual participants. An edited volume was then proposed, and was reviewed by Edward Elgar's external referees, then final revisions were made prior to submitting the manuscript for publication.

Part I (Chapters 1–3) of the volume deals with theoretical and methodological issues that arise in the investigation of agricultural sustainability and related policy formation. Part II (Chapters 4–6) addresses these issues specifically in the context of EU agriculture. Part III (Chapters 7–11) presents the experience of some EU member countries. Part IV (Chapters 12 and 13), finally, looks at future developments in an enlarged EU context, as well as in the context of the forthcoming WTO conference in 1999.

We gratefully acknowledge the financial support of the European Commission, ESRC, the Hellenic Ministry for Agriculture, the Hellenic Ministry for Environment, Physical Planning and Public Works, and the University of Crete, the help of the reviewers of this volume, and the moral support of our publisher Edward Elgar. The views presented in this volume are those of the individual authors and do not necessarily reflect those of our sponsoring agencies.

John M. Antle
Joseph N. Lekakis
George P. Zanias

Introduction: Free trade, agriculture and the environment with a view to the European Union

John M. Antle, Joseph N. Lekakis and George P. Zanias

Prior to the recent World Trade Organization (WTO) agreement, concern over its likely impacts precipitated an international scientific and policy debate on 'trade and the environment'. The General Agreement on Traffic and Trade (GATT) issued special reports and also appointed a working group, the Organization for Economic Cooperation and Development (OECD) formed a joint committee, the World Bank released an extensive discussion paper, the International Agricultural Trade Research Consortium (IATRC) initiated relevant work, the American Journal of Agricultural Economics hosted a discussion of US agricultural economists, and the journal *Ecological Economics* devoted a special issue on this debate. The relevant literature is now surpassing its infancy, basically suggesting research topics such as the impact of free trade on the environment, the employment of environmental policies as non-tariff protectionist policies, and the relationship between international agreements intersecting on trade and environmental policies (Runge, 1994).

The impact of free trade on the environment is usually tied to ecological sustainability questions, although the recent notion of sustainability surpasses biophysical considerations. Environmentalists advocate that by raising the scale of economic activity, trade liberalization leads to higher levels of investment and consumption and hence a greater demand for environmental resources (Røpke, 1994).

In response to environmentalists' arguments against trade liberalization, economists have argued in general terms that economic growth and trade liberalization need not lead to environmental degradation (Low, 1992), and these arguments have also been made in the context of agricultural trade liberalization (Anderson and Blackhurst, 1992). However, these economists' arguments have typically been made in the context of aggregate (i.e., national) analyses, and data used to support these views were national aggregates. There is also an evolving theoretical and empirical literature on the interface between agriculture and the environment at the farm and regional level. A central theme of this literature is that the environmental impacts of agriculture are location specific and highly variable over the landscape. It follows that the effects of policy changes on the environment are also variable over the landscape, and that their regional or national effects often cannot be inferred from aggregate data (Just and Antle, 1990; Antle *et al.*, 1996).

This volume is intended to contribute to the growing literature on the relationship between the economic and environmental sustainability of agriculture, with a focus on European Union (EU) agriculture. As the 21st century approaches, EU agriculture faces significant challenges that span the spectrum of issues underpinning its economic and environmental sustainability.

Historically, after attaining self sufficiency, the European Community realized production surpluses, increasing budgetary costs due to subsidized exports, and environmental decay. This, along with pressures towards freer international trade, led to the famous MacSharry Reform in 1992 which was subsequently used by the European Commission as the instrument for mediating the EU's agricultural trade policy. Measures such as land set-aside programmes (similar to the US Acreage Reduction Programs, ARP), the abolition of input subsidies, and the reduction of export subsidies, aim to control production. The impact of these programmes is not always complete. For example, set-aside schemes are affected by ineffective monitoring, use of more variable inputs per unit of land and increased land productivity.

The WTO and international environmental agreements changed the dynamics around European agriculture which has to face competition both within the EU and internationally. In addition, it must face not only the impact of the EU's legal obligations to the WTO but also domestic sustainability issues which have been carved by the European Commission's 'Fifth Environmental Action Programme, Towards Sustainability'. All of these forces signal a new era of competition for agriculture within the EU and between the EU and the rest of the world. When considered in the context of the economic protections that earlier policies afforded European agriculture, these changes raise significant questions about how the transition to the new economic environment will occur. What sectors of EU agriculture can compete in the global marketplace? How will the transition affect the structure of agriculture, in light of policies designed to protect smaller, less efficient farms? In short, what segments of EU agriculture are economically sustainable in the present and likely future economic environment?

At the same time that the economic forces associated with policy change are coming into play, there is a continuing and growing demand by the public for agriculture to be sustainable in a broader social and environmental sense. The convergence of these economic and social forces raises some very profound questions about public policy design for agriculture that parallel the broader debate about economic growth and environmental quality. Is the movement towards agricultural policy liberalization compatible with the goal of achieving economic and environmental sustainability of EU agriculture? Or are there trade-offs that must be made between economic and environmental goals?

Overview of the book

The book is divided into four parts. Part I (Chapters 1–3) explore theoretical and methodological issues that arise in the investigation of agricultural sustainability and related policy formation. Part II (Chapters 4–6) address these issues specifically in the context of EU agriculture. Part III (Chapters 7–11) present the experience of some EU member countries. Part IV (Chapters 12 and 13), finally, address future developments in an enlarged EU context.

In Chapter 1, Panos Fousekis investigates the effects of agricultural trade liberalization on global pollution, using a two-country, one commodity, two-factor model. Pollution is generated by production in each of the trading partners through the use of land and chemicals. Solving the model explicitly yields the elasticity of aggregate pollution with respect to the level of trade restrictions which is the key variable studied. This variable has been found to assume a positive or negative value, which formally supports propositions or hypotheses that freer trade may increase or decrease global pollution. The author then investigates factors that can determine this outcome. These factors include the relative size of each of the trading partners, the product demand elasticities, the input supply elasticities, and the characteristics of the production process in each country reflected in the elasticities of substitution between chemicals and land. The effect of each of these factors is examined by performing comparative statics analysis on the elasticity of aggregate pollution with respect to the level of trade restrictions.

Chapter 2, by John Antle and Susan Capalbo, discusses quantitative methods for the assessment of agriculture–environment tradeoffs for policy analysis at the firm, regional, and national levels. The presentation begins with the premise that reliable analyses of the environmental impacts of agricultural production practices must be based on model integration at the level of aggregation compatible with the models describing the environmental processes. Typically this level of aggregation (or in environmental science jargon, the scale of analysis) is at the field or farm scale. The authors propose a statistical procedure that provides the basis for construction of relatively simple yet sophisticated stochastic simulation models. These simulation models are used to construct statistical distributions of economic and environmental outcomes that can be aggregated to regional or national levels for analysis of economic–environmental tradeoffs associated with alternative technology and policy scenarios. The chapter also discusses the implications of this approach for the construction of aggregate environmental indicators such as those recently proposed by the OECD. The authors illustrate this methodology with a review of several case studies in which it was applied, and conclude with a discussion of the potential for this approach to be applied in European settings.

Based on work by Miranowski, Grossman, Krueger and others, the OECD developed a simple framework for decomposing the effects of trade on the environment. Subsequent OECD work enlarged the original framework to take more complete account of the potential effects of trade. David Abler and James Shortle find both frameworks to be of limited value. In Chapter 3, they discuss the limitations of the OECD frameworks and then offer an alternative approach. The Abler–Shortle approach divides the environmental effects of trade on a country into five mutually exclusive and exhaustive categories: scale, mix, externality, policy and technology.

The objectives of Chapter 4, by Floor Brouwer and Siemen van Berkum, are threefold: a) to summarize existing linkages which are currently known among CAP and the Environment in the EU, b) to assess the linkages between the reform in 1992 of the cereals regime and of the beef regime with the environment – effects on the environment of market and price policies regarding cereals and beef are reviewed, as well as the present environmental requirements in the framework of agricultural policy – and, c) to assess linkages between the environment and Council Regulation 2078 (EEC) on agricultural production methods compatible with the requirements of the protection of the environment and the maintenance of the countryside. Conclusions are drawn on the inclusion of environmental requirements in agricultural policy, as well as on the importance of environmental policies by member states to allow for meeting targets. Finally, the chapter reports on the effects of the Common Agricultural Policy (CAP) on the environment of the EU and assesses the existing environmental conditions on policy.

Alain Carpentier, Hervé Guyomard, and Chantal Le Mouël, in Chapter 5, examine the extent to which the 1992 CAP reform may be viewed as a first response to the problem of chemical input inefficiency in the crop sector and induced non-point source pollution. They develop an analytical framework of producer behaviour which considers land as a fixed but allocatable factor between two enterprises corresponding to an 'intensive' and to an 'extensive' technology. The latter uses low levels of fertilizers and pesticides per hectare. It is assumed that pre-reform CAP parameters led the farmer to allocate all the land to the intensive technology only. In that context, the effects of the new CAP arrangements are analysed in the crop sector (i.e., lower support prices, compensatory payments per hectare and set-aside) on output supply, input use, intensification, and quasi-fixed factor (land and labour) returns. It is shown that yields and farming intensity are likely to decrease due to support price cuts, but that the set-aside programme may counterbalance a large part of this effect. The analytical framework is then used to analyse the various parameters which may influence conversion of land from the intensive to the extensive technology, i.e., to analyse the changes at the extensive margin of production.

In Chapter 6, Steve McCorriston and Ian Sheldon explore the linkages between the agricultural sector and the downstream food-processing sectors. While recent research has identified that these sectors are imperfectly competitive, the implications of market structure for the outcomes of policy reform have not been considered. Furthermore, research on the industrial organization of the food sector has assumed that the farm-retail spread comprises a single downstream sector. However, there are likely to be several downstream sectors, such that the food sector may be more appropriately characterized as successive oligopoly. The chapter therefore considers the implications for agriculture and agricultural policy reform of oligopoly in a multi-stage food sector in a consistent theoretical framework, and presents empirical results from recent research.

In Chapter 7, Franz Sinabell addresses the question of whether measures of protection and environmental externalities of agriculture are linked together. The impact of agricultural policies on consumers and taxpayers, as well as trading partners are captured in transfer indicators like the producer subsidy equivalent (PSE) and the aggregate measure of support (AMS). From a general as well as partial equilibrium perspective an integration of external effects (both positive and negative) fits into their underlying theoretical concept. The theoretical part of the chapter shows how to deal with externalities in a consistent manner and makes proposals to adapt the way of calculation of the PSE to capture the effects of externalities unambiguously. A simple model shows the inter-linkages of agricultural production and negative external effects from a welfare perspective and the consequences for a transfer indicator like the PSE. Since the environmental costs of agricultural production in Austria are unknown, the nitrate content in groundwater serves as a proxy for the environmental damage which has occurred. The results of a regression analysis show that transfers to crop producers (measured by a PSE-like Regional Transfer Indicator) have significant influence on the level of nitrate content in groundwater and presumably on the extent of the related environmental damage.

In Chapter 8, Nick Hanley, Hilary Kirkpatrick, David Oglethorpe and Ian Simpson are concerned with policies aimed at supplying public environmental goods from the agricultural sector. In particular, they characterize the buying of these goods by the public from farmers using the 'Provider Gets Principle'. The principle is applied in a case study addressing the conservation of heather moorland in northern Scotland where an environmental good is identified, as perceived by ecologists, which can be indirectly created through reductions in agricultural intensity. As the basis of the study, the authors present an ecological–economic modelling framework, allowing the physical consequences and financial returns of alternative management scenarios to be appraised. Then they provide results from the models regarding the necessary changes in management required to create the desired environmental good and the possible exchequer costs of implementing such an environmental policy. The chapter provides a method of identifying and costing spatially-differentiated ecological targets, but concludes that policies aimed at providing such public goods also possibly require an assessment of the demand for such goods on narrow-economic efficiency grounds.

In Chapter 9, Margaret Loseby maintains that Italian agriculture has enjoyed a long period of protection from competition from foreign suppliers. For some products, such as fruit, vegetables and fresh dairy products, this protection was due, in the past also, to the lack of technical know-how for conservation and transportation. For other less perishable products, it relied on a specific policy, implemented before World War II and continued afterwards. Under the CAP, for a variety of reasons, a higher degree of formal protection appears to have been enjoyed by products common to Northern Europe, unlike Mediterranean products which experienced a lower level of protection. For this reason, different productive sectors and geographical areas associated with them will experience varying reactions as a consequence of agricultural policy reform under way. The effects of the reduction in protection due to the Uruguay Round are likely to be felt by increasing competition on home markets and on export markets for both processed and unprocessed products. This Chapter assesses whether this trend can be expected to continue if, as predicted, public support to the primary agricultural sector is reduced, creating negative multiplier effects in rural areas.

In Chapter 10, Consuelo Varela-Ortega analyses the influence of the CAP on Spanish agriculture and the environment. First, it focuses on the analytical overlook of the environmental consequences of the implementation of CAP programmes in Spain. Then, it analyses, as a case study, the regional consequences of the application of agricultural policy programmes linking economic and environmental effects. The analysis focuses on the impacts of CAP on the farmers' decisions and on the environment. The methodology integrates an agronomic model and a mathematical programming model, which takes into account simultaneously the economic and environmental impacts of the policy programmes. By defining different policy scenarios, the analysis enables the prediction to be made of variations in the choice of techniques, crops grown, and environmental damage at the regional level, considering risk and market imperfections. The results indicate a trend towards a subsidy-guided agriculture, technical extensification, and farm income sustainability heterogeneously distributed across regions. The conclusions point to the need to undertake regional studies for decision-making in agricultural and environmental policies.

In Chapter 11, Joseph Lekakis studies the productivity of agrochemicals which constitute the main production inputs associated with the question of competitiveness and ecological sustainability in modern agriculture. In Greece, agrochemicals may have been used at an environmentally damaging/unproductive rate. While this remains a plausible hypothesis, no work has attempted to explore and qualify this issue using quantitative analysis to date, even at the sectoral level. In addition, given the recent GATT agreement, the economic sustainability of Greek agriculture in the future depends to a large extent on how productively agrochemicals will be combined in production. This requires some knowledge of past agrochemical productivities. This chapter evaluates the productivity of fertilizers and pesticides in the Greek agricultural sector during the period 1971–1995, using single factor productivity analysis. The results verify the above hypothesis, showing that the productivity indexes of fertilizers and pesticides, from 100 in 1971, declined to about 48 and 22 respectively in 1995.

In Chapter 12, Tim T. Phipps and Paavo Eliste propose that agricultural policy reform, trade liberalization, and economic transition will influence the structure of European agriculture and have implications for the environment. Economic transition will bring forth special problems including incomplete land and capital markets, shifting price margins, restructuring, and uncertain trade relationships. Phipps and Eliste analyse the effects of transition on the intensive and extensive margins of production and the environment. They then apply the analysis to the Estonian agricultural sector, the focus being on the issue of wetlands restoration and conversion. This issue is of particular interest because wetlands in Estonia create a transboundary positive externality since they support migratory waterfowl. Currently agricultural land is undervalued compared with its expected post-transition level.

Chapter 13, finally, by George Zanias, paints the picture of the CAP by looking both back and forward. The traditional mechanisms of supporting EU agriculture under the CAP resulted in very high taxpayer (budgetary) and consumer costs, problems with trade partners, and pressures on the environment. Simultaneously, that policy did not manage adequately to support farm incomes which constituted a dominant target. The relatively recent CAP reform, assisted by developments in the international markets, reduced considerably the intensity of a number of problems that the previous regime had contributed to, and eased, for the time being, the pressure for further reform. However, this pressure will escalate, given the prospective entry of Central and Eastern European countries into the EU which constitutes a major long-term determinant of the CAP and its policy mix. In addition, any policy adjustments need to observe the recent GATT and thus they constitute also a blueprint for future policy measures. A new round of talks under the WTO will be another major determinant factor. It seems that the result of these multiple influences will be a policy framework for EU agriculture which will further disassociate support from production, enhance the role of the quality criterion including the observance of environmental goals, and promote a more integrated approach to dealing with the problems of the rural economy.

Conclusions
Based on the chapters presented in this volume, we conclude that there are few generalizations or stylized facts that emerge about answers to the questions raised about trade and the environment, and this conclusion is particularly true for agriculture in a region as economically and environmentally diverse as Europe.

Perhaps the one generalization that can be made is that because environmental conditions vary spatially over the landscape, impacts of human activity also vary spatially, and as a result there is a loss of information about this variability as one aggregates from a specific location, such as a farmer's field, to the regional or national level. As a result, the environmental impacts of national policies are likely to be spatially variable and are likely to have different impacts in different places. This observation suggests that efficient policies for environmental management in the EU need to be tailored to fit local conditions; any attempt to impose uniform policies across a region as environmentally and economically diverse as Europe will have widely divergent, and no doubt unintended, consequences.

On the theoretical and methodological front, this volume demonstrates that a wide range of analytical and quantitative tools are relevant to the investigation of these issues. To assess the environmental impacts of agricultural activities accurately, highly disaggregate data are needed combined with microeconomic analyses that can assess change in input use intensity and changes in land use (in traditional economic jargon, the distinction must be made between intensive margin and extensive margin effects). To address policy issues at the regional and national scale, it is necessary to utilize aggregate data and models as well. Indeed, most trade policy research is conducted at the national scale. Bridging the gap between the spatially explicit, microeconomic analyses of environmental impact and the national scale policy analyses remains a challenge to researchers. Yet until this gap is bridged, it will be difficult to assess how the various national policy initiatives will affect environmental quality and other aspects of welfare at the disaggregate level.

A related theme that emerges from the contributions to this volume is that advances are needed in how economists conceptualize and measure indicators of economic and environmental conditions. Simple aggregate indicators of input use are not likely to provide useful information about site-specific environmental impacts of changes in policy. Likewise, measures of policy intervention such as the PSE and the AMS may need to be linked to environmental impacts and generalized to take social costs into account.

A broader view of agricultural sustainability that goes beyond environmental impacts also seems to be particularly relevant for the European setting. Many of Europe's agricultural policies have been designed to maintain rural landscapes and communities. Further work on the implications of trade liberalization for changes in the structure and organization of European agriculture seem to be needed to understand this transition and its social and environmental consequences. Again, the diversity of the economic, social, and environmental conditions in Europe mean that it may be difficult to draw broad generalizations. Rather, more detailed, country-specific and region-specific case studies may be needed.

Looking ahead, one can see additional issues on the research agenda that this volume did not address. One area that is of great significance concerns the broader issues of human nutrition, food safety, and their linkages to market structure, environmental conditions, and international trade. The Uruguay Round agreements laid a foundation for addressing sanitary and phytosanitary issues, and the next round of multilateral trade negotiations may take on the difficult question of how to distinguish between scientifically justified regulations for the protection of health and safety and non-tariff barriers to trade. We trust that the contributions made in this volume will provide the foundations for further advances in our understanding of these complex issues.

References

Anderson, K. and R. Blackhurst (eds) (1992), *The Greening of World Trade Issues*, London: Harvester Wheatsheaf.

Antle, J.M., C.C. Crissman, J. Hutson and R.J. Wagenet (1996), 'Empirical foundations of environment–trade linkages: evidence from an Andean study', in M.E. Bredahl, N. Ballenger, J.C. Dunmore and T.L. Roe (eds), *Agricultural Trade and the Environment: Understanding and Measuring the Critical Linkages*, Boulder, Colorado: Westview Press.

Just, R.E. and J.M. Antle (1990), 'Interactions between agricultural and environmental policy: A conceptual framework,' *American Economic Review*, **80**(2), 197–202.

Low, P. (1992) (ed.), *International Trade and the Environment*, Washington, DC, World Bank Discussion Paper No. 159.

Røpke, I. (1994), 'Trade, Development, and Sustainability – A Critical Assessment of the Free Trade Dogma', *Ecological Economics*, **9**, 13–22.

Runge, C. Ford (1994), *Freer Trade, Protected Environment: Balancing Trade Liberalization and Environmental Interests*, New York: Council of Foreign Relations Press.

PART I

1 Comparative statics on a two-country, one-commodity, two-factor agricultural trade model with process-generated pollution

Panos Fousekis

1.1 Introduction

In the early parts of the present decade, an international debate emerged on 'Trade and the Environment', which has been receiving extensive attention and publicity (Low, 1992; GATT, 1992; Anderson and Blackhurst, 1992; Folke *et al.*, 1994; Johnstone, 1995). The debate was mainly a response to concerns about the economic and environmental effects of the recent round of GATT negotiations. One of the critical research needs which the literature points to is the impact of free trade on the environment (Antle, 1993; Harold and Ford Runge, 1993; Ford Runge, 1994).

Proponents of freer trade insist that, by leading to higher growth rates and per capita incomes, trade increases the demand for environmental quality and helps poor countries escape the 'poverty generated pollution gap'. Countering this position, political economists attempt to unveil the worsening distribution of trade incomes among rich and poor countries, and the environmentalists advocate that by raising the scale of economic activity, freer trade implies higher levels of investment and consumption and hence a greater demand for natural resources and environmental services.

The literature on 'Trade and Environment' recognizes that, at least in the short-run, trade liberalization will result in a redistribution of pollution levels among trading partners. Specifically, if pollution is process generated, countries which have a market competitive advantage will experience environmental degradation due to higher production for exports while less efficient countries will experience environmental gains since free trade will shrink domestic polluting activities. Capturing this spirit, Steininger (1994) uses a geometric two-country, one-commodity trade model to conclude that beyond redistributing the pollution load, free trade can result in higher or lower levels of aggregate pollution compared to a situation with no trade at all. He acknowledges, however, that it may be both possible and worthwhile to try to identify factors which work towards raising or lowering the global pollution level following trade liberalization.

Regarding agriculture, which has been traditionally a highly protected sector of national economies, McCalla (1993) provides an excellent review of the unsuccessful attempts made in the past to promote trade liberalization and obstacles to achieving it. Agricultural policies have been criticized for stimulating farmers to use excessive levels of polluting inputs such as fertilizers and pesticides (Bonnieux and Rainelli, 1988; Daberkow and Reichelderfer, 1988; Madden, 1988; Weinschenck, 1987). Abler and Shortle (1992), and Harold and Runge (1993) provide empirical evidence that agricultural policy reforms can be beneficial to the environment. Abler and Pick (1993) find that the North American Free Trade Agreement (NAFTA) may result in lower total agricultural pollution in North America through shifting horticultural production from Florida (USA) to Sinaloa (Mexico). Antle (1993) employs a concave transformation frontier to trace out tradeoff between agricultural and environmental services. While appearing optimistic that changes in production technology, spatial distribution of production, and the rise in incomes due to free trade can eventually improve global environmental conditions, Antle admits that it is in fact difficult to draw generalizations about the environmental impact of trade liberalization.

The purpose of this chapter is, first, formally to examine propositions/ hypotheses that the global pollution level may rise or fall as a result of trade liberalization. Second, going a step further, the chapter identifies factors which work towards raising or lowering the global pollution level. These are pursued through a two-country, one-commodity, two-factor agricultural trade model with process generated pollution. The formalization is general enough to accommodate both product and factor markets as well as technical production characteristics (e.g. elasticities of factor substitution among environmentally harmful and other production inputs) in each country. A key variable for the analysis is the elasticity of aggregate pollution with respect to the level of trade restrictions. This variable is derived here from an explicit solution of the model. Although the sign of this variable is generally unknown, comparative statics analysis with respect to model parameters does indicate the direction of change in total pollution due to trade liberalization.

The rest of the chapter is structured as follows. Part 2 outlines the theoretical model. Part 3 derives the elasticity of aggregate pollution with respect to trade restrictions. Comparative statics are finally performed in part 4, before drawing conclusions in part 5.

1.2   The theoretical model
Let the agricultural good Y be produced and consumed in two countries, country 1 and country 2. The production functions of Y in these two countries are given by,

$$Y^i = F^i(L^i, X^i), \ i = 1,2 \tag{1.1}$$

where L stands for the land input and X for the chemical input. F^i is assumed to be twice differentiable, increasing and concave in L^i and X^i. It is also assumed that F^i exhibits constant returns to scale. The domestic supply functions of L and X are given by,

$$L^i = L^i(v^i) \tag{1.2}$$

$$X^i = X^i(w^i) \tag{1.3}$$

where w^i and v^i, $i = 1,2$, are the prices of chemicals and land, respectively. L^i and X^i are assumed twice differentiable and increasing in v^i and w^i, respectively. The use of the chemical input generates pollution Z^i according to[1]

$$Z^i = Z^i(X^i), \ i = 1,2. \tag{1.4}$$

Z_i is assumed to be twice differentiable and increasing in i. Therefore, the process generated aggregate pollution in the two countries from using levels of chemical input X^1 and X^2 is

$$Z(X^1, X^2) = Z^1(X^1) + Z^2(X^2). \tag{1.5}$$

In the absence of trade restrictions, consumers and producers in these two countries face the international price, p, determined by the total supply and total demand in 1 and 2. Here, it is assumed that country 1 protects its domestic producers by means of import restrictions which raise domestic price to bp, where $b > 1$.[2] Given country 1's trade policy, the international price p is determined by

$$Y^1(bp) + Y^2(p) = D^1(bp) + D^2(p). \tag{1.6}$$

Relation (1.6) is an accounting identity implying that total production (given the trade restrictions) equals total consumption (given the trade restrictions) or alternatively excess supply equals excess demand.

1 The amount of agricultural land and the way this land is used and managed by farmers may influence the environment. The properly managed land can provide environmental amenities such as flood and soil water protection, fostering of water resources, air purification, and maintenance of biodiversity (OECD, 1996). Here, the environmental effects from the amount and the management of agricultural land have not been considered in order to keep the model and the ensuing analysis tractable.
2 This is scheme implies that producers and consumers in country 1 face the same price. Alternative schemes may involve 'deficiency payments', applied currently for some agricultural products in the US and in the UK (before the accession of this country in the EU) or export subsidies used by several developed and developing countries.

A step towards trade liberalization can be thought as a decrease in b which determines the degree to which the domestic price in country 1 differs from the international price. Let $\hat{b} = db/b$ be the percentage reduction in b and $\hat{Z} = dZ/Z$ be the percentage change in Z due to the reduction in b. Given this notation, the objective of this chapter may be formally stated as the investigation of the sign and the magnitude of the elasticity, ξ, of the aggregate pollution, Z, with respect to b, where

$$\xi = \frac{\hat{Z}}{\hat{b}}. \tag{1.7}$$

This objective is pursued in the next section.

1.3   Derivation of the elasticity of aggregate pollution with respect to trade restrictions

Since the production functions exhibit constant returns to scale the respective cost functions may be written as

$$C^i(w^i, v^i, Y^i) = \Phi^i(w^i, v^i)Y^i \tag{1.8}$$

where Φ^i is the average and marginal production cost. Application of Shepard's lemma to (1.8) yields the demand functions for inputs X^i and L^i as

$$\hat{X}^i = S_L^i \sigma^i \hat{v}^i - S_L^i \sigma^i \hat{w}^i + \hat{Y}^i \tag{1.9}$$

$$\hat{L}^i = S_X^i \sigma^i \hat{w}^i - S_X^i \sigma^i \hat{v}^i + \hat{Y}^i, \tag{1.10}$$

where S_L and S_X stand for cost shares and σ stands for the elasticity of substitution between inputs X and L. The supply functions of inputs can be written as

$$\hat{X}^i = e_X^i \hat{w}^i \tag{1.11}$$

$$\hat{L}^i = e_L^i \hat{v}^i \tag{1.12}$$

where e_L and e_X are input supply elasticities.

Production efficiency requires that marginal cost equals output price, that is,

$$S_X^i \hat{w}^i + S_L^i \hat{v}^i = \hat{p}^i \tag{1.13}$$

where

$$\hat{p}^1 = \hat{p} + \hat{b} \tag{1.14}$$

and

$$\hat{p}^2 = \hat{p}. \tag{1.15}$$

Changes in the aggregate pollution level are brought about by changes in the use of chemicals in the two countries. The percentage change in Z can be expressed as

$$\hat{Z} = de_Z^1\hat{X}^1 + (1 - d)e_Z^2\hat{X}^2, \tag{1.16}$$

where d stands for the share of country 1 in the total level of pollution prior to easing trade restrictions, and e_Z^1 and e_Z^2 stand for the elasticities of pollution with respect to chemical use in each country.

Imposing or easing restrictions in a two-country trade model affects the level of the world price, which in this chapter is the price prevailing in country 2. The elasticity of world price, p, with respect to b can be derived by differentiating logarithmically the accounting identity (1.6) as

$$\rho = \frac{\hat{p}}{\hat{b}} = \frac{ge_Y^1 + he_D^1}{-ge_Y^1 - (1-g)e_Y^2 - he_D^1 - (1-h)e_D^2} \tag{1.17}$$

where e_Y^i and e_D^i are the supply and demand elasticities in each country and g and h are the shares of country 1 in total production and consumption of commodity Y prior to easing trade restrictions. From (1.17) it follows that the elasticity of world price with respect to trade restrictions is negative and less than one (in absolute value). Combining (1.17) and (1.14) obtains

$$\frac{\hat{p}^1}{\hat{b}} = \rho + 1, \tag{1.18}$$

while combining (1.17) and (1.15) obtains

$$\frac{\hat{p}^2}{\hat{b}} = \rho. \tag{1.19}$$

Having derived expressions for the price elasticities in each country with respect to b one may proceed to determine the elasticities of chemical use with respect to b. This exercise is performed in the Appendix. It turns out that

$$\frac{\hat{X}^1}{\hat{b}} = e_Y^1(\rho+1)\frac{S_L^1\sigma^1 e_X^1 + e_L^1 e_X^1 + e_X^1 S_X^1 \sigma^1}{e_L^1 e_X^1 + e_X^1 S_X^1 \sigma^1 + e_L^1 S_L^1 \sigma^1} \qquad (1.20)$$

$$\frac{\hat{X}^2}{\hat{b}} = e_Y^2\rho\frac{S_L^2\sigma^2 e_X^2 + e_L^2 e_X^2 + e_X^2 S_X^2 \sigma^2}{e_L^2 e_X^2 + e_X^2 S_X^2 \sigma^2 + e_L^2 S_L^2 \sigma^2} \qquad (1.21)$$

where

$$e_Y^1 = \frac{e_L^1 e_X^1 + e_L^1 S_L^1 \sigma^1 + e_X^1 S_X^1 \sigma^1}{S_X^1 e_L^1 + S_L^1 e_X^1 + \sigma^1} \qquad (1.22)$$

and

$$e_Y^2 = \frac{e_L^2 e_X^2 + e_L^2 S_L^2 \sigma^2 + e_X^2 S_X^2 \sigma^2}{S_X^2 e_L^2 + S_L^2 e_X^2 + \sigma^2}. \qquad (1.23)$$

Notice that given the sign and magnitude of ρ the elasticity of X^1 with respect to trade restrictions is positive while that of X^2 is negative. The elasticity of Z with respect to b is given by,

$$\frac{\hat{Z}}{\hat{b}} = d e_Z^1 \frac{\hat{X}^1}{\hat{b}} + (1-d)e_Z^2 \frac{\hat{X}^2}{\hat{b}}, \qquad (1.24)$$

where the elasticities of input use with respect to b are given by (1.20) and (1.21).

1.4   Comparative statics analysis

Comparative statics are concerned with the effects of parameter changes on the elasticity of aggregate pollution, Z, with respect to trade restrictions as reflected in b. The analysis will provide some indication about which of these two effects (positive or negative) in (1.24) is likely to prevail under certain circumstances. For example, if an increase in a given parameter leads to an increase of the elasticity of Z with respect to b one may conclude that higher values of this particular parameter are likely to bring about a decrease in total pollution when steps towards trade liberalization are taken. The reverse will be true when an increase in a given parameter leads to a decrease in the elasticity of Z with respect to b. This type of analysis requires the differentiation of $\xi = \hat{Z}/\hat{b}$ with respect to every parameter appearing in (1.24). However, given the number of involved parameters in the model, differentiation will, in most of the cases, lead to expressions which are too complicated to evaluate. On the basis of these considerations, the analysis needs to concentrate selectively on a number of special cases. The selection of these cases draws mainly on the characteristics of the agricultural production such as fixity of the amount of agricultural land available in the short-run, and/or on perfect elasticity of supply chemicals with respect to chemical prices. At the same time, whenever direct differentiation leads to tractable expressions it is used for the purpose of analysis as well.

a) An increase in d
As stated above d is the share of country 1 in total pollution Z prior to reducing trade restrictions. The derivative of (1.24) with respect to Z is

$$e_Z^1 \frac{\hat{X}^1}{\hat{b}} - e_Z^2 \frac{\hat{X}^2}{\hat{b}} > 0.$$

Therefore, higher contribution of country 1 in aggregate pollution prior to taking steps for freer trade works towards a net reduction of total pollution following trade liberalization. The result makes absolute sense. The higher the share of country 1, the larger the reduction in pollution which will result from a given decrease (as a percentage) in the use of chemicals in this country when trade restrictions are eased.

b) An increase in e_Z^1
e_Z^1 is the elasticity of pollution in country 1 with respect to the use of chemicals. The derivative of (24) with respect to this parameter is

$$d \frac{\hat{X}^1}{\hat{b}} > 0.$$

Therefore, higher e_Z^1 works towards reducing the level of aggregate pollution when trade becomes freer. This is reasonable, since higher e_Z^1 leads to higher reduction of pollution in country 1 from a given fall in the use of chemicals. An increase in e_Z^2 works in the opposite direction.

c) An increase in $\hat{X}^1/\hat{b}$
The derivative of (1.24) with respect to the elasticity of chemical use with respect to trade restrictions is

$$de_Z^1 > 0.$$

Therefore, higher $\hat{X}^1/\hat{b}$ works towards a reduction in aggregate pollution following trade liberalization. An increase in $\hat{X}^2/\hat{b}$ (lower absolute value) is likely to bring about lower total pollution as well.

The elasticity of demand for chemicals with respect to trade restrictions is itself a function of a number of parameters related to product demand and to the production conditions in each country. Given that higher demand elasticities of chemicals with respect to b work towards a decrease in aggregate pollution one may determine the influence of supply and demand parameters on Z by simply examining their effects on $\hat{X}^1/\hat{b}$ and $\hat{X}^2/\hat{b}$.

c1) An increase in e_D^1   This is the elasticity of demand for commodity Y in country 1 and affects the elasticities of demand for chemical inputs with respect to trade restrictions through the elasticity of international price with respect to b given in (1.17). Differentiating (1.17) with respect to e_D^1 yields

$$\frac{-(1-g)e_Y^2 - (1-h)e_D^2}{\left(-ge_Y^1 - (1-g)e_Y^2 - he_D^1 - (1-h)e_D^2\right)^2} < 0.$$

This result together with (1.20) (1.21) and (1.24) implies that a higher (in absolute value) demand elasticity in country 1 works towards a decrease in the aggregate level of pollution. An intuitive explanation for this follows. As trade barriers are eased, the price in country 1 tends to decrease while the price in country 2 increases. Higher elasticity of demand in country 1 implies that the expansion of Y consumption in this country will be larger than with a smaller demand elasticity. Thus, higher e_D^1 keeps the overall demand and, in turn, the international price higher than with a lower demand elasticity. This implies that, for a given change in b, the decrease in production of country 1 will be lower and the increase in country 2 will be higher. The latter, taken together, work towards a higher Z. In contrast, higher (in absolute value) e_D^2 works towards a lower Z. An intuitive explanation can be obtained in same way as that for e_D^1.

The production conditions in each country are reflected in the own-price elasticities of commodity Y. Relations (1.22) and (1.23) suggest that e_Y^1 and e_Y^2 depend on the own-price supply elasticities of inputs as well as the elasticities of factor substitution. Differentiating (1.25) with respect to these parameters gives expressions that are too complicated to evaluate. Notice, however, that a reasonable assumption for the agricultural sector is that supply elasticities of the land input are zero, in the short-run. Imposing this condition, one may be able to get some meaningful results by considering certain special cases arising from different assumptions about elasticities of factor substitution and about the own-price supply elasticities of the chemical input in each country.

d) Special cases

d1) $e_L^i = 0$ *and* $F^i = 0$ *(Leontief Production Functions)* $I=1,2$.   Under these circumstances, own-price supply elasticities of Y in both countries are zero. Using (1.22), (1.23) and (1.25) leads to $\hat{Z}/\hat{b} = 0$, that is, trade liberalization leaves aggregate pollution as well as pollution in each country unchanged.

d2) $e_L^i = 0$, $I = 1,2$, *and* $\sigma^I = 0$, $0 < \sigma^2 < \infty$.   Then, elasticity of total pollution with respect to b is negative and equal to the elasticity of pollution in country 2. In the same way, when elasticity of factor substitution in country 2 is zero, but in country 1 it is different from zero then, the elasticity of aggregate pollution with respect to b is positive and equal to the elasticity of pollution in country 1. It appears, therefore, that if supply elasticities of land are zero then the sign of $\hat{Z}/\hat{b}$ is likely to be determined by the country in which the substitution elasticity between land and chemicals is higher. When land is fixed, larger adjustments to a change in b will take place in the country where substitution between the fixed and the variable input is higher. In this country producers enjoy higher flexibility in production relative to those in the country where substitution possibilities are low.

   In the context of d2) investigation of the role of the own-price supply elasticities of chemicals is straightforward. When $e_L^i = 0$, $I=1,2$, and $\sigma^I = 0$, $0 < \sigma^2 < \infty$ the elasticity of X^1 with respect to b is zero. The elasticity of X^2 with respect to b, however, may be written as

$$\frac{\hat{X}^2}{\hat{b}} = e_Y^2 \frac{ge_D^1}{-1 - ge_Y^2 - he_D^1 - (1-h)e_D^2} \frac{1}{S_X^2}. \tag{1.25}$$

The derivative of this term with respect to e_Y^2 is negative. The derivative of e_Y^2 with respect to e_X^2, however, is positive. Therefore, $\hat{X}^2/\hat{b}$ is negative and so is that of the elasticity of Z with respect to b. In other words, high own-price elasticity of chemicals in country 2 works towards an increase in aggregate pollution. An intuitive explanation follows. High own-price supply elasticity of chemicals implies that the increase in the price of this input due to higher demand in country 2 will be lower relative to the case of a smaller elasticity. This works towards a higher increase in this input's use and, in turn, towards a higher pollution level. Performing the same exercise for e_X^1 obtains that higher e_X^1 works towards a lower aggregate pollution level.

1.5 Summary

This chapter investigated the effects of trade liberalization on aggregate pollution by analysing the market of a tradable agricultural commodity produced by land and environment damaging inputs (agricultural chemicals). Pollution has been assumed to be generated by the production process of the agricultural commodity in each of the trading patterns. The analysis shows that freer trade will increase pollution in the exporting country, will reduce the pollution in the importing country but it may increase or decrease aggregate pollution. This outcome depends on the number of factors attesting to the relative size of each of the trading partners, the product demand elasticities, the input supply elasticities, and the characteristics of the production process in each country as reflected in the elasticities of substitution between chemicals and land.

The effect of each of these factors has been examined here by pursuing comparative statics on the elasticity of aggregate pollution with respect to level of trade restrictions. The analysis shows that, if under trade restrictions the importing country's share in the aggregate pollution load was large, trade liberalization will work towards lowering that load. The same holds for higher elasticity of pollution with respect to chemicals in that country, as well as for a high elasticity of demand for the chemical input with respect to trade restrictions. However, a high elasticity of commodity demand in the importing country works towards raising aggregate pollution. Given that the importing and the exporting countries enter the model symmetrically, high values of the above parameters in the exporting country work in the opposite direction compared to high values of the same parameters in the importing country. Input supply elasticities and elasticities of substitution between land and agricultural chemicals are technological constraints faced by producers in each country. The comparative statics analysis, with reference to these parameters, suggests that changes in aggregate pollution following trade liberalization are likely to be determined by the trading partner whose producers enjoy greater flexibility in their production decisions.

In this chapter, free trade has been assumed to affect price but not production technologies in each country. However, in the longer-run, free trade may force producers to alter their production technologies by moving along a meta-production function in accordance with the Hayami and Ruttan induced-innovation hypothesis. This will not only change the allocation of production and pollution among trading partners but also the level of aggregate pollution. Therefore, attempts to extend the model to accommodate technical change are certainly warranted.

Appendix: Elasticities of chemical input use with respect to trade restrictions
Setting (1.9) = (1.11) and (1.10) = (1.12) yields a system of equations in $\hat{w}^i$ and $\hat{v}^i$ in terms of $\hat{Y}^i$ as

$$\begin{bmatrix} \hat{w}^i \\ \hat{v}^i \end{bmatrix} = \frac{1}{\Theta} \begin{bmatrix} e_L^i + S_X^i \sigma^i & S_L^i \\ S_X^i & e_X^i + S_L^i \sigma^i \end{bmatrix} \begin{bmatrix} 1 \\ 1 \end{bmatrix} \hat{Y}^i \tag{A1.1}$$

where

$$\Theta = S_X^i e_L^i + S_L^i e_X^i + \sigma^i > 0.$$

Solving (A1.1) obtains

$$\frac{\hat{w}^i}{\hat{Y}^i} = \frac{1}{\Theta} \left(e_L^i + \sigma^i \right) \tag{A1.2}$$

and

$$\frac{\hat{v}^i}{\hat{Y}^i} = \frac{1}{\Theta} \left(e_X^i + \sigma^i \right). \tag{A1.3}$$

Using (1.18) and the definition of output supply elasticity we get

$$\frac{\hat{Y}^1}{\hat{b}} = e_Y^1 (\rho + 1). \tag{A1.4}$$

Using (1.19) and the definition of supply elasticity we get

$$\frac{\hat{Y}^2}{\hat{b}} = e_Y^2 \rho. \tag{A1.5}$$

For country 1 the combination of (A1.2) and (A1.3) with (A1.4) yields the elasticities of input prices with respect to b as

$$\frac{\hat{w}^1}{\hat{b}} = (\rho + 1) e_Y^1 \frac{1}{\Theta^1} \left(e_L^1 + \sigma^1 \right) \tag{A1.6}$$

and

$$\frac{\hat{v}^1}{\hat{b}} = (\rho + 1) e_Y^1 \frac{1}{\Theta^1} \left(e_X^1 + \sigma^1 \right), \tag{A1.7}$$

where Θ^1 is just Θ for $i = 1$. Finally, substituting (A1.4), (A1.6) and (A1.7) into (1.9) and collecting terms yields (1.20). The derivation of (1.21) is achieved performing the same substitutions as above for country 2.

References

Abler, D. and D. Pick (1993), 'NAFTA, agriculture and environment in Mexico', *American Journal of Agricultural Economics*, **75**, 794–8.

Abler D. and J. Shortle (1992), 'Potential for environmental and agricultural policy linkages and reforms in the European Community', *American Journal of Agricultural Economics*, **73**, 775–81.

Anderson, K. and R. Blackhurst (eds) (1992), *The Greening of World Trade Issues*, London: Harvester-Wheatsheaf.

Antle, J. (1993), 'Environment, development and trade between low and high income countries', *American Journal of Agricultural Economics*, **75**, 784–8.

Bonnieux F. and P. Rainelli (1988), 'Agricultural policy and environment in developed countries', *European Review of Agricultural Economics*, **15**, 363–80.

Daberkow, S. and K. Reichelderfer (1988), 'Low-input agriculture: trends, goals, and prospects for input use', *American Journal of Agricultural Economics*, **69**, 1159–66.

Folke, C., P. Ekins, and R. Costanza (1994), 'Trade and the environment', *Ecological Economics'*, **9**.

Ford Runge, C. (1994), 'Freer Trade, Protected Environment: Balancing Trade Liberalization and Environment Interests', New York, Council of Foreign Relations.

GATT (1992), *International Trade 90–91*, Vol. 1, including Special Topic, Geneva: Trade and Environment.

Harold, C. and C. Ford Runge (1993), 'GATT and the environment: policy research needs', *American Journal of Agricultural Economics*, **75**, 789–93.

Johnstone, N. (1995), 'Trade liberalization, economic specialization, and the environment', *Ecological Economics*, **14**, 165–73.

Low, P. (ed.) (1992), *International Trade and the Environment*, Washington, DC: World Bank Discussion Paper no. 159.

Madden, P. (1988), 'Low-input/sustainable agricultural research and education-challenges to the agricultural economics profession', *American Journal of Agricultural Economics*, **69**, 1167–72.

McCalla, A. (1993), 'Agricultural trade liberalization: the ever-elusive grail', *American Journal of Agricultural Economics*, **75**, 1102–22.

OECD (1996), Seminar on Environmental Benefits from a Sustainable Agriculture: Issues and Policies, Helsinki, Finland, 10–13 Sept. (several case studies).

Steininger, K. (1994), 'Reconciling trade and environment: towards a comparative advantage for long-run policy goals', *Ecological Economics*, **9**, 23–42.

Weinschenck, G. (1987), 'The economic or the ecological way? Basic alternatives for the EC's agricultural policy', *European Review of Agricultural Economics*, **14**, 49–60.

2 Quantifying agriculture–environment tradeoffs to assess environmental impacts of domestic and trade policies

John M. Antle and Susan M. Capalbo

A reorientation of public agricultural research institutions towards sustainable agricultural practices began in the 1980s and continues today (Bouma *et al.*, 1995). At the same time, the movement towards domestic and trade policy liberalization has intensified competition in world agricultural markets. Most governments, including those of the European Community and the United States, have established goals of enhancing both the sustainability and the competitiveness of their agricultures. The widespread acceptance of the goal of sustainable agricultural systems along with intensifying international competition has created the demand for analyses that can quantify the tradeoffs that inevitably must exist between the goals of sustainable agriculture and competitiveness.

This chapter reports on a general approach to assess quantitatively the economic, environmental, and human health tradeoffs associated with the use of agricultural technologies. Using the methods presented here, researchers can quantitatively assess how domestic or trade policy liberalization may move a region or country along the tradeoff curve between economic and environmental outcomes associated with a specified production technology, and also how those tradeoffs may be changed through the adoption of new technologies, including more sustainable practices. This approach is designed to account for key measurement issues that arise in agricultural impact assessment. These issues include: the temporal and spatial variability of agricultural impacts; the need to integrate disciplinary models and data at a small scale or level of aggregation, such as the field scale, at which impacts can be reliably modelled; and the need to assess impacts at a large scale or level of aggregation, such as the regional or population level, for purposes of risk assessment and policy analysis. Using this approach, it is possible to quantify aggregate tradeoffs between economic outcomes and environmental and health risk, and to assess the effects of aggregation on the measured tradeoffs.

To illustrate the feasibility and limitations of this approach, we describe several case studies where it is currently being utilized. We conclude with an assessment of the data needs and other research developments that are needed to make this method widely applicable.

2.1   A conceptual framework for quantifying tradeoffs in agricultural production systems

Following Antle *et al.* (1996), this section describes a conceptual framework for agricultural technology impact assessment that incorporates essential features of agriculture–environment interactions. We begin with a review of a conceptual framework suggested by recent research on modelling agricultural production decision-making on a location-specific basis (e.g., Antle and Just, 1991; Antle, Capalbo and Crissman, 1994; Crissman, Antle and Capalbo, 1998). The motivation for the development of this approach was the recognition that it was not possible to conduct environmental impact analysis with the regional or national units of analysis typically used by economists. Whereas economists use aggregate constructs such as market supply and demand, analogous constructs are not used in the physical and biological sciences. For example, economists typically use equations representing the regional or national demand for pesticides to estimate how pesticide use would change in response to, say, a price change. But from the soil science perspective, it would not make sense to use an 'average soil' to predict leaching of a pesticide into groundwater at a regional or national scale. Rather, soil scientists would disaggregate the study area into units of analysis with recognized soil types and other geophysical characteristics, and estimate leaching for each of these units. The approach described here is to disaggregate the economic analysis in a manner compatible with the soil science analysis, to estimate economic and environmental impacts at that disaggregate scale of analysis, and then statistically to aggregate impacts to the regional level needed for policy analysis.

Although the following discussion will focus on agriculture–environment interactions for brevity, the same logic can be applied to interactions between agriculture and certain health consequences such as farm worker exposure to pesticides.

2.1.1   A static spatial model of agriculture–environment interactions

In the conceptual framework for agricultural–environmental analysis developed by Antle and Just, prevailing market prices, policies, and the physical attributes of land affect farmers' management decisions in terms both of land use and input use. These decisions affect agricultural production, but also may affect the environment through two distinct but interrelated mechanisms. Decisions at the extensive margin determine which particular acres of cropland are put into production and which crops are grown. Management decisions at the intensive margin determine the application rates of chemicals, water use, and tillage practices. Physical relationships between the environmental attributes of the land in production and management practices then jointly determine the agricultural output and environmental impacts associated with a particular unit of land in production. The distribution of farm and environmental characteristics induces a joint distribution of input use, outputs, and environmental impacts. This joint distribution provides the basis for aggregation of the field–specific impacts to the regional level for policy analysis. The structure of this model is summarized in Figure 2.1.

The construction of the disaggregate model begins by defining a population of land units (referred to henceforth as a field) in relation to an environmentally meaningful geographical unit, such as an aquifer or watershed. A vector ω^i represents the ith field's physical characteristics (e.g., soil types, climate) that affect both crop productivity and environmental impact. Environmental impact

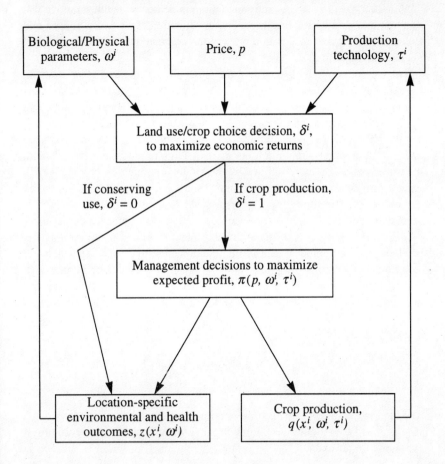

Source: Antle (1996)

Figure 2.1 *A static spatial model of land use and crop management decision-making*

is represented with a stylized physical model $z^i = z(x^i, \omega^i)$, where x^i is a vector of management actions taken on the ith field measured per unit area (stochastic effects due to weather and dynamics are embedded in ω), and z^i is the environmental impact measured in physical units per unit area. The function $z(x, \omega)$ is assumed to be increasing in x, and its convexity properties will generally depend on the type of physical process involved. This function is a static representation of a reduced-form process model of the type that is developed by physical and biological scientists to quantify environmental processes on a site-specific basis (Wagenet and Rao, 1990).

Note that z could also be interpreted as an indicator of health status. In this case $z(x, \omega)$ would be a health production function (see, e.g., Cropper and Freeman, 1991) and ω would represent the characteristics of an individual exposed to a health risk.

The economic model is based on the allocation of land and other inputs to maximize expected economic returns (which may be adjusted for risk attitudes in a more general presentation). Let a farmer manage the ith field of a^i acres that has environmental characteristics ω^i. The indicator δ^i is defined to be equal to 1 if the field is in crop production and equal to zero if the field is in a non-crop use (e.g., fallow, pasture, or conserving use). Crop production on the ith field, measured per unit area, is defined by the production function $q^i = q(x^i, \omega^i, \tau^i)$, where constant returns to scale are assumed and x^i is a vector of inputs measured per unit area. For simplicity, the production process with technology τ^i is represented as static and deterministic. If the crop is produced, the farmer's management problem is to maximize expected returns. The solution to this problem is represented by the profit function $\pi(p, \omega^i, \tau^i)$ and input demand functions $x(p, \omega^i, \tau^i) = \partial \pi(p, \omega^i, \tau^i)/\partial p^i$, where p is a vector of input prices normalized by the output price. Farmers allocate each field between crop and non-crop use at the beginning of each production period according to its highest valued use. Letting c^i be the return to the non-crop use, farmers make land-use decisions to solve:

$$\max_{\delta^i} \{\delta^i \pi(p, \omega^i, \tau^i) + (1-\delta^i)c^i\}.$$

The land-use decision is therefore a step function depending on the form $\delta^i = 1$ if $\pi^i > c^i$ and $\delta^i = 0$ otherwise, implying that the land allocation decision is a function of p, ω^i and c^i.

2.1.2 Deriving agriculture–environment tradeoffs

The model outlined in the previous section implies that the environmental impacts of agriculture are determined by two fundamental factors. First, farmers' land use decisions determine which parcels of land are in crop production. This decision determines the environmental characteristics of the land in production. Second, farmers' input use decisions on the land in production, combined with the land's environmental characteristics, determine the environmental outcomes z^i on each parcel of land. In other words, both the extensive margin decisions of farmers and the intensive margin decisions of farmers play a role in determining the location-specific environmental impacts of agricultural production.

The physical characteristics ω^i of fields are distributed in the population according to a distribution $f(\omega|\Omega)$, and production technologies are distributed according to $g(\tau|T)$. These distributions induce a joint distribution of input use, land use, crop production, and environmental impact through the input demand functions, the production function, and the physical process model.

Given the goals of balancing agricultural production against environmental impacts, the joint distribution of crop production and environmental impact is of particular interest. Using this joint distribution, two basic types of information can be obtained. First, it is possible to assess tradeoffs between crop production and environmental outcomes as prices are varied and physical characteristics of land in production and the production technology are held constant. Because these tradeoffs are derived from the underlying distribution of location-specific outcomes, the tradeoffs can be defined in terms of total production and environmental outcomes in a region, and also in terms of risk measures such as probability that an environmental outcome will exceed a critical value in the region. Note that this tradeoff relationship between crop output and environmental outcomes is a probabilistic analogue to the conventional production possibilities curve in economic theory. An example of such tradeoff relationships is presented in Figure 2.2.

Second, it is possible to estimate the shifts in the output–environment tradeoff that occurs when either the resource base (land attributes) or production technology change. This shift is analogous to a shift in the production possibilities frontier that occurs in response to changes in resource endowments or production technology.

Formally, for a given price vector p faced by all farmers in the region, output and environmental impact are jointly distributed random variables. For example, the mean crop output and mean environmental impact can be derived as:

$$\mu_q(p,\Omega,T) = \iint q(x(p,\omega,\tau),\omega,\tau)\, f(\omega|\Omega)\, g(\tau|T))\; d\omega d\tau$$

$$\mu_z(p,\Omega,T) = \iint z(x(p,\omega,\tau),\omega)\, f(\omega|\Omega)\, g(\tau|T)\; d\omega d\tau.$$

Under the assumption that q and z are increasing in x, it follows that changes in p induce changes in mean output and mean environmental impact so as to

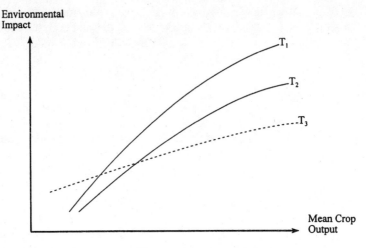

Environmental
Impact

Mean Crop
Output

Figure 2.2   Output–environment   tradeoffs   associated   with   alternative technologies

trace out a positive relationship between the two as in Figure 2.2. Moreover, a change in either the distribution of physical characteristics of land in the region (a change in Ω), or a change in the technology used in production (a change in T) will cause a shift in this tradeoff relationship. Figure 2.2 shows that a technology T_1 causes more environmental impact than technology T_2.

There may also be cases where a technology such as T_3 causes more impact at low output levels but less impact at high levels. Situations where these relationships cross over could occur, for example, with the use of different combinations of tillage and weed management systems. No-till systems used in the United States reduce soil erosion but increase pesticide use and potential for surface and groundwater contamination, especially where pesticide use rates are high, whereas conventional tillage systems rely more heavily on mechanical weed control. So if both erosion and chemical contamination were considered as environmental impacts, the total impact of no-till systems might be less at low output levels but might be more than conventional tillage systems at high levels of output.

Similar tradeoff relationships can be derived for measures of production or environmental risk that are generated by spatial or temporal variability. In many cases of environmental and human health impact, mean measures of impact are inadequate because the concern is to achieve a sufficiently low probability of an adverse outcome. For example, if z is increasing in x, then the probability distribution of z shifts in the positive direction as x increases, and the probability that z will exceed a critical value increases with x. Consequently, a positive tradeoff is observed between mean crop production and the probability that environmental impact exceeds the critical level. This means that we could also interpret the vertical axis in Figure 2.2 as measuring the risk that an environmental impact exceeds a critical value.

2.1.3 Dynamic considerations

The preceding derivation of tradeoffs is presented in static terms. But in the analysis of sustainability of agricultural production systems, long-run dynamics of the system are often the critical concern. The preceding model can be cast in dynamic terms, for example as in Antle (1996). Here we simply note that in cases such as the long-term sustainability of the soil resource, the physical characteristics of land in the region represented by Ω may evolve over time as a function of farmers' land use and management decisions. Also climate change may impact Ω over long periods of time. By explicitly incorporating these dynamic elements into the model, the long-term issues of sustaining productivity and environmental quality can be addressed.

Important temporal variability can occur within a growing season of a crop. In the case of pest management, for example, farmers apply pesticides at points in time to manage the risk of pest damage. These intra seasonal dynamics determine when and to what extent farmers apply pesticides and thus have an important influence on environmental impacts. These intra seasonal dynamics are the focus of the analysis of pesticide use in the potato-pasture system discussed in the remainder of this chapter.

2.1.4 Integrated simulation models for construction of tradeoffs

To construct tradeoffs like the ones illustrated in Figure 2.2, integrated economic–environment–health simulation models can be constructed utilizing various disciplinary models. The key feature of the modelling approach being proposed is that it is based on a statistical representation of the relevant populations of production units, environmental units, and exposed groups of humans. By sampling from these populations and simulating impacts at the disaggregate level, economic, environmental and health outcomes can be accurately represented while accounting for the spatial and temporal heterogeneity in the populations. The outcomes can then be aggregated in a statistically representative manner to construct tradeoffs for the population as a whole. As in Figure 2.2, these tradeoffs can be defined in terms of total or average outcomes, or in terms of other distributional characteristics. The structure of one such integrated model, corresponding to the Ecuador case study discussed below, is presented in Figure 2.3. A policy or technology scenario – e.g., alternative pesticide prices or pest management technologies – is input into the economic model described in the preceding section (Figure 2.1). The economic model generates three types of output that are used subsequently. First, pesticide

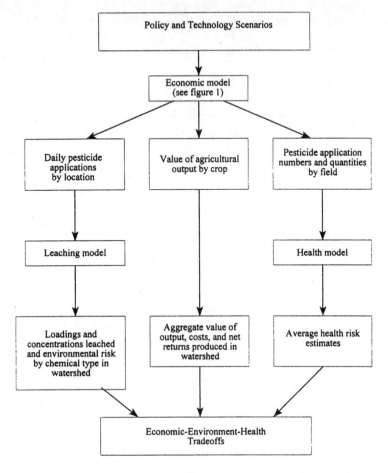

Figure 2.3   An integrated simulation model for tradeoff analysis

applications are generated on a daily time step, by agroecological zone, to be input into the pesticide leaching model. A pesticide leaching model generates outputs in the form of loadings into the environment (the total mass leached into groundwater), water concentrations leached below the root zone, and estimates of the risk of loadings or concentrations exceeding critical values. Second, the value of agricultural output by field is output so that it can be aggregated for policy analysis. Third, numbers of quantities of pesticide applications by field are generated to be used in the health simulations that are based on the analysis of the health data at the farm level. The health simulations generate estimates of the effect of pesticide exposure on the farm population. The last step in the simulation model aggregates the economic, environmental and health outcomes to the watershed level and constructs tradeoff relationships.

2.2 An integrated economic–environment–health simulation model: the impacts of pesticides in the Andean potato-pasture production system

In this section we illustrate the implementation of the framework described in the preceding section with an integrated economic–environment–health simulation model constructed to assess tradeoffs for the potato-pasture production system in the Andean highland of Ecuador. For a detailed presentation of this study, see Crissman, Antle and Capalbo (1998). Several factors make the economic, environmental and health tradeoffs potentially important in this setting. The equatorial climate exhibits little seasonality so potato production is continuous. Potato production is management intensive, and there are as many as 20 distinct operations during the six-month crop cycle. In economic terms, potato production is a high-value, high-risk crop for farmers, with much of the production risk associated with important crop pests. The late blight fungus (*Phytophthora infestans*) is the principal disease and the tuber boring Andean weevil (*Premnotrypes vorax*) and several foliage damaging insects are the principal insect pests affecting production. The control of these three threats requires distinct strategies relying primarily on chemical pesticides. Late blight can be a devastating disease where in a susceptible variety entire fields can be destroyed overnight. Farmers apply as many as 12 applications of fungicides and 12 applications of insecticides during the growing season. Combined with the continuous production of the crop, the potential for both environmental and human health risk is potentially high.

We now provide an overview of each component of the integrated simulation model that was constructed.

2.2.1 The economic model

The economic component of the simulation model is composed of four main steps, following the model structure presented in Figure 2.1:

Initialization. Physical characteristics of the field are drawn from empirical distributions estimated with the sample data (field size, agroecological zone representing soil and moisture characteristics, elevation, day of the year when the production cycle begins). At the beginning of each production cycle for each field, a set of prices is sampled from empirical price distributions.

Extensive margin decisions. For each field for each production cycle, a land use decision is made based on the comparison of net returns to the two competing uses (potato and pasture). These net returns distributions are based on econometric estimation of Cobb–Douglas revenue and cost functions. When more than one potato crop is produced on a field without being rotated with pasture, the net returns distribution for potatoes is adjusted downward to reflect pest build-up and diminished soil productivity.

Intensive margin decisions. When potato production is selected as the crop activity, a sequence of pesticide application decisions is selected. For this purpose pesticides are classified as fungicides, insecticides used to treat the Andean weevil, and insecticides used to treat foliage pests. For each type of pesticide, a pair of reduced-form, dynamic factor demand equations representing both the quantity and timing of pesticide applications was estimated econometrically, following the procedures described in Antle, Capalbo and Crissman (1994). This econometric model is unique in that it represents both the quantity of an input decision as well as the time intervals between application decisions. The application time can then be expressed as the number of days after crop planting. This information is needed as input into the physical process models that estimate environmental impact, because the timing of application decisions in relation to rainfall plays an important role in determining the environmental impact.

Output realization. At the end of the production cycle, the input realizations are combined with other data generated about the production process to estimate the value of crop production on the field. An econometrically estimated Cobb–Douglas restricted revenue function and cost function are used to estimate the value of output, cost and net returns.

2.2.2 The environmental model

Based on field observations in the study watersheds, the environmental science members of the research team concluded that the principal environmental impact of pesticide use would be through leaching of pesticide through the root zone into groundwater and through return flows of groundwater to surface water. The LEACHA simulations model (Hutson and Wagenet, 1993) was parameterized with data measurements made in each of the four agroecological zones in the study area to represent both the mass of chemical leached below the crop root zone and the chemical concentration in water leaving the crop root zone. The simulations were run using historical weather data that was collected at weather stations in the area.

To facilitate integration of the economic and physical simulations models, a statistical meta-model was estimated to represent the simulation outcomes of the LEACHA model runs. The LEACHA model was executed multiple times for each month of the year for each agroecological zone, for standardized applications of each type of pesticide. The distributions of the leaching outcomes were found to be highly skewed, with many observations at or near zero but also with a long positive tail. This distribution was estimated using Heckman's two-stage econometric procedure for censored distributions, by defining a cut-off point below which all observations were interpreted to be effectively equal to zero. All observations above the cut-off were interpreted as representing positive outcomes. Following the Heckman procedure, the probit technique was used to estimate the probability that a positive amount of leaching occurred, as a function of location (agroecological zone) and month of year (a proxy for weather, particularly rainfall). The second stage of the Heckman procedure was used to estimate a regression relating the quantity of leaching to weather and physical characteristics, corrected with the Mill's ratio for the probability of zero leaching.

These two equations from the Heckman procedure were used to represent the leaching process in the physical model component of the simulation model. Output from the economic model indicating the date and the quantity of pesticide applied was input into the physical simulation model. The physical simulation model then determined, for each field and for each pesticide application, whether a positive leaching event occurred, and if so, how much pesticide mass and what concentration of pesticide leached beyond the root zone.

2.2.3 The health model

To examine the health impacts of this pesticide use, the health research team conducted a survey of the farm population and an age- and education-matched referent group not exposed to pesticides. All participants answered questions on pesticide use and medical problems, received a clinical examination by a field physician, completed a series of tests of nervous system function and underwent blood tests. These tests were oriented towards those effects most likely to be associated with the insecticide and fungicide exposures that the agricultural team had documented. Crissman, Cole and Carpio (1994) report on the higher rates of skin problems (dermatitis), reduced vibration sensation, lower cholinesterase levels and generally poorer neuro-behavioural test results among the farm population compared to the referent group.

Preliminary analyses revealed that the neuro-behavioural tests demonstrated the most consistent relationship with recent use of pesticides within the farm population. Neuro-behavioural tests were chosen because psychiatric literature indicated problems among those with chronic exposure to organophosphate compounds, epidemiological work has documented central nervous system effects of acute poisoning episodes and assessments of neuro-behavioural function are sensitive measures of such problems in non-clinical populations. Standardized neuro-behavioural scores for the farm population were significantly lower than those of the referent non-farming population, taking account of differences in age, education and verbal intelligence level. The mean standardized score was almost one standard deviation less than the population not directly exposed to pesticides and substantially lower than that currently observable in other working populations exposed to neuro-toxic substances. The mean minimums for the various functions were over three standard deviations lower, indicating substantial, clinically important deficits in the basic cognitive tasks. Such levels of dysfunction would correlate with considerable difficulties carrying out the daily tasks of running a household and making rational decisions in farm management and would be comparable to the levels found in the neuro-cognitively impaired on disability pensions. The quality of home and working life of these farm members would thus be expected to be substantially reduced.

The health component of the simulation model is based on an econometrically estimated health production function that specifies health (measured as an individual's mean neuro-behavioural score) as a function of the total number of applications and total quantity applied of neuro-toxic substances that the individual was exposed to, the total quantity of potatoes consumed by the individual during the period (to control for possible exposure through the consumption of potatoes by farm workers), and the individual's verbal intelligence scores (to control for individual differences in neuro-behavioural function not associated with pesticide use). In the simulations, the intelligence scores are set at sample means, so the results can be interpreted as the variations in neuro-behavioural health explained by variations in exposure to pesticides. The estimates of the health production function indicated that pesticide use was statistically significant in explaining the neuro-behavioural health of the farm population.

2.2.4 Economic, environmental and health tradeoffs

Using the simulation model described above, tradeoffs between economic, environmental and health outcomes were generated by varying output and input prices. Tradeoff relationships were generated to test hypotheses about the properties of the tradeoff relationships of the observed technology, as well as to quantify the effects of some alternative technology scenarios. Here we will summarize a few of the findings of that study to illustrate some key aspects of the approach.

Figure 2.4 presents the results of simulations designed to generate tradeoffs between agricultural output and environmental impacts. In the Figure, each data point represents the aggregate outcome from a set of fields simulated to represent the physical and economic populations in the Carchi region. For each technology and price setting, the simulation was replicated 30 times. To generate output/environment tradeoffs, pesticide prices were varied from the base case (observed prices) to 90 per cent above the base prices, and the potato crop price was increased from the base case to 90 per cent above the base. The Figure shows the outcomes for the tradeoff between crop production and the total mass of an important insecticide, carbofuran, leached below the crop root zone from the carbofuran applications made during the production process. Note that the resulting tradeoff has a positive slope as illustrated in Figure 2.2. The Figure also shows that the dispersion of the leaching events increases as the output level increases, demonstrating that the risk of environmental impact increases as the

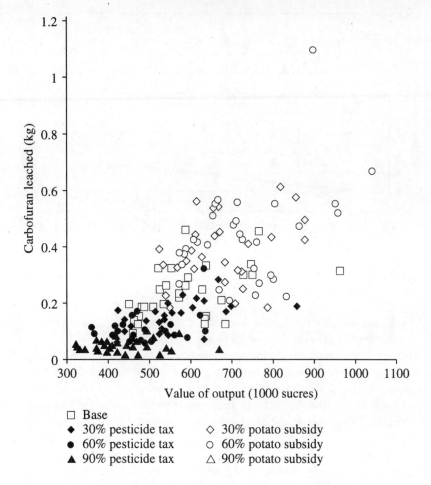

Figure 2.4   *Output–leaching tradeoff in an Ecuadorian study*

output level increases. This finding means that a simple mean tradeoff relationship (e.g., a line fit through the points in the Figure) would be an incomplete representation of the distribution of potential environmental impacts.

Figure 2.5 shows the output-leaching tradeoffs by the four agroecological zones represented in the data. The key result here is that Zone 4, the highest and wettest one in the watershed, exhibits much higher vulnerability than the other zones. Note that a representative farm model parameterized on one of the 'representative' zones, such as zone 2, would miss the key source of environmental vulnerability in zone 4.

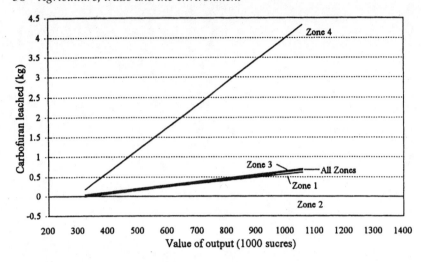

Figure 2.5   Carbofuran leaching–output tradeoffs for agroecological zones in an Andean study

2.3   Economic–environmental tradeoffs of dryland agriculture in the Northern Plains of the United States

In this section we illustrate the integrated framework on a scale of analysis that encompasses more than one watershed area. The setting is the dryland cropping agricultural system which is characteristic of the Northern Great Plains area of the United States. The study covers three sites in the eastern half of Montana: Northeast Montana (NE), the Southern Triangle area (ST), and the Northern Triangle area (NT). The latter two areas are part of what is commonly referred to as Montana's Golden Triangle, because of the productivity and the importance of grains to the region's economy. For purposes of discussion we will focus only on two areas, the NE and the ST, and make comparisons with respect to the economic and environmental tradeoffs associated with different production technologies and different physical and climatic conditions. A more complete description of the study is found in Antle *et al.* (1995).

The predominant crops grown in the areas are winter and spring wheat, barley, other minor grain crops and fallow. Winter wheat and spring wheat production is generally more profitable than barley production in Montana. Based on the relative ranking of the returns for wheat and barley, producers tend to plant wheat to the limiting constraint of the available fallow land or commodity programme acreage allowance. If wheat base remains after planting to the fallowed acres, the producer will typically plant a crop of wheat into stubble, i.e. re-crop. After enough acreage has been planted to wheat to the extent of available wheat base, producers will fill their barley base utilizing remaining fallow, if any, then planting the remainder of their barley onto re-crop acres. In dry years, producers may reduce the amount of re-crop areas that are planted.

In Montana, some farmers have been experimenting with dryland legume/cereal grain rotations. Other alternative dryland crops currently being grown in Montana include safflower and canola.

For this study we have modelled dryland crop production as involving one of three types of land use intensities. These three categories of land use intensities can be viewed as points on a spectrum of possible intensities. At one extreme is the 50/50 crop/fallow system. The 50 per cent crop and the 50 per cent fallow system has a crop planted on a field in alternate years. At the other extreme of the land use spectrum lies continuous cropping. In continuous cropping systems, one crop follows another without an intervening fallow period. For these two cropping systems, explicit consideration of plant-available soil moisture or expected growing season precipitation is not included in the planting decision rule.

The third category of land use intensities that we modelled is referred to as a flexible cropping system. Under this system the decision to re-crop or fallow is based on available soil moisture prior to the planting date and an evaluation of expected growing season precipitation (government programme constraints, e.g. Acreage Reduction Programme acres and programme crop base acres, are also considered in the crop acreage allocation decisions made by the producers). Through time, there will be fallow under a flexible cropping system, but the expected percentage of the fallow would be less than 50 per cent of the total tillable acres. Thus, the flexible cropping system represents the spectrum of cropping intensities that lie between the 50/50 crop/fallow system and continuous cropping and is perhaps most depictive of management decisions.

Each of the cropping systems can utilize one of the 'generic' categories of tillage for the acreage that is fallowed. The *mechanical tillage* method relies on farm implements to control weeds on the fallowed land and to prepare the seed-bed. In most cases, mechanical tillage results in the least amount of surface residue when compared to the other categories of tillage methods. *Minimum tillage* methods use a combination of herbicides and mechanical tillage to control weeds and, generally, increases the residue on the soil surface thereby reducing soil erosion. *No-till tillage* methods employ a more significant level of herbicide use in an attempt to eliminate mechanical tillage passes for the purposes of weed control and seed-bed preparation.

In the discussions of the environmental and economic tradeoffs we will focus primarily on the flexible cropping system under two tillages, minimum tillage and mechanical tillage, since these technologies are most representative of farms in the region. Each tillage practice implies different chemical applications and different amounts of soil disturbance, thus providing a tradeoff among the environmental indicators of erosion, leaching, and runoff.

2.3.1 Model overview

The simulation model developed for this study is basically what we refer to as a Level I simulation model. In a Level I model the economic and physical models are simulated independently, and then the outputs from both models are combined to infer environmental impacts. This type of model integration is compatible with certain types of physical conditions, such as chemical leaching, where the physical processes do not feed back to affect production decisions in future periods.

For the Great Plains study, the Level I characterization is not quite correct, since some of the environmental impacts would feed back into future management decisions, such as the residual moisture content that is influenced by tillage as well as other factors. However, the complexity of the physical model that was used in this study did not, to date, lend itself to dynamic, period by period feedback. The only feedback that we have incorporated is to utilize the estimated yields that are output from the physical simulation model into the net revenues calculations.

2.3.2 Physical model

The Erosion-Productivity Impact Calculator (EPIC) model is a continuous simulation model, developed by the US Department of Agriculture, that is used to determine the effects of management strategies on agricultural production and soil and water resources. The major components in EPIC are weather simulation, hydrology, erosion-sedimentation, nutrient cycling, pesticide fate, plant growth, soil temperature, tillage, and plant environment control.

Each of the rotation/tillage systems analysed in the study was simulated thirty times by EPIC for a thirty-year production period. For each system analysed, an observation for a given EPIC environmental output variable consisted of the mean of the annual output values for the given variable computed over the thirty-year simulation period. Crop yield observations for a given production system were computed as the mean annual yield for those years that the given crop was produced in the thirty-year simulation period.

The EPIC model outputs numerous environmental variables along with the estimates of annual yields. These environmental variables include measures of water and wind erosion, pesticide and nitrate movement through various surface levels, leaching of chemicals through the root zone, and so on. In section 2.3.4 we will discuss two environmental measures from EPIC, soil erosion as measured by the universal soil loss equation (USLE), and nitrate movement through the subsurface layer (SSFN).

2.3.3 Economic model

The economic component for this study is far less sophisticated than the model developed for the Ecuador study. This was in part dictated by the nature of the data collected for the farmers in the Great Plains area. The data are not representative in any statistical sense of farmers in these areas. The data were collected from a non-random survey of 22 farmers. Current efforts are underway to expand the sample to over 600 farmers.

For each area, individual crop budgets were developed for all cropping systems and for each tillage method. The information in the budgets was based on discussions with the 22 farmers included in the survey and combined with economic information developed by economic specialists.

Net revenue calculations were based on 1993 input and output prices, and based on the EPIC estimates of yields. A net revenue calculation was made for each crop produced in the given crop production system at the end of each thirty-year period. Since each production system was simulated thirty times, the net revenue variable is also an average of the 30 thirty-year simulations. In general we found that for a given level of fertilizer use, net returns across tillage/cropping practices are approximately the same for a given area. Thus there is no *a priori* basis to prefer one tillage/rotation over another. A similar pattern emerges when we decrease the fertilizer usage to approximately 50 per cent of current levels: net returns are not discernibly different among the tillage/rotation methods.

2.3.4 Environmental – net returns tradeoffs

The environmental–net returns tradeoffs that we discuss in this section are with respect to two environmental indicators: USLE (soil loss), and mineral nitrate loss in the subsurface flow (SSFN). The mean values and standard deviations for other environmental variables can be found in Antle *et al.* (1995). Based on the information we have available, there is no defensible way to aggregate the environmental indicators into a single index of environmental damage, and thus the tradeoffs are presented in terms of each indicator.

Figure 2.6 presents the tradeoff between USLE and net returns for the flexible cropping system for both minimum tillage and mechanical tillage practices in the NE area. Each technology tradeoff relationship was based on the mean values for both the environmental indicator and net returns as discussed above. With reduced fertilizer use we observe a reduction in the mean net returns for both technologies. However, as fertilizer use declines, there is an increase in the USLE within tillage practices.

Figure 2.7 represents the tradeoff between SSFN and net returns also for the NE area. The general conclusion reached here is the opposite from the USLE case: as fertilizer use falls, there are decreases in the mean amount of mineral N loss in subsurface flows. This can be explained by thinking of the amount

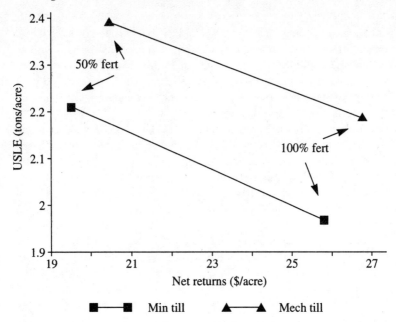

Figure 2.6   USLE vs net returns for Northeast MT

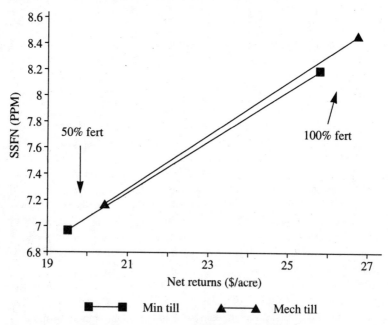

Figure 2.7   SSFN vs net returns for Northeast MT

of mineral N remaining in the soil as a function of the amount applied and the amount used by the plant. At lower fertilizer levels, there is a lower biomass which implies a lower usage of mineral N, but at the same time there is less applied. In a comparative sense, the EPIC model is indicating that the high fertilizer use, and thus higher biomass, is associated with increased amounts of mineral N loss; the higher fertilizer applications more than offset the increased usage of mineral N by the plants, and thus we obtain more potential environmental damage.

A similar set of tradeoffs are shown in Figures 2.8 and 2.9 for the ST area of the study. Once again the direction of change in the environmental indicators depends upon the specific indicator.

One last set of comparisons can be made by examining the USLE/Net returns tradeoffs in the NE and ST areas (Figures 2.6 and 2.8). It appears that the environmental benefits in the ST of reducing fertilizer use as measured by the USLE are less relative to the NE area. In general this can be explained by the productivity of the soil and the more favourable moisture conditions. Sites with poorer and drier soil may realize larger environmental benefits associated with reduced tillage.

Finally, the tradeoffs presented in this section are meant to be illustrative of the types of analyses that an integrated economic and physical simulation model can provide. Much research remains to be done on improving the data and model integration before these results can be meaningful in a policy setting.

2.4   Aggregate analysis of economic–environment tradeoffs

The preceding case studies illustrate how it is possible to generate valid tradeoffs between economic and environmental outcomes at the watershed or regional level. Ultimately, however, most policy analyses related to competitiveness, domestic agricultural policy and trade policy, are focused at the national level. There have been some attempts to link changes in domestic or trade policies to changes in aggregate input use, and to draw inferences about environmental impact (e.g., Anderson, 1994). However, Antle and Just's (1991) analysis of the interaction between agricultural and environmental policies demonstrates that existing agricultural and environmental policies can have either positive or negative effects on nonpoint source pollution, and that to infer an aggregate effect requires data that does not currently exist in most cases. Antle *et al.* (1994, p. 1) extend this point to the context of trade policy:

> Will the movement towards trade and domestic policy liberalization in agriculture lead to environmental degradation? The location-specific nature of the interactions between agricultural production and the environment, and the changes in the intensity and location of production brought about by policy liberalization, suggest that the answer to this question is to be found in careful empirical research, not in stylized generalities.

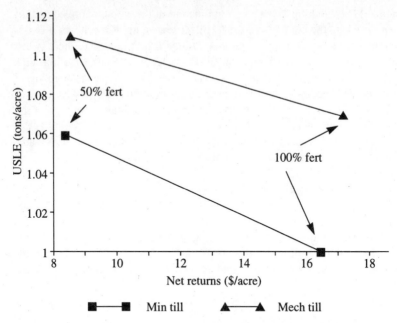

Figure 2.8   USLE vs net returns for the Southern Triangle of MT

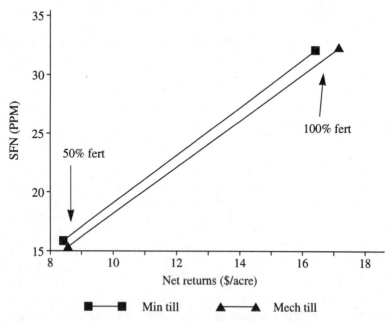

Figure 2.9   SSFN vs net returns for the Southern Triangle of MT

As the Andean and Northern Plains case studies illustrate, disaggregate analysis of the relationship between agricultural production and environmental quality can generate a large amount of detailed information, too much information to be comprehended and used in aggregate policy analysis. The aggregation of the detailed, disaggregate data into a transformation frontier provides a means to summarize the disaggregate data in a form that is valid from the point of view of the underlying scientific disciplines and also intuitively appealing to policy analysts. But as we aggregate to regional and national levels of analysis, we cannot take prices as exogenous to the analysis. We clearly need to integrate the environmental impact analysis into a partial or general equilibrium framework. In addition, as the scale of analysis is increased, the list of environmental impacts to be considered becomes longer, making aggregation increasingly problematic.

To illustrate the various issues that arise in attempting to bridge the gap between disaggregate and aggregate analyses, we consider here the approach being taken by the OECD to conduct national analyses of the environmental impacts of policy change. The OECD approach is based on the construction of aggregate 'environmental indicators'. We first discuss the approach proposed by the OECD, and then contrast it with the disaggregate approach described earlier in this chapter.

The OECD (1994) proposed a set of 18 agri-environmental indicators (AEIs) for collection by OECD countries, representing:

1. Indicators of agricultural trends of environmental significance:
   a. input use;
   b. productivity and efficiency;
   c. management practices.
2. Indicators of the impacts of agriculture on the environment:
   a. soil, water, and air;
   b. biodiversity;
   c. landscape.
3. Indicators of agricultural and environmental policy and market interactions:
   a. trends in agricultural price relationships;
   b. public expenditure on agri-environmental measures;
   c. quantifying the links between environmental impacts and agricultural policies.

As noted in that report, '...the key question is, what is the effect of change in policy measures on the environment in agriculture?' We now consider how the proposed indicators can be used to quantify the impact of policy on environmental quality.

2.4.1 Using agri-environmental indicators to measure the effects of policy change

Suppose that the goal of policy is to increase societal well-being measured as an index $W(Z,Q)$ where Z is a vector of measures of environmental impact and Q is aggregate output. Suppose further that we can define aggregate functions for land use and input use $X(S,\psi)$, aggregate production $Q(X,S)$, and environmental quality $Z(X,S)$, where S represents all of the fixed factors such as land characteristics, climate, prices, etc, and ψ is a policy parameter. We can write a change in social welfare associated with a policy change as

$$\Delta W = \{\Sigma_j \, (\partial W/\partial Z^j)(\partial Z^j/\partial X)(\partial X/\partial \psi) + W_Q Q_X X_\psi\}\Delta \psi.$$

The first set of terms on the right-hand side represent the value of the environmental change associated with the policy change. Each of these terms is made up of three components: the change in land use and input use induced by the policy change $(\partial X/\partial \psi)$; the environmental change caused by the change in land use and input use $(\partial Z/\partial X)$; and the marginal social value of the environmental change $(\partial W/\partial Z)$. The information available to the OECD will not permit valuation of environmental impacts (the terms $\partial W/\partial Z$ in the above expression are not available) so it will not be possible to construct a single aggregate indicator of environmental impact based on social valuation of impacts. At best it is possible with the available data to measure the changes in the physical environment caused by policy change, i.e., the terms $\partial Z/\partial \psi$.

Recall from the preceding discussion, the aggregate environmental impact indicators are functions $Z(X,S)$, where X represents the inputs into the production process, including input use and patterns of land use, and the state variables S are land characteristics, prices, technology, and farm characteristics. Therefore the observed changes in environmental indicators over time are:

$$dZ^j/dt = (\partial Z^j/\partial X)(\partial X/\psi)(d\psi/dt)$$

change in environmental indicator effects of policy change on input use

$$+ \{(\partial Z^j/\partial X)(\partial X/\partial S) + (\partial Z^j/\partial S)\}(dS/dt)$$
effects of changes in state variables

Thus, the change in an environmental indicator over time can be decomposed into several parts:

1. the effect of policy change on input use, which is equal to the product of:
   a. the effect of input use on environmental quality $(\partial Z^j/\partial X)$;
   b. the effect of policy change on aggregate input use $(\partial X/\partial \psi)$; and,
   c. the change in policy, $d\psi/dt$.

2. the effect of changes in state variables on input use, equal to the product of:
   a. the effect of input use on environmental quality $(\partial Z^i/\partial X)$;
   b. the effect of state variables on input use $(\partial X/\partial S)$; and,
   c. the change in state variables, dS/dt.
3. the effect of changes in state variables on the aggregate environmental impact function, equal to the product of:
   a. the effect of changes in state variables on the aggregate environmental quality function $(\partial Z^i/\partial S)$; and,
   b. the change in state variables (due to changes in policy or other factors), dS/dt.

This analysis shows that there are two possible approaches to the measurement of the effect of policy change on environmental quality. One approach is to measure the total change in environmental quality over time, dZ^i/dt, and the effects of changes in state variables on environmental quality, and then to infer the policy change effect as a residual. The difficulty with this approach is that all of the components of S must be identified, and their changes and their effects on input use and on environmental impact must be quantified.

The other approach to measure the effect of policy on environmental quality is to measure the terms $(\partial Z^i/\partial X)$, $(\partial X/\partial \psi)$ and $(d\psi/dt)$. The proposed OECD AEIs include measurements of X, Z^i, and ψ over time, hence it is possible to determine $(d\psi/dt)$ but not $(\partial Z^i/\partial X)$ or $(\partial X/\partial \psi)$. Changes in input use attributable to policy change, $(\partial X/\partial \psi)$, could be estimated using estimates of input demand equations available in the literature and the values of X and ψ collected as part of the AEIs. The effects of input changes on environmental quality, $(\partial Z^i/\partial X)$, is the most difficult component to quantify. As noted earlier in this chapter, environmental scientists generally have not constructed estimates of this type of aggregate impact relationship, although work is moving in that direction in the environmental sciences. However, in many countries field-level studies have been conducted, and it would be possible to construct an estimate of this term using available data. This point is elaborated in the example discussed below.

In summary, it can be concluded that the aggregate effects of policy change on environmental quality can be estimated using the OECD's proposed AEIs, if they are supplemented with the information needed to estimate the effects of policy change on input use, and with estimates of parameters relating changes in environmental quality to changes in aggregate input use and land use.

2.4.2 A water quality example

We illustrate the preceding discussion with the following example. Consider the use of the AEI data to quantify the impact of policy liberalization on contamination of groundwater with the insecticide carbofuran discussed in the Andean study. Let ΔL measure the change in total mass of carbofuran that leaches below the root zone in the region, and define environmental quality change as $\Delta Z = -\Delta L$. The policy liberalization is assumed to have occurred at time t_1. Prior to the liberalization, policies had the effect of encouraging the production of subsidized crops that required carbofuran as an input, and also had the effect of intensifying carbofuran use on those crops. Thus, up to time t_1 groundwater quality was progressively declining, but after liberalization carbofuran use declined and leaching of carbofuran was reduced.

Our challenge is to utilize the AEIs to infer the effects of the policy liberalization on groundwater quality. In this example, the data available from the AEIs would be time series of measurements of groundwater quality and pesticide use, prices, and information about the changes in policy. This data would be sufficient to know the total changes in insecticide use and the total changes in water quality from time t_1 to some subsequent time t_2. Under the assumption that no other factors affecting pesticide use or their environmental impacts had changed from t_1 to t_2 it would be possible to infer that the policy liberalization reduced carbofuran use by the amount $\Delta X = X_2 - X_1 < 0$, reduced leaching by the amount $\Delta L = L_2 - L_1 < 0$, and thus improved environmental quality by the amount $\Delta Z = -\Delta L > 0$. But unless all other factors affecting leaching remained the same over the period t_1 to t_2, the observed change in leaching could not be attributed only to policy change. Therefore, it is generally necessary to estimate the component of environmental change attributable to policy change in the manner outlined in the preceding section.

In our example of carbofuran leaching, let policy liberalization result in a percentage change p in the price of the crop on which carbofuran is used (assume a single crop for simplicity). Letting the output price elasticity of carbofuran demand be θ, it follows that the policy-induced change in input use relative to input use at the time of policy liberalization is $\Delta X = X_1 \theta p$.

The term $\partial Z/\partial X = -\partial L/\partial X$ measures the effect of changes in aggregate input use on the mass of carbofuran leached. This term can be estimated using available information on carbofuran leaching by soil type and climate. Dividing crop production regions into $I = 1,...,n$ soil/climate classes, existing physical models can be used to estimate the average fraction of carbofuran predicted to leach below the root zone in each land class. Define this fraction as r_i, and defining the share of land area in each soil/climate class as $a_i = A_i/A$, where capitals represent total land in each class and in the region. Under these assumptions, the marginal impact of a change in pesticide use on water quality can be estimated as $\partial L/\partial X = \Sigma_I r_i a_i = r$. Under the additional assumption that input use changes by $\Delta X/A$ on each hectare of land in production, the change in environmental quality induced by a change in carbofuran use is

$$\Delta Z = A(-\partial L/\partial X)(\Delta X/A) = -r(\Delta X) = -rX_1 \theta p.$$

This example shows that the set of indicators proposed by the OECD is not adequate to support analysis of environmental impacts of policy change because parameters such as r, θ and p are not typically included in the indicator data that is collected by the OECD or other governmental organizations.

2.4.3 Implications for aggregate environmental impact assessments

The preceding discussion leads us to several conclusions and implications for the construction of aggregate environmental impact analyses designed to be integrated with aggregate economic analyses in order to develop aggregate tradeoff relationships.

A first general observation is that disaggregate analyses are data intensive and thus costly, consequently there will be attempts to construct and use summary statistics (aggregate environmental indicators) in aggregate analyses. Generally, the data are not available to construct aggregate environmental indicators that reflect social valuations derived from valuation studies, and hence will necessarily be *ad hoc*. At the present time, available data will permit certain physical impacts to be quantified, and even then, adequate data may not exist to quantify impacts at the disaggregate level and then aggregate them to the national level. Thus, researchers will invariably resort to using environmental indicators constructed with available data. Until such indicators are in some way validated by showing that they correlate in a meaningful way with estimates of environmental impact derived from disaggregate data, these types of analysis will have to be viewed with some scepticism.

An important implication of the theoretical derivation of agriculture–environment tradeoffs in section 2.1.2 is that aggregate economic and environmental outcomes are functions of the underlying distributions of physical, climatic, technology, and other 'state variables' that define an individual economic agent's decisions. To the extent that these state variables themselves may change over time and space, aggregate outcomes cannot be viewed as stable functions of aggregate variables. In particular, large changes in policy will cause significant changes in economic behaviour of farmers, in land use, and in the environmental impacts of agricultural activities over time. For example, a significant change in the subsidy policy for a crop could result in significant changes in factor demand elasticities, as well as changes in the location of production that would change the relationship between pesticide use and groundwater quality. Use of parameters estimated under a subsidy regime to predict environmental impacts of a policy liberalization could result in highly inaccurate predictions of the environmental effects of liberalization.

Analysts are tempted to use annual time series on aggregate input quantities and environmental quality indicators as indicators of the environmental effects of policy change. The analysis of section 2.4.1 shows that only under the implausible assumption that the state variables (prices, technology, farm characteristics, policy) are constant is it possible to infer that observed aggregate changes over time in environmental quality are attributable to observed changes in agricultural practices such as aggregate input use.

Another concern is that changes in aggregate input quantities may be misused to infer changes in environmental quality over time and to infer differences in environmental quality across regions or countries. Each country has different relationships between agricultural activity and environmental quality, and therefore it is not valid to infer differences in environmental quality across countries from differences in agricultural input use.

2.5   Conclusions

We conclude by observing that the state of the art in quantifying economic–environment tradeoffs involves the integration of models and data from the relevant disciplines at a disaggregate level, and the aggregation of the resulting measurements to the level appropriate for policy analysis. While in principle these methods can be used to assess the environmental impacts of any domestic or trade policy, the problem we currently face in using these methods is that adequate data does not exist to conduct disaggregate analyses across the entire landscape of most countries. Hence there remains a gap between the demand for information about environmental impacts at the national level and our capability to deliver scientifically sound estimates of such impacts.

We conclude that the solution to this problem is for each country or region where such analyses are needed to follow a systematic approach to filling the existing data gaps. We see great potential for the development of geographic information systems to remedy the current data limitations. Nevertheless, for the foreseeable future, the data demands will far outstrip our data resources for agricultural–environmental policy analysis. Based on experience working on these challenges, we offer the following principles to facilitate the development of data suitable to support policy analysis:

1. Specific, feasible goals for use of the agri-environmental indicators must be set before the indicators are collected.
2. Data collection must be based on a coherent theoretical framework of the process through which policy change causes environmental change. This theoretical framework must be consistent with the economic processes governing farmer behaviour and the biophysical processes governing environmental change.
3. The choice of economic and environmental data to be included in a set of aggregate indicators must be guided by scientific and policy analysis requirements for meeting policy analysis goals. The indicator set must

include information needed to estimate the impacts of policy on land use and management practices that affect environmental quality, and information needed to estimate the impacts of land use and management practices on environmental quality.

References

Anderson, K. (1994), 'On measuring the environmental impact of liberalizing agricultural trade'. Paper presented at the International Agricultural Trade Research Consortium meetings, Toronto, June, in M. Bredhal and T. Roe (eds), *Agricultural Trade and the Environment: Understanding and Measuring the Critical Linkages*, University of Minnesota Press.

Antle, J.M. (1996), 'Methodological issues in assessing potential impacts of climate change on agriculture', *Agricultural and Forest Meteorology*, **80**, 67–85.

Antle, J.M. and R.E. Just (1991), 'Effects of commodity program structure on resource use and the environment', in N. Bockstael and R.E. Just (eds), *Commodity and Resource Policy in Agricultural Systems*, New York: Springer-Verlag, pp. 97–127.

Antle, J.M., S.M. Capalbo and C.C. Crissman (1994), 'Econometric production models with endogenous input timing: An application to Ecuadorian potato production', *Journal of Agricultural and Resource Economics*, **19**, July, 1–18.

Antle, J.M., S.M. Capalbo, J.B. Johnson and W.E. Zidack (1995), 'Economics and Sustainability of Crop and Livestock Agriculture in the Northern Plains and Foothill Mountain Environments', unpublished report to US Department of Agriculture, Montana State University, December.

Antle, J.M. C.C. Crissman, J. Hutson and R.J. Wagenet (1996), 'Empirical foundations of environment – trade linkages: evidence from an Andean study', in M.E. Bredahl, N. Gallagher, J.C. Dunmore and T.L. Roe (eds), *Agricultural Trade and the Environment: Understanding and Measuring the Critical Linkages*, Boulder, CO: Westview Press.

Bouma, J., A. Kuyvenhoven, B.A.M. Bouman, J.C. Luyten and H.G. Zandstra (1995), *Eco-Regional Approaches for Sustainable Land Use and Food Production*, Kluwer Academic Publishers in cooperation with International Potato Centre, Dordrecht, The Netherlands.

Crissman, C.C., J.M. Antle and S.M. Capalbo (eds) (1998), *Economic, Environmental, and Heath Tradeoffs in Agriculture: Pesticides and the Sustainability of Andean Potato Production*, Boston: Kluwer Academic Publishers.

Crissman, C.C., D.C. Cole and F. Carpio (1994), 'Pesticide use and farm worker health in Ecuadorian potato production', *American Journal of Agricultural Economics*, **76**, August, 593–7.

Cropper, M.L. and A.M. Freeman, III (1991), 'Environmental health effects' in J.B. Braden and C.D. Kolstad (eds), *Measuring the Demand for Environmental Quality*, Amsterdam: North-Holland.

Hutson, J.L. and R.J. Wagenet (1993), 'A Pragmatic field-scale approach for modeling pesticides', *Journal of Environmental Quality*, **22**, 494–9.

OECD (1994), Joint Working Party of the Committee for Agriculture and the Environment Policy Committee, *The Use of Environmental Indicators for Agricultural Policy Analysis*, Paris, 25 October.

Wagenet, R.J and P.S.C. Rao, (1990), 'Modeling pesticide fate in soils', in H.H Cheng *et al.* (eds), *Pesticides in the Environment: Processes, Impacts and Modeling*, Soil Science Book Series No. 2. American Society of Agronomy, Madison, Wisconsin.

3 Decomposing the effects of trade on the environment

David G. Abler and James S. Shortle

Concern for the environmental impacts of agricultural production has grown significantly in Europe in recent years. Environmental problems often linked with agricultural production in European countries include nonpoint surface water and groundwater pollution by fertilizers, pesticides and animal manure; sedimentation of surface waters by eroded soils; loss of flora and fauna due to pesticide runoff and overspray; acidification of the atmosphere due to nitrogen in fertilizers and manure; soil and water pollution from heavy metals in fertilizers and manure; loss of biodiversity due to conversion of forests and wetlands to farm land; salinization and waterlogging from irrigation; and greenhouse gas emissions from deforestation and livestock.

Several European countries have adopted environmental policies directed at agriculture (OECD, 1993). Pesticide registration is the principal method for protecting the environment, workers, and consumers from pesticide hazards (US General Accounting Office, 1993). This policy instrument regulates which pesticides may be marketed and establishes conditions of use through labelling requirements. A number of European governments have also implemented programmes to encourage 'low-input', 'sustainable', 'alternative', or 'organic' fruit and vegetable production methods. These methods vary widely but their common goal is to reduce (or in some cases eliminate) the use of pesticides and inorganic fertilizers. Existing programmes include research and development on alternative production techniques, information and education programmes for producers, subsidies to adopt alternative techniques, and certification schemes for organic produce.

However, designing cost-effective environmental policies that can adequately address environmental problems associated with agricultural production is a difficult problem (Shortle and Abler, 1997). Agricultural pollutants are nonpoint source pollutants, meaning that they reach surface water, groundwater, and the atmosphere by diffuse and indirect pathways that are very difficult to predict or model in advance. The timing, frequency, and intensity of precipitation, which of course are unknown in advance, are critical in this regard. Soil characteristics (e.g., depth, density and permeability) are also critical, and although these are measurable in theory, they are often unknown in practice. For these reasons, agricultural pollutants are very site- and time-specific: under identical farm management conditions, environmental problems can be very severe at particular times or locations but virtually non-existent at other times or locations. In some cases, there may also be long time lags (years or even decades) between polluting activities and the actual movement of pollutants into water resources.

The nonpoint character of agricultural pollution places constraints on the options available to policy makers. One cannot control nonpoint pollution in the way that one can control point sources of pollution, such as the flow of sewage out of a pipe or pollutants from a smoke stack. In contrast to point source pollution, the assignment of responsibility is also difficult or impossible. How much a particular farm is polluting, or even whether it is polluting at all, is usually very uncertain. Moreover, the feasibility, effectiveness, and cost of pollution prevention and control technologies tend to vary significantly from one location to another. These considerations tend to hinder the design and implementation of cost-effective environmental policies for agriculture along the lines of the polluter pays principle.

Because of the difficulties in designing environmental policies for agriculture, one cannot count on environmental policies to fully buffer any negative environmental impacts of other public policies and programmes. By the same token, other public policies and programmes may have positive environmental impacts in the agricultural sector that environmental policies, because of their intrinsic design difficulties, could not achieve in a cost-effective manner.

Trade liberalization is an excellent case in point. Should the current trend toward agricultural trade liberalization continue in future global and regional trade agreements, significant shifts in agricultural production patterns among countries are likely. The amounts and types of agricultural commodities that European countries produce, as well as the techniques of production employed, may change substantially. These changes may give rise to a whole host of environmental impacts, some positive and some negative. The objective of this chapter is to decompose the ways in which trade may affect the environment in a single country and, in particular, the environment as it relates to European agriculture.

3.1　A critique of existing decomposition frameworks

The negotiations and debates over the Uruguay Round Agreement (URA) and the North America Free Trade Agreement (NAFTA) in the late 1980s and early 1990s spawned considerable interest among policy makers, environmental groups and economists over trade–environment interactions. Based on earlier work by John Miranowski, Gene Grossman, Alan Krueger, and others (e.g., Miranowski, Hrubovcak and Sutton, 1991; Grossman and Krueger, 1992), the Organization for Economic Cooperation (OECD) initiated a series of work directed at decomposing the environmental effects of trade.

In a well-known report, OECD (1994a) distinguished between so-called product effects, scale effects, and structural effects of trade on the environment. Product effects refer to trade in specific products that have particularly beneficial or harmful environmental impacts. For example, positive product effects may result from 'environmentally friendly' consumer goods or inputs into production, while negative product effects may result from trade in such things as hazardous wastes.

Scale effects refer to positive or negative environmental impacts caused by changes in the overall scale of economic activity. On the one hand, negative scale effects can arise because additional production and consumption can lead to environmental degradation. On the other hand, positive scale effects may arise if, as some evidence suggests, wealthier countries are more likely to adopt environmental protection policies. The structural effects category is not clearly defined by OECD (1994a). Essentially, however, it appears to be a residual, encompassing all effects not classified as product or scale effects. It would include, among many other things, international changes in the location, intensity and mix of production and consumption activities.

While this framework is a useful initial effort, dividing the environmental effects of trade into only three broad categories causes a variety of quite distinct effects to be lumped into each category. The negative effects of an expansion in the total scale of economic activity operate through economic channels that are very different from the political channels through which positive scale effects operate. Depending on economic and political institutions, there could also be significant differences in the time horizons over which these positive and negative effects manifest themselves. For example, if political institutions are slow to respond, the negative scale effects could occur well before the positive scale effects. In addition, as we will see when we lay out our own decomposition framework, many effects do not fall under the product or scale effects headings. In the OECD (1994a) framework, one would be forced to lump all of these effects together under the heading of structural effects. These effects turn out to be quite distinct from each other in the ways that they operate and in the degree to which they are environmentally beneficial or harmful.

A subsequent report by OECD (1994b) contains a revised framework that comes somewhat closer to describing the full range of potential environmental effects of trade and to putting distinct effects in distinct categories. This framework divides the potential effects of trade into five categories: product, scale, structural, technology, and regulatory.

Product and scale effects in the revised OECD framework are defined in essentially the same way as in the initial framework and, as such, the limitations of the original framework apply here as well. Like the initial framework, product effects in the revised framework refer to trade in specific products that have particularly beneficial or harmful environmental impacts. In addition, like the initial framework, scale effects in the revised framework are associated with changes in the overall level of economic activity.

Unlike the initial OECD framework, structural effects are not defined as a residual in the revised framework. Instead, they are effects associated with changes in the pattern or mix of economic activity. While the revised definition is clearer, the structural effects category now overlaps to some extent with the product effects category. Changes in the mix of economic activity in one country (structural effects) could manifest themselves as, among other things, increased trade in environmentally beneficial or harmful products (product effects) by that country. The result is that product effects are double-counted.

Technology effects refer to changes in production processes for goods and services. Positive technology effects may occur if multinationals transfer 'clean' technologies from one country to another, or if firms in one country purchase inputs embodying cleaner technologies from some other country. Negative technology effects can occur if, for some reason, dirty technologies are transferred instead of clean ones. Regulatory effects refer to the legal and policy effects of a trade agreement on environmental regulations or standards. For example, a trade agreement may include environmental provisions. Alternatively, a trade agreement might conceivably prevent a government from enacting certain types of environmental regulations. Perhaps surprisingly, the regulatory effects category does not include changes in environmental regulations due to the effects of trade on aggregate income and, in turn, societal demands for environmental quality. In the OECD's revised framework, these changes continue to be classified as scale effects.

3.2   An alternative decomposition framework

The purpose of any decomposition framework is to break a complex problem into smaller, more manageable and more understandable pieces. In order for a framework to make sense, the pieces must be mutually exclusive and exhaustive; in other words, they should not overlap and should, when added up, give us the whole picture. It is also a great aid in understanding the original problem if each piece consists of similar effects rather than dissimilar effects. In this way, even if the original problem is highly complex, we can understand and clearly interpret each of the individual pieces. On both these grounds, the frameworks proposed by OECD (1994a, 1994b) are lacking. In this section, we lay out an alternative decomposition framework designed to better meet these two criteria, and illustrate the framework within a two-sector economic model.

Our framework decomposes the environmental effects of trade within a country into five mutually exclusive and exhaustive categories: scale, mix, externality, policy, and technology. As will become apparent, while much can be said both in theory and in practice about scale and mix effects, much less can be said about the other four effects. Paradoxically, the remaining three effects, especially technology effects, could turn out to be the most important.

3.2.1 Scale and mix effects

Scale effects are environmental effects arising from a change in the total scale of economic activity, holding constant the mix of goods produced and consumed. Unlike the OECD (1994a, 1994b) frameworks, however, the effects of trade on aggregate income and, in turn, societal demands for environmental quality are not classified as scale effects in our framework. Instead, they are part of the policy effects category. The mix effects category captures environmental impacts owing to changes in the mix of goods produced and consumed, holding constant the total scale of economic activity. Both scale and mix effects hold constant the impacts of environmental externalities or other externalities on production and consumption (externality effects), environmental policies and other public policies (policy effects), and the technologies used in production (technology effects).

In order to better understand mix and scale effects, it is helpful to consider a relatively simple model that can be illustrated diagrammatically. Consider a market economy containing two sectors, which for expositional purposes we will refer to as agriculture (subscript A) and non-agriculture (subscript N). Some factors of production can be used in either agriculture or non-agriculture, while there may be other factors specific to one of the two sectors. In anticipation of the discussion below, we assume that the government, if it chooses, can adopt environmental policies toward producers in either or both sectors. For the sake of simplicity, the government is not assumed to adopt any other policies toward producers. In addition, in anticipation of the discussion to follow, we assume that environmental externalities from production may impair production possibilities in either or both sectors.

Output supply in sector i ($i = A,N$) is $S_i = S_i\,(p,\bar{E}_A,\bar{E}_N,Z_A,Z_N,A_A,A_N)$, where $p = p_A/p_N$ is the relative price of agricultural goods, $\bar{E}_i$ is the stock of environmental capital used in production in sector i, Z_i is a scalar or vector of environmental policies toward sector i, and A_i is a scalar or vector of technologies used in sector i. We can trace out the economy's production possibilities frontier (PPF) by varying p and plotting the resulting combinations of S_A and S_N.

We have $\partial S_A/\partial p \geq 0$, $\partial S_N/\partial p \leq 0$, $\partial S_i/\partial \bar{E}_i \geq 0$, $\partial S_i/\partial Z_i \leq 0$, and $\partial S_i/\partial A_i \geq 0$. The sign of $\partial S_i/\partial A_j$ ($j \neq i$) is in general ambiguous. It depends on whether technical change in one sector draws factors of production into that sector from the other sector, or whether it pushes them out. For similar reasons, the sign of $\partial S_i/\partial \bar{E}_j$ ($j \neq i$) is ambiguous. The effect of environmental policies in one sector on output in the other sector ($\partial S_i/\partial Z_j$, $j \neq i$) is also ambiguous in sign. On the one hand, environmental policies in one sector may reduce returns to factors of production in that sector, causing factors to move to the other sector. On the other hand, many environmental policies require firms to devote inputs to pollution abatement. These inputs are no longer available for production in either sector. The potential environmental effects of changes in $\bar{E}_i$, Z_i, and A_i are taken up below in the sections on externality effects and policy effects. For now, we assume that these variables are fixed at their initial (superscript 0) values $\bar{E}_i^0$, Z_i^0, and A_i^0.

On the consumer side, there is an aggregate indirect utility function $u = u(p,Y,\bar{E})$, where $Y = pS_A + S_N$ is aggregate income in units of the non-agricultural good and $\bar{E}$ is the total stock of environmental capital. In this respect, the environment is a public good that positively affects utility. From Roy's identity, we can obtain domestic consumer demands for agricultural and non-agricultural goods, $D_i = D_i(p,Y,\bar{E})$. Both goods are assumed to be normal, so that $\partial D_A/\partial p \leq 0$ and $\partial D_i/\partial Y \geq 0$. The effect of a change in p on D_N is ambiguous, as are the effects of a change in $\bar{E}$ on D_A and D_N. The potential effects of a change in $\bar{E}$ are taken up below in the section on externality effects. For the moment, we assume that $\bar{E}$ is fixed at its initial value $\bar{E}^0$.

Initially, assume that there is no trade, so that $S_i^0 = D_i^0$. Once the economy is opened up to trade (superscript 1), assume that it becomes a net importer of agricultural goods ($S_A^1 < D_A^1$) and a net exporter of non-agricultural goods ($S_N^1 > D_N^1$). These directions of change in trade for agriculture and non-agriculture as a whole are consistent with projections of the effects of global trade

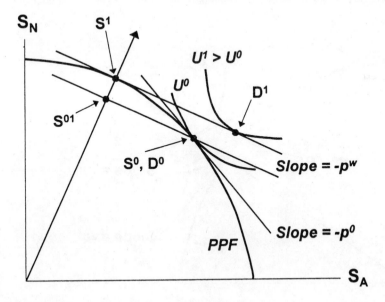

Figure 3.1   Scale and mix effects in production

liberalization on the European Union (e.g., Goldin, Knudsen, and van der Mensbrugghe, 1993; Anderson and Strutt, 1996). They imply that the relative domestic price of agricultural goods, which is now equal to the world price (p^w), falls because of trade ($p^1 = p^w < p^0$). To keep things simple and focused, assume that the country is 'small' in a trade sense, so that p^w is exogenous.

Domestic production and consumption before and after trade are illustrated diagrammatically in Figure 3.1. As a result of trade, domestic agricultural output falls from S_A^0 to S_A^1, while non-agricultural output rises from S_N^0 to S_N^1. In order to decompose these movements into scale and mix effects, draw a ray from the origin in Figure 3.1 that goes through the point $S^1 = (S_A^1, S_N^1)$. Along this ray, the mix of goods produced is the same as the post-trade mix, in the sense that $S_N/S_A = S_N^1/S_A^1$; only the scale of production varies. At the same time, draw a line in Figure 3.1 that intersects the point $S^0 = (S_A^0, S_N^0)$ and has a slope of $-p^w$. Along this line, the scale of production is the same as in the pre-trade situation, in the sense that $p^w S_A + S_N = p^w S_A^0 + S_N^0$; only the product mix varies. The intersection of this line and the ray from the origin define a new point $S^{01} = (S_A^{01}, S_N^{01})$. The movement from S^0 to S^{01} is then the mix effect on domestic production, while the movement from S^{01} to S^1 is the scale effect. A similar decomposition can be carried out on the demand side and is illustrated in Figure 3.2.

To analyse the environmental impacts of changes in mix and scale, we need to describe how the stock of environmental capital is affected by production

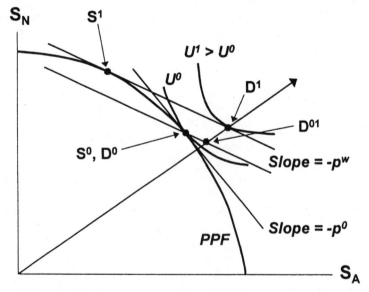

Figure 3.2 Scale and mix effects in consumption

and/or consumption in each sector. For the sake of simplicity, the total environmental capital stock is assumed to be the sum of the stocks used as inputs in each sector ($E = E_A + E_N$). Each sector's stock is negatively affected by production in that sector but is not affected by production in the other sector or by consumption. Environmental policies reduce pollution at any given level of production. Technical change might reduce or increase pollution at any given level of production, depending on the technologies employed. The result is that $E_i = E_i(S_i, Z_i, A_i)$, with $\partial E_i / \partial S_i \leq 0$ and $\partial E_i / \partial Z_i \geq 0$. Note that $\bar{E}_i$ and $\bar{E}$ are used as arguments in the supply and demand functions above, but E_i and E are used here. In the section below on externality effects, we will bring them together by setting $\bar{E}_i = E_i$ and $\bar{E} = E$, thereby allowing $\bar{E}_i$ and $\bar{E}$ to vary. For the time being, however, $\bar{E}_i$ and $\bar{E}$ are held fixed even though E_i and E vary.

The environmental impacts of changes in the mix of production depend on the relative impacts of changes in production in each sector on the total stock of environmental capital. Trade causes agricultural production to decrease and non-agricultural production to increase. If agricultural production is less polluting at the margin than non-agricultural production (in a sense to be made clear below), the mix effect on the environment is negative. On the other hand, if agricultural production is more polluting at the margin, the mix effect is positive. The environmental impacts of changes in the scale of production are always negative, because the scale effect works to increase both agricultural and non-agricultural output.

Starting at some point along the production possibilities frontier (PPF), consider the tradeoffs that we face between agricultural and non-agricultural production if the total stock of environmental capital is held constant in the equation $E = E_A + E_N$. The slope of this 'environment-constant' tradeoff curve is $(dS_N/dS_A)|_E = - (\partial E_A/\partial S_A)/(\partial E_N/\partial S_N)$. The corresponding slope for the PPF is $(dS_N/dS_A)|_{PPF} = (\partial S_N/\partial p)/(\partial S_A/\partial p)$. If the slope of the environment-constant tradeoff curve is less in absolute value than the slope of the PPF, then a small upward movement along the PPF must reduce E. If this holds at all points on the PPF between S^0 and S^1, then over the relevant range we can say that agricultural production is less polluting at the margin than non-agricultural production. Alternatively, if the slope of the environment-constant tradeoff curve is greater in absolute value than the slope of the PPF at all points between S^0 and S^1, then over the relevant range agricultural production is more polluting at the margin.

The two possibilities are illustrated in Figures 3.3 and 3.4, respectively. In the case where agricultural production is less polluting at the margin (Figure 3.3), the mix effect on the environment is negative ($E^{01} < E^0$) because trade shifts the composition of products toward more polluting products. The scale effect leads to a further loss in environmental capital ($E^1 < E^{01}$). In the case where agricultural production is more polluting at the margin (Figure 3.4), the mix effect

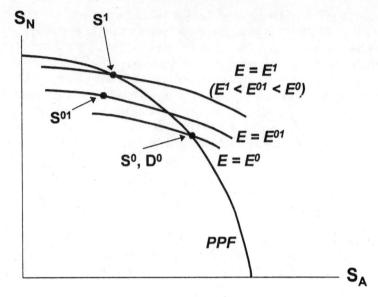

Figure 3.3   Scale and mix environmental effects (agriculture less polluting at the margin)

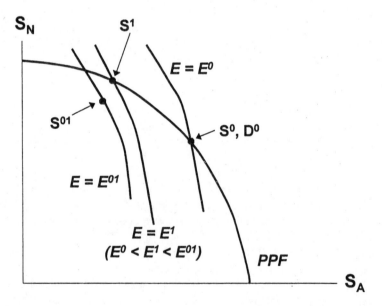

Figure 3.4   Scale and mix environmental effects (agriculture more polluting at the margin)

on the environment is positive. The scale effect is negative, but the sum of the scale and mix effects is still positive ($E^1 > E^0$).

Whether agriculture is more polluting or less polluting at the margin than non-agriculture, in Europe or elsewhere, is an empirical question that is beyond our scope here. In the case of Europe, one might reasonably argue that agriculture is less polluting in total than non-agriculture. Non-agriculture includes industry, and European industry is responsible for a wide array of water pollution, anthropogenic air pollution, greenhouse gas emissions, hazardous wastes, solid wastes, etc. (OECD, 1997). However, what is relevant is not total pollution but rather changes in pollution from each sector in response to additional trade. In this regard, empirical evidence is lacking.

Simulation analyses of trade liberalization almost uniformly show very small impacts on the total scale of economic activity. For example, Nguyen, Perroni and Wigle (1993) estimate that the Uruguay Round Agreement will lead to about a 1 per cent increase in national income in Australia, Canada, New Zealand and the US, and about a 2 per cent increase in the EU and Japan. For the world as a whole, their estimated increase in total income is about 1 per cent. Simulations by Goldin, Knudsen and van der Mensbrugghe (1993) indicate that full global trade liberalization would lead to about a 3 per cent increase in aggregate income in the EU and Japan, and no significant change in Eastern Europe, Canada, or the US.

Simulation analyses also tend to show only moderate effects of trade liberalization on product mix in most countries, at least at the aggregate level of agriculture and non-agriculture (e.g., Goldin, Knudsen and van der Mensbrugghe, 1993; Anderson and Strutt, 1996). The major exception to this statement would be Japan. However, the story is very different in most countries if one looks at specific commodities that are highly protected from imports.

3.2.2 Externality Effects

Externality effects refer to the feedback effects on production and/or consumption of environmental externalities or other externalities caused by production and/or consumption. In the two-sector model above, production in each sector generates environmental externalities and, in turn, negative feedback effects on production in that sector. These feedback effects were set aside in the discussion of scale and mix effects by holding $\bar{E}_i$ and $\bar{E}$ constant. It is now time to bring these feedback effects into the picture by allowing $\bar{E}_i$ and $\bar{E}$ to vary, with $\bar{E}_i = E_i$ and $\bar{E} = E$.

Due to the nature of the externalities in the model, the method outlined above to measure scale and mix effects does not change once externality effects are brought into the picture. However, starting from any point such as S^0 in Figure 3.1, the shape of the PPF changes and, as a result, the scale and mix effects change. There are a large number of possibilities. Suppose, to help illustrate this point, that externalities are stronger at the margin at S^0 in non-agricultural production than in agricultural production. This causes the slope of the PPF at S^0 to be smaller in absolute value than it would be if $\bar{E}_A$ and $\bar{E}_N$ were held constant, because externalities limit what we can gain in non-agricultural output by giving up agricultural output. Moreover, if $\partial^2 E_i / \partial S_i^2 < 0$, the gap between the two slopes must grow as the economy moves toward more S_N and less S_A (the opposite would occur if the economy moved in the other direction). The result, as shown in Figure 3.5, is that post-trade agricultural output is larger (point $(S^1)^*$) than it would be if $\bar{E}_A$ and $\bar{E}_N$ were held constant (S^1), while the opposite holds for non-agricultural output.

Changes in domestic consumption have no environmental implications in the model here because there are no externalities from consumption. In any event, the method shown in the diagram in Figure 3.2 to decompose scale and mix effects on consumption still holds once externality effects are brought into the picture. However, externality effects would cause the post-trade consumption point (D^1) to differ from the corresponding point in the absence of externality effects for two reasons. First, externality effects will in general lead to a change in the post-trade production point (S^1) and thus post-trade aggregate income. Second, the total stock of environmental capital enters the utility function as a public good. The effects of a change in E on D_A and D_N are uncertain.

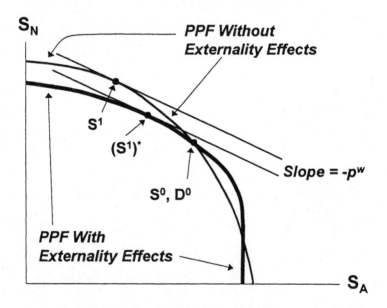

Figure 3.5   Externality effects and the production possibilities frontier

A richer model would permit many other types of externalities, both environmental and non-environmental. Consumers might be significant sources of environmental externalities in some cases – for example, because of household wastes or automobile emissions. These externalities tend to be substantial in developing countries, so that any study of a developing country would need to take them into account (World Resources Institute, 1996; World Bank, 1992). Alternatively, there might be externality effects in production that spill over from one sector to another. As Baumol and Oates (1988) discuss, these types of intersectoral spillovers, if they are sufficiently strong, can lead to non-convexities in the production possibility set that can cause the usual efficiency properties of market equilibria to break down.

3.2.3 Policy effects

Policy effects refer to changes in environmental policies and other public policies induced by trade. Our policy effects category encompasses the OECD (1994b) regulatory effects category, as well as changes in environmental policies that the OECD (1994a, 1994b) puts in its scale effects category. In analysing policy effects, we allow production, consumption, and environmental capital to vary in response to environmental policies along the lines modelled above. However, technologies (the A_i) are still treated as constant and equal to their initial values A_i^0.

Within the confines of our two-sector model, consider the social welfare-maximizing choices for the environmental policies, and how those choices respond to trade. Beginning with the aggregate indirect utility function $u = u(p,Y,\bar{E})$, the marginal social benefit of some environmental policy Z_i is the gain in utility due to an increase in the total environmental capital stock, or $MSB_i = (\partial u/\partial \bar{E})(dE/dZ_i)$. The marginal social cost is the loss in utility due to a decrease in aggregate income and any change in the relative price of agricultural goods, or $MSC_i = - (\partial u/\partial p)(dp/dZ_i) - (\partial u/\partial Y)(dY/dZ_i)$. In the post-trade situation, $dp/dZ_i = 0$ because p is exogenous and equal to p^w. Attaining the social optimum requires that $MSB_i = MSC_i$ for all environmental policies adopted (some might not be adopted at all because marginal social costs exceed marginal social benefits even at a minimal level of adoption).

Marginal social cost might well be negative at low levels of Z_i because environmental policy, if properly designed, can correct for harmful externalities. Beyond a certain point, however, losses in output due to costs imposed by pollution abatement and pollution prevention requirements outweigh gains from correction of externalities.

The impacts of trade on the marginal social benefit and marginal social cost curves are, in general, uncertain. Consequently, policy effects on the environment are also uncertain. The change in Z_i depends on how each of the components of the marginal social benefit and marginal social cost equations above responds to the economic changes caused by trade. The change in the environmental capital stock depends on whether changes in the Z_i reinforce or offset the change in E that occurs with environmental policies held fixed.

If there is diminishing marginal utility to income $(\partial^2 u/\partial Y^2 < 0)$, the increase in aggregate income caused by trade will, by itself, push down the marginal social cost curve for every environmental policy. Beyond this, changes in the Z_i depend in part on which sector is more polluting at the margin (see the discussion above on scale and mix effects). Suppose that non-agriculture is more polluting at the margin, so that E declines in the absence of any offsetting changes in environmental policies (see Figure 3.3). If there is diminishing marginal utility to environmental capital $(\partial^2 u/\partial \overline{E}^2 < 0)$, the reduction in E will, by itself, push out the marginal social benefit curve for every environmental policy. On the other hand, suppose that agriculture is more polluting at the margin, so that E increases in the absence of any changes in environmental policies (see Figure 3.4). If there is diminishing marginal utility to environmental capital, the increase in E will, by itself, push out the marginal social benefit curve for every environmental policy.

Of course, real-world environmental policies are not determined solely by social welfare but rather are based in part, sometimes in large part, on political considerations. Economists and political scientists have not yet come up with any widely accepted model of public choice. For the time being, the best approach for the trade practitioner is probably an empirical one.

In this regard, several studies in recent years have estimated the relationship between per capita income and a variety of indicators of environmental degradation and environmental quality. These studies are relevant to the trade–environment debate to the degree that trade raises per capita income. Three of the better-known studies are Antle and Heidebrink (1995), Grossman (1995), and Lucas (1996). These studies suggest an 'inverted-U' relationship between per capita income and several types of environmental degradation, a relationship widely known as the environmental Kuznets curve. However, there are other types of environmental degradation that either become uniformly worse as per capita income increases, become uniformly better, or show no apparent relationship to per capita income. Moreover, for those types of environmental degradation that do appear to follow the environmental Kuznets curve, the level at which more income turns from environmental harm to improvement varies substantially from one type of degradation to another.

In general, the policy effects category includes not only changes in environmental policies but also changes in a whole host of other public policies. While environmental policies might be the most important for our purposes here, changes in other policies could also have environmental impacts. For example, trade liberalization could increase or decrease a country's total government revenue. A reduction in import tariffs would tend to decrease government revenue, while a reduction in export subsidies and an increase in total tax collections (due to an increase in national income) would tend to increase government revenue. If the net result of all these changes were a decrease in government revenue, the result might be offsetting increases in other taxes or reductions in government expenditures on certain programmes. If the net result were an increase in revenue, that might pave the way for reductions in other taxes or increases in government expenditures. Depending on the taxes and expenditures affected, there could (at least in principle) be significant environmental impacts.

3.2.4 Technology effects

Technology effects refer to impacts of trade on the environment caused by the development and adoption of new products, new production processes, or new pollution abatement technologies. New products or new production processes might be entirely new or might be ones already in use in other countries. New products might be sold directly to consumers or might be used as capital equipment or intermediate inputs in the production of other goods. In analysing technology effects, we allow production, consumption, environmental capital, and public policies to vary in response to technology along the lines modelled above. Our technology effects category is similar to the OECD's (1994b) category of the same name, but somewhat broader in the kinds of changes in technology that we consider.

Trade can lead to changes in technology for at least four reasons. First, trade can lead to the international diffusion of technologies, potentially including so-called 'environmentally friendly' technologies (Grossman and Helpman, 1991; Low, 1992). Trade enables a country to purchase a larger variety of capital equipment and intermediate inputs embodying technologies not previously available. Trade also provides channels of communication through which producers can learn about, and then copy or adapt, technologies used in other countries. Coe and Helpman (1995) and Coe, Helpman and Hoffmaister (1997) find that spillovers in research and development (R&D) between countries are significant, and that they are stronger the more open an economy is to trade. Ben-David (1993) finds that trade openness has increased the speed at which EU countries have converged toward each other in terms of per capita income.

Second, by enlarging potential market sizes, trade can enable firms to better exploit scale economies in R&D. Many innovations are characterized by substantial up-front R&D costs, followed by production costs that are small or trivial in comparison with R&D costs. In agriculture, biotechnology tends to follow this pattern.

Third, by changing relative output prices, trade alters the incentives to do research in one sector versus another because the rate of return to output-increasing R&D depends positively on output prices. For example, if trade lowers relative agricultural product prices, then the incentives to invest in agricultural research fall relative to the incentives to invest in non-agricultural research. In a simulation analysis of the effects of elimination of government programmes for maize in the US, Abler (1996) finds this type of effect at work for private-sector R&D on maize.

Fourth, changes in relative output prices due to trade can have Stolper–Samuelson effects on factor prices. A decline in the relative output price in a sector tends to decrease the prices of factors in which that sector is relatively intensive and increase the prices of other factors. These changes in factor prices could in turn lead to changes in technologies along the lines predicted by the induced innovation model (Hayami and Ruttan, 1985). In this model, technologies tend to be developed and adopted which conserve on relatively expensive factors of production.

Agricultural production throughout the world is intensive in land relative to other sectors, except perhaps forestry in some cases. In the case of Europe, this means that trade liberalization, by reducing relative agricultural product prices, would tend to reduce land rents. Simulations in Abler and Shortle (1992) suggest that the decline in land rents in the EU could in fact be substantial. Historically, agricultural researchers in the public and private sectors have conserved on land by developing and improving inputs that increase yields – fertilizers, pesticides, hybrid seeds, and irrigation technologies (Hayami and Ruttan, 1985). The future might or might not be the same. In any event, these are the very inputs that are associated with environmental degradation in many cases. Lower agricultural output prices could diminish the tendency toward yield-increasing technologies.

Within the confines of our two-sector model, technical change in one sector can have a direct effect on the stock of environmental capital in that sector, holding constant output and environmental policies (recall that $E_i = E_i(S_i,Z_i,A_i)$). It can also have indirect effects that operate through changes in S_i and Z_i. In addition, changes in technology in one sector can potentially affect output and environmental policies in the other sector. All of these effects would need to be taken into account in computing the change in the total stock of environmental capital ($E = E_A + E_N$).

Even in the case of environmentally friendly technical change ($\partial E_i/\partial A_i > 0$), the total effect (the direct effect plus indirect effects in both sectors) could be environmentally harmful. Like all types of technical change, environmentally friendly technical change will increase output in the sector benefiting from the change. This, by itself, is environmentally harmful because $\partial E_i/\partial S_i \leq 0$. Essentially, we have less pollution per unit of output but more output. Under many circumstances, the negative impact on E_i of the increase in S_i could actually outweigh the positive impact of the increase in A_i (Abler and Shortle, 1995).

The situation becomes even cloudier when we consider the possibility that environmental policies could change. By increasing aggregate income, technical change would tend to lead to stricter environmental policies for reasons discussed above in the policy effects section. Environmentally friendly technical change could lead regulatory authorities to adopt stricter environmental regulations for another reason as well. Environmentally friendly technologies reduce the costs to producers of stricter environmental regulations, thereby making stricter regulations more politically feasible. This process is sometimes referred to as 'ratcheting' in the environmental economics literature.

3.3 International issues

The framework for decomposing the environmental effects of trade outlined above pertains to a single country. An international assessment of trade and the environment would require one to apply this framework to several countries. Shifts in production between countries, especially production of pollution-intensive goods, could have important environmental implications. Environmental damages from any given level of production could differ from one country to another. The economic loss attached to any given level of damages could also differ. Although this issue is quite important, it is beyond our scope here. Copeland and Taylor (1994, 1995) discuss some of the impacts of trade on the international location of polluting industries and on global pollution in the case of transboundary pollutants. Abler and Pick (1993) provide an empirical illustration of the location issue in the case of fruit and vegetable production in the US versus Mexico under NAFTA.

An international assessment of trade–environment interactions would also require consideration of environmental externalities from international transportation. Gabel (1994) discusses some of the impacts that trade liberalization can have on the volume and modes of international transportation and, in turn, the environment.

3.4 Conclusions

In this chapter, we outlined a framework for dividing the environmental effects of trade on a country into scale, mix, externality, policy, and technology. It should be clear from inspection of this framework that a comprehensive environmental assessment of trade would be a difficult task. It would require analysing the environmental effects of trade on a sector-by-sector basis and then expressing these effects in monetary terms in order to make comparisons across sectors. Each of these effects can be quite complex, and different effects tend to move in different directions, even within a single sector. Paradoxically, the effects about which we know the least, and the effects most commonly left out of trade–environment analyses – externality, policy, and technology – could be the most important. Technology, in particular, is the 'wild card' that has the potential to dominate all other effects.

Nevertheless, environmental data collection and environmental valuation in Western Europe, North America, and some other parts of the world have progressed to the point where a comprehensive, reasonably accurate environmental assessment of trade is now feasible. As the world moves toward more liberalized trade, including liberalized agricultural trade, the challenge for researchers and for governments is to bring the available data and methodology to bear on this important problem.

References

Abler, D.G. (1996), 'Environmental policies and induced innovation: the case of agriculture', in *Agricultural Markets: Mechanisms, Failures and Regulations*, Amsterdam, Netherlands: Elsevier.

Abler, D.G. and D. Pick (1993), 'NAFTA, agriculture, and the environment in Mexico', *American Journal of Agricultural Economics*, **75**, 794–8.

Abler, D.G. and J.S. Shortle (1992), 'Environmental and farm commodity policy linkages in the US and EC', *European Review of Agricultural Economics*, **19**, 197–217.

Abler, D.G. and J.S. Shortle (1995), 'Technology as an agricultural pollution control policy', *American Journal of Agricultural Economics*, **77**, 20–32.

Anderson, K. and A. Strutt (1996), 'On measuring the environmental impacts of agricultural trade liberalization', in *Agriculture, Trade and the Environment: Discovering and Measuring the Critical Linkages*, Boulder, Colorado, US: Westview Press.

Antle, J.M. and G. Heidebrink (1995), 'Environment and development: theory and international evidence', *Economic Development and Cultural Change*, **43**, 603–25.

Baumol, W.J. and W.E. Oates (1988), *The Theory of Environmental Policy*, Cambridge, UK: Cambridge University Press.

Ben-David, D. (1993), 'Equalizing exchange: trade liberalization and income convergence', *Quarterly Journal of Economics*, **108**, 653–79.

Coe, D.T. and E. Helpman (1995), 'International R&D spillovers', *European Economic Review*, **39**, 859–87.

Coe, D.T., E. Helpman and A. W. Hoffmaister (1997), 'North-South R&D spillovers', *Economic Journal*, **107**, 134–49.

Copeland, B.R. and M.S. Taylor (1994), 'North–South Trade and the Environment', *Quarterly Journal of Economics*, **109**, 755–87.

Copeland, B.R. and M.S. Taylor (1995), 'Trade and Transboundary Pollution', *American Economic Review*, **85**, 716–37.

Gabel, H. (1994), 'The environmental impacts of trade in the transport sector', in *The Environmental Effects of Trade*, Paris: OECD.

Goldin, I., O. Knudsen and D. van der Mensbrugghe (1993), *Trade Liberalisation: Global Economic Implications*, Paris: OECD.

Grossman, G.M. (1995), 'Pollution and growth: what do we know?' in *The Economics of Sustainable Development*, Cambridge, UK: Cambridge University Press.

Grossman, G.M. and E. Helpman (1991), *Innovation and Growth in the Global Economy*, Cambridge, Massachusetts, US: MIT Press.

Grossman, G.M. and A. Krueger (1992), *Environmental Impacts of a North American Free Trade Agreement*, Discussion Paper, John M. Olin Program for the Study of Economic Organization and Public Policy, Princeton University.

Hayami, Y. and V.W. Ruttan (1985), *Agricultural Development: An International Perspective*, Baltimore: Johns Hopkins University Press.

Low, P. (ed) (1992), *International Trade and the Environment*. Discussion Paper No. 159. Washington, DC: World Bank.

Lucas, R.E.B. (1996), 'International Environmental Indicators: Trade, Income, and Endowments', in *Agriculture, Trade, and the Environment: Discovering and Measuring the Critical Linkages*, Boulder, Colorado, US: Westview Press.

Miranowski, J., J. Hrubovcak and J. Sutton (1991), 'The effects of commodity programs on resource use', in N. Bockstael and R.E. Just (eds), *Commodity and Resource Policies in Agricultural Systems*, New York: Springer-Verlag.

Nguyen, T., C. Perroni and R. Wigle (1993), 'An evaluation of the draft final act of the Uruguay Round', *Economic Journal*, **103**, 1540–49.

OECD (1993), *Agricultural and Environmental Policy Integration: Recent Progress and New Directions*, Paris: OECD.

OECD (1994a), *The Environmental Effects of Trade*, Paris: OECD.

OECD (1994b), *Methodologies for Environmental and Trade Reviews*, Paris: OECD.

OECD (1997), *Environmental Data Compendium 1997*, Paris: OECD.

Shortle, J.S. and D.G. Abler (1997), 'Nonpoint Pollution', in *International Yearbook of Environmental and Resource Economics*, Cheltenham, UK and Lyme, US: Edward Elgar.

US General Accounting Office (1993), *Pesticides: A Comparative Study of Industrialized Nations' Regulatory Systems*, Washington, DC: Government Printing Office.

World Bank (1992), *World Development Report 1992: Development and the Environment*. New York: Oxford University Press.

World Resources Institute (1996), *World Resources 1996–97*. New York: Oxford University Press.

PART II

4 Effects of CAP reform on the environment in the European Union[1]

Floor Brouwer and Siemen van Berkum

4.1 Introduction

Deterioration of the environment resulting from the leaching of minerals is a subject gaining increasing public concern. A Directive was accepted by the Council of Ministers in 1991 concerning the protection of waters against pollution by nitrates from agricultural sources. Measures need to be taken by Member States to reach targets on the quality of drinking water, as formulated in the Nitrates Directive. Also, there is some empirical evidence that the use of plant protection products poses a threat to the environment (Faasen, 1995). Use of plant protection products is greatest in intensively farmed areas, because of the risks of pests and diseases. The agricultural sector is one of the principal contributors to water pollution, mainly from plant protection products and nitrate (CEC, 1992).

The Common Agricultural Policy (CAP) has been the main driving force behind the increase in agricultural production in the European Union during the past three decades. The intensive methods employed in agriculture and the subsequent use of agricultural inputs (fertilizers, feed concentrates and plant protection products) have increased partly in response to the price support measures. CAP also provided incentives for the consolidation of farm structures, which have led to extensive rationalization of the landscape, as well as pressures on semi-natural habitats. Farming practice intensified in some areas and specialization of agriculture increased as well. The subsequent deterioration of the environment is one of the main issues of concern to the public, local authorities, Member States and the European Commission. However, the impact of agriculture on the environment also has a positive side, and it certainly also contributes to nature conservation aspects. The animal sectors are of major importance to nature conservation, as they occupy most of the areas of Europe with high nature values. Also, low-intensity livestock farming has created

1 This chapter is the result of work undertaken in a project 'CAP and environment in the European Union: Analysis of the effects of CAP on the environment and an assessment of existing environmental conditions in policy'. The project was part of a study contract with the European Commission (DG XI), contract B4-3040/94/0093/MAR/B2. This support is gratefully acknowledged. The European Commission does not take responsibility for the content of the chapter.

large areas of semi-natural grassland, scrubland and other grazed areas of nature conservation value (Beaufoy *et al.*, 1994). Beneficial effects of agricultural policy on the environment are also being explored (e.g. OECD, 1997a), and agricultural policy may compensate farmers for taking specific measures in implementing landscape and nature conservation measures and for improving pollution control.

The objectives of the chapter are threefold:

1. To summarize the currently known links between CAP and the environment in the European Union;
2. To assess the linkages between the 1992 reform of the cereals regime and of the beef regime with the environment. Effects on the environment of market and price policies regarding cereals and beef are reviewed, as well as the present environmental requirements in the framework of agricultural policy.
3. To assess linkages between the environment and Council Regulation 2078 (EEC) which aims to encourage the use of agricultural production methods compatible with the protection of the environment and the maintenance of the countryside.

We will draw conclusions about the incorporation of environmental requirements in agricultural policy, and assess the importance of Member States' environmental policies in allowing targets to be met. Empirical work to assess the environmental effects of CAP reform measures so far remains limited (Brouwer and Van Berkum, 1996).

4.2   The Common Agricultural Policy

The original objectives of the Common Agricultural Policy are specified in the well-known Article 39 of the 1957 Treaty of Rome. These objectives were described as follows (Tracy, 1989):

1. to increase agricultural productivity by promoting technical progress and by ensuring the rational development of agricultural production and the optimal utilization of the factors of production, in particular labour;
2. thus to ensure a fair standard of living for the agricultural community, in particular by increasing the individual earnings of persons engaged in agriculture;
3. to stabilize markets;
4. to ensure stability of supplies;
5. to ensure that supplies reach consumers at reasonable prices.

The main reason for government intervention policies was (and still is) considered to be to encourage agricultural productivity thereby ensuring farmers a satisfactory and equitable standard of living and to stabilize agricultural markets and farmers' incomes. No objectives relating to the environment and nature are specified in Article 39 of the Treaty of the European Union, nor in other Articles of the separate agricultural section of the Treaty (Articles 38–47). The only place where indirect reference is made to environmental concerns in relation to agriculture is Article 43. This Article states that the Council may grant authorization to lend support in order to protect farming disadvantaged by structural or natural conditions. This formulation opens the way for measures directed at protecting and managing the environment, nature and landscape. An important example of this kind of policy to protect the environment and landscape can be seen in the agri-environmental measures established under Council Regulation (EEC) 2078/92.

The main objectives of CAP are traditionally achieved by price support, and are therefore very much dependent on production levels of crops and livestock. CAP covers a wide range of measures, including:

- CAP market and price support measures;
- Accompanying measures;
- Horizontal socio-structural measures (Objective 5a);
- Regional and rural policy (Objectives 1 and 5b);
- Other policies like incentives for alternative crops, quality and (eco-) label policy, biomass production, farm diversification, etc.

The European Commission concluded in 1991 that there was a need for a fundamental change of the CAP (CEC, 1991). It was recognized that existing price guarantees, through their direct link to production, lead to output growth, adding to already excessive intervention stocks or to already oversupplied world markets. Reference was also made at the time to the fact that the inbuilt incentives to greater intensity and a rise in production, provided by the market and price policy mechanisms, put the environment at increasing risk. Therefore, lowering prices should result in less (surplus) production. Less intensive production methods could be encouraged by direct payments subject to conditions regarding the intensity of farming and the use of inputs. In the so-called Reflection Paper of 1991, the Commission also stressed that the farmer plays an important role in the maintenance and protection of the environment, landscape and nature.

The CAP reform of 1992 – based on the Reflection Paper of 1991 – was aimed among other things at improving the competitiveness of EU agriculture, restoring market balance and encouraging less intensive production methods. Measures were adopted in order to reduce surplus production, reduce price support (together with more targeted direct income support), and to improve environmental soundness of agricultural production (CEC, 1993). The Commission was well aware that the shift in policies could result in an increase in the agricultural budget but was prepared to accept this.

Table 4.1   Main features of the 1992 CAP reform

Arable sector:
1) A reduction – in three stages – of about one third in the cereal intervention price, which is to fall by 1995/96 to 100 green ECUs per ton. The threshold price will be 155 green ECUs per ton;
2) Elimination of the price support for oilseeds and protein crops;
3) Compensation through direct area payments based on historical base areas and regional yields, subject to set-aside for such crops grown by all farmers except the relatively small ones with a production level which does not exceed 92 tonnes of cereals equivalent. A certain percentage of set-aside is decided each year by the Council of Ministers. Fifteen per cent rotational set-aside was introduced in 1993/94. In 1994/95, farmers were given the option of choosing non-rotational set-aside, at 18 or 21%.

Livestock sector:
1) In two stages a 2% cut in milk quota, optional to the market situation; 5% reduction of the butter intervention price, also in two stages;
2) A 15% reduction in the intervention prices for beef from July 1993, in three stages;
3) Compensation through direct headage payments (premiums) subject to a maximum stocking rate (two livestock units (LU) per hectare of forage crops by 1996);
4) Increased male bovine and suckler (beef) cow premiums. Male bovine premiums are subject to an individual limit of (2 times) 90 bovine animals per holding, while the ceiling for suckler cow premiums is equal to the number of animals for which a premium was granted in the reference year (1990, 1991 or 1992). Premiums are granted within the limits of regional ceilings which, if exceeded, reduce the number of eligible animals per producer. There are extra headage premiums if a producer reduces the stocking rate to below 1.4 LU per hectare of forage crops;
5) A reduction in the ceiling for normal beef intervention buying from 750 000 to 350 000 tonnes by 1997;
6) Individual limits of full ewe premium based on eligible claims made in 1991. Full ewe premiums for no more than 1000 animals in LFAs, and for 500 animals in other areas.

Accompanying measures:
1) An agri-environmental package aimed at more extensive means of production and the use of land for natural resource protection and public leisure;
2) Aid for forestry investment on agricultural land and management with up to 20 years' compensation for income loss;
3) Various forms of compensation for early retirement, including lump sum and/or annual payments, for farmers and farm workers aged over 55;
4) Implementation through Member States programmes with 50% of the cost (75% in Objective 1 regions) borne by the CAP budget.

The most fundamental change resulting from the CAP reform concerned cereals. Intervention prices are to be reduced by around one third. In order to compensate cereal producers for income losses following price decreases, a direct payment is provided on a per hectare basis. Large scale producers (with production levels which may exceed the equivalent of 92 tonnes of cereals on their land under cereals, oilseeds and protein crops) are only eligible for hectare compensations if they set aside a certain percentage, decided each year by the Council of Ministers, of their so-called base area. This area includes the average acreage utilized to grow cereals, oilseeds, fodder maize and protein crops in the period 1989–91. Producers with production levels below 92 tonnes of cereals or equivalent are exempted from this set-aside rule.

The reform proposals were much less radical for animal products than they were for arable crops. The intervention price for beef is to be reduced by fifteen per cent in three stages. After a transitional period, farmers may in 1996 apply for premiums for bulls and suckler cows up to a stocking rate of two livestock units per hectare of fodder area. Small scale producers are exempted from the stocking rate requirement. If stocking rates do not exceed 1.4 livestock units per hectare, farmers receive an additional premium. The reform also introduces a measure aimed at curbing the rapid increase in expenditures on sheep, by putting a maximum on the amount of support individual producers are able to receive.

The main features of the 1992 CAP reform are summarized in Table 4.1.

Accompanying measures as formulated in Council Regulation 2078/92 are adopted because 'measures to reduce agricultural production in the Community must have a beneficial impact on the environment'. Therefore, an aid scheme has been introduced to encourage farmers to introduce or to continue farming practices compatible with the increasing demand of protection of the environment and natural resources and upkeep of the landscape and the countryside. For instance, farmers are eligible for compensation when they reduce the use of inputs, or change to more extensive forms of production. The agri-environmental measures are elaborated at national, regional and local level.

4.3   Effects of the reform of the cereal regime
The basic regulation 120/67 of the cereal regime covers the common internal pricing system and the system of the regulation of trade with third countries. This regulation was succeeded by Regulation 2727/75 which was, in turn, succeeded by Regulations 1765/92 and 1766/92. There it is said that the new support system for producers of certain arable crops is established 'in order to ensure better market balance' and must lead to a better competitive position of the European Union. No direct reference is made to environmental concerns being a reason to change the cereal regime. The objective of a better market balance is achieved by the lowering of institutional prices, which are compensated for

by direct payments to producers. To be eligible for the compensatory payments under the so-called 'general scheme', producers must set aside a predetermined percentage of their arable area. Furthermore, '... the land set aside would have to be cared for so as to meet certain minimum environmental standards'. However, these minimum environmental standards are not explained in these two regulations.

Environmental objectives are formulated in Commission Regulation 762/94 of 6 April 1994. As outlined in the Regulation, the set-aside scheme is primarily meant to control production. Some conditions or provisions are imposed regarding maintenance and use of the areas set aside. These provisions are laid down for environmental reasons (Article 3(3)). Measures must be taken to ensure the protection of the environment. These measures may involve use of a green cover. In this case it is stipulated that the plant cover may not be used for seed production and that it may on no account be used for agricultural purposes before 31 August or produce crops, before the following 15 January, which are intended for commercial use. As an alternative to set-aside, non-food crops can be grown. Bound to certain requirements the producers' obligation to put land aside may be transferred to another producer in the same Member State. Member States may submit plans to the European Commission permitting transfers of set-aside obligations between producers within a 20 km radius, and/or within areas where specific environmental objectives are sought. In Denmark, for example, farmers may transfer their set-aside obligation to someone situated in an environmentally sensitive agricultural (ESA) area pointed out by the local authorities.

To get compensatory payments for land set aside, the conditions specified at the national level must be complied with. Member States can decide the penalties 'which are appropriate and proportional to the seriousness of the environmental consequences of not observing the said measures' (Commission Regulation 762/94). All measures to protect the environment in relation to set-aside land are agreed upon at the Member State level. Management rules on set-aside also differ between Member States, for instance with respect to restrictions on the application of plant protection products, fertilizers and animal manure. In the United Kingdom, for example, farmers are allowed to apply slurry, manure or organic waste to set-aside land from their own holding. Also, some types of herbicides may be used on set-aside land. A selective use of herbicides is permitted in order to encourage farmers not to cut their green cover. In the past, no herbicides were allowed to be used. Farmers were then cutting their green cover which caused problems for nesting birds. In general, a farmer may not apply any manure or organic waste on guaranteed set-aside land (MAFF, 1994). This restriction could make non-rotational set-aside less attractive to the British farmer than rotational set-aside. A summary of management restrictions on set-aside in Denmark, France, Germany and the United Kingdom is provided in Table 4.2.

Table 4.2 Management rules on chemical use of set-aside land in Denmark, France, Germany and the United Kingdom

Denmark:	None allowed until the following 20 October. The application of fertilizers is allowed after 15 July, in case set-aside is to be followed by winter crop.
France:	Selective and non-selective use of herbicides is allowed. Chemicals are allowed to be used after 15 July if set-aside is to be followed by winter crop.
Germany:	None allowed during set-aside period. Chemicals are allowed to be used after 15 July if set-aside is to be followed by winter crop.
United Kingdom:	Non-residual herbicides are allowed provided that, before 15 April, the green cover is not destroyed (except if replacing cover). Thus spot applications, the use of wick applicators or the use of non-residual herbicides that leave the majority of cover intact are allowed before that date. After 15 April, no restriction on the use of herbicides.

Source: Ansell and Vincent (1994) pp. 12,13.

Farmers have two options under the 1992 set-aside scheme: rotational and non-rotational. The rotational set-aside specifies that each year a different piece of land must be kept aside for a period of at least seven months, between 15 January and 15 August. Non-rotational set-aside allows producers to fallow their least productive land on a multi annual basis. In the first two years of the reform, the non-rotational rate was higher than the rotational rate (see Table 4.1), but the difference was abolished in 1995/96. For 1995/96 the rotational and non-rotational set-aside rates are the same, i.e. 10 per cent. According to Williamson (1993), non-rotational set-aside provides more consistent benefits than rotational, mainly related to the achievement of soil conservation benefits. Under the rotational option, farmers must prepare the set-aside land for production the next year which could require additional inputs, particularly herbicides. When farmers rotate their land which is put aside, it may prove difficult to establish an effective green cover. If the green cover fails to fill in before the first significant rainfall, the farmer risks considerable erosion damage to the set-aside land (Williamson, 1993: 66). Non-rotational set-aside is also the better choice for counteracting runoff and leaching problems. Other benefits of non-rotational set-aside are mentioned by Hawke and Kovaleva (1994) who stress that the agreement to set aside land on a semi-permanent basis (for at least five years) allows for the restoration of a greater variety of habitats than is possible under rotational set-aside. Such a system would also contribute to the build-up of local populations of plants and animals, and so is, in general, better for wildlife. A more detailed analysis on the environmental effects of set-aside schemes in the European Union is provided in OECD (1997b).

The potential impact of the 1992 reform of the cereal regime on the environment and landscape comes from changes in price support as well as from the set-aside regulation. Lower prices may induce farmers to reduce their use of fertilizers and plant protection products. However, farmers may change their cropping plan towards products using agro-chemicals more intensively (fruit, vegetables, potatoes). On the other hand, experiences in Spain show that, because of a decline in cereal prices, the production pattern on irrigated lands changes so that water is increasingly used for crops with lower water demand. The conclusion is that lower prices have complex implications for the agricultural system, and environmental benefits on the one hand may be offset by increased costs. Differences across Member States are largely due to different farming systems and biophysical conditions.

The set-aside scheme can be applied on a rotational and a non-rotational basis. Farm-specific features, like soil productivity and cropping plan, affect the farmer's decision whether to opt for one form or the other. Of both options, the non-rotational form appears to have a more favourable impact on the environment and landscape. A greater diversity of plant species is likely to develop, and this will subsequently support a greater variety of fauna. The management rules on the treatment of land which is put aside are, however, crucial to the environmental impact of both forms of the set-aside scheme.

The area eligible for the arable payment scheme was limited to the area of arable crops used in the period 1989–91. This condition, which was introduced by the European Commission for budgetary reasons, also had a positive effect on the environment as it prevents farmers from reverting extensive grassland to arable land. On the other hand, fixation of the base area may also imply that regions with intensive production methods and high yields remain on that level.

4.4   Effects of the reform of the beef regime

The basic regulation (805/68) includes a system of price support which is aimed to keep Community market prices as close as possible to an agreed common price level. The main support mechanisms are internal price support measures such as support buying and private storage, premium payments, import measures and export refunds.

The common organization of the market in beef has been reformed because 'of the structural imbalance between the supply and demand on the Community market'. A compensation for lowering the intervention price for beef is granted in the form of premiums, subject to a limit on the number of eligible male animals. Furthermore the special premium for beef producers and the premium for maintaining suckler cow herds continue. Therefore the schemes are adapted to the new situation by redefinition of the conditions of the grant. Conditions of major importance are the restriction of the total number of animals eligible for the premiums and the stocking density on the holding. Because 'the reorientation of the premiums should not be reflected in an increase in overall production, ... the number of animals eligible for premiums should be limited by applying regional and individual ceilings respectively to be determined in accordance with reference years' (Council Regulation 2066/92). In order 'to encourage extensive production, the grant of such premiums should be subject to compliance with a maximum stocking density on the holding, and an additional amount should be granted to producers who do not exceed a minimum stocking rate'. Although support by premiums is subject to a certain degree of intensity of production, no reference is made explicitly to an environmental clause when applying for support under this scheme. However, by an amendment CR 3611/93 the option to Member States to include environmental conditions is given:

> Member States may apply appropriate environmental measures which correspond to the specific situation of the land used for the production of male bovine animals or suckler cows qualifying for premium. Member States which avail themselves of this possibility shall decide the penalties which are appropriate and proportional to the seriousness of the ecological consequences of not observing the said measures. These penalties may provide for a reduction or, where appropriate, cancellation of the benefits accruing from the premium schemes... (article 4a).

In EUR 12, total livestock density on holdings with fattening bulls and suckler cows is 1.7 LU/ha of forage crops (Table 4.3). Looking at the livestock eligible for support under the beef scheme (i.e. dairy cows, suckler cows, male cattle and ewes, so excluding pigs and poultry) density per hectare of forage crops is only 0.9 LU. So, generally speaking, the average EU holding with beef and suckler cows is eligible for the premiums under this scheme. However, on 283 000 holdings stocking rate exceeds 2 LU/ha forage crops. Stocking density of livestock eligible for support on that group of farms on average is 3.1 LU/ha. Dairy cows dominate on these relatively intensive farm holdings.

Country as well as regional differences within the EU Member States are significant. Livestock density on farms with beef and suckler cows is highest in Greece (7.2). Stocking rate also exceeds 2 LU/ha of forage crops in Belgium, Denmark, Germany and the Netherlands. Only in Greece, however, does the average livestock density on holdings with fattening bulls and suckler cows exceed the limit of two when looking at the animal types which are eligible for support. Regions in EU Member States potentially mostly affected by the scheme are Macedonia (Greece), Galicia (Spain) and Central North (Portugal).

Table 4.3   *Structure and livestock density on farms with fattening bulls and suckler cows*

Country/region	Density per hectare of forage crops		Farms with density > 2 LU eligible for support per ha forage crops[a]						
	Total livestock	Livestock eligible for support	Number of farms represented (×1000)	Density per ha of forage crops		Share in livestock population (%)			
				Total livestock	Livestock eligible for support	Male cattle	Suckler cows	Dairy cows	
Belgium	3.5	1.6	10	5.8	2.6	18	15	67	
Denmark	4.2	1.7	9	6.9	2.7	8	9	83	
Germany	2.7	1.2	15	5.4	2.6	42	1	57	
Greece Makedonia	7.2	5.1	28	10.3	7.4	10	45	32	
Thraki	7.9	5.6	18	10.0	7.2	12	26	53	
Spain	1.3	0.9	44	7.1	4.6	2	53	34	
Galicia	3.0	1.7	31	5.8	3.9	0	55	38	
France	1.6	0.9	10	6.1	2.8	53	16	30	
Ireland	1.3	0.8	1	2.7	2.2	39	3	50	
Italy	1.6	1.1	71	5.1	3.5	22	9	66	
Piemonte	2.2	1.5	12	4.8	3.4	24	15	60	
Luxembourg	1.9	1.0	–	–	–	–	–	–	
Netherlands	3.2	1.7	7	4.5	2.3	2	–	97	
Portugal	0.9	0.5	79	7.2	4.6	28	30	40	
Norte-Centro	1.3	0.8	71	7.3	4.8	30	31	38	
United Kingdom	1.3	0.8	7	4.0	2.4	27	4	63	
EUR 12	1.7	0.9	283	5.4	3.1	22	16	59	

Note: [a]   Livestock eligible for support are suckler cows, male cattle and ewes. Total livestock refers to livestock eligible for support, plus dairy cows, pigs and poultry.
Source: FADN-CCE-DG VI/A-3; adaptation LEI-DLO, data 1990/91

In Italy, there are three regions (Lombardia, Veneto and Campania) where the potential impact may also be high because of a relatively high share of holdings with stocking density exceeding 2 LU/ha. In all regions of other Member States, the share of holdings which exceed the threshold of two livestock units eligible for support per hectare is (much) less than those in the four Southern Member States mentioned above.

Member States' experience with the scheme so far indicates the relative unattractiveness of the premium to the farmer and the ineffectiveness of the measure to reduce livestock density. The measure is said to be rather complex in nature and to the farmer, it is rather difficult to assess its benefits. Furthermore, farmers in countries with a currency devaluating against the ECU were not affected at all by the institutional beef price decline. On the contrary, beef producers in all Southern EU countries experienced an increase of real prices in their national currency. Such a trend did not encourage them to reduce their stocking density in order to be eligible for the beef premium. And last but not least, dairy cows dominate the holdings with beef and suckler cows. As long as milk production is considered to be rather attractive, dairy cows will not be disposed of easily. The milk quota regulation is effective in stabilizing the milk production while production per cow increases. Therefore, fewer cows are needed to produce the quota. But because most producers seem to have no other attractive alternative than to use their land for cattle, the resulting excess production capacity in the livestock sector happens to be allocated to a great extent to non-dairy cattle. This explains the relative popularity of this activity despite declining real prices.

4.5 Effects of the agri-environmental measures

Regulation (EEC) 2078/92 is an aid scheme which is aimed to encourage farmers to introduce or to continue with agricultural production methods compatible with the protection of the environment and the maintenance of the countryside. The regulation aims to

> encourage farmers to make undertakings regarding farming methods compatible with the requirements of environmental protection and maintenance of the countryside, and thereby to contribute to balancing the market; whereas the measures must compensate farmers for any income losses caused by reductions in output and/or increases in costs and for the part they play in improving the environment.

The agri-environmental measures under Regulation (EEC) 2078/92 have three general purposes:

1. To accompany the changes to be introduced under market organization· rules;
2. To contribute to the achievement of the Community's policy objectives regarding agriculture and the environment;
3. To contribute to providing an appropriate income for farmers.

The agri-environmental programmes, elaborated at national, regional and local level, include aid to farmers who undertake (Article 2, paragraph 1 of Regulation (EEC) 2078/92):

1. to reduce substantially, or maintain reduction in their use of fertilizers and/or plant protection products, or to introduce or continue with organic farming methods;

2. to change, by means other than those referred in 1), to more extensive forms of crop production, or to convert arable land into extensive grassland;
3. to reduce the proportion of sheep and cattle per forage area;
4. to use other farming practices compatible with the requirements of protection of the environment and natural resources, as well as to maintain the countryside and the landscape, or to rear animals of local breeds in danger of extinction and plants endangered by genetic erosion;
5. to maintain abandoned farmland or woodlands for environmental protection;
6. to set aside farmland for at least 20 years with a view to its use for purposes connected with the environment, in particular for the establishment of biotope reserves or natural parks or for the protection of hydrological systems;
7. to manage land for public access and leisure activities.

In addition (Article 2, paragraph 2 of Regulation (EEC) 2078/92), the scheme also includes measures to improve the training of farmers with regard to farming or forestry practices compatible with the environment.

The implementation of programmes under Regulation (EEC) 2078/92 is based on proposals developed by national and regional authorities in the Member States. The programmes which have been accepted by the STAR Committee (Comité des Structures Agricoles développement et du Rural) have recently been summarized (De Putter, 1995). Participation of the programmes is assessed to range across Member States between 3 per cent of UAA (Utilized Agricultural Area) (the Netherlands) and 25 per cent of UAA (Germany). Participation by farmers of the programmes submitted by Austria is assessed to be very high (91 per cent of UAA) (Table 4.4).

A successful implementation of the programmes under the agri-environmental scheme depends on many items including organization, provision of information, monitoring of progress, integration with other policy objectives and the financial resources available. These aspects are discussed in more detail below.

Administrative units at different levels are in charge of the implementation of programmes. The agricultural sector may also be involved in the development and implementation of programmes. The implementation of programmes requires major expertise by regional authorities in coordination and delegation of tasks. Furthermore, knowledge of policies concerning environmental protection may also contribute to the achievement of the objectives of the agri-environmental programmes. It seems likely that the lack of organizational capacity and experience may limit the potential of this programme, especially in countries which have never implemented national schemes whereby farmers are paid in return for undertaking specific environmental practices. In such a situation programme implementation becomes even more difficult when the Member State has a highly complex and large variety of farming systems and habitats to deal

Table 4.4   Characteristics of programme budget of Council Regulation (EEC) 2078/92 by Member State

Country	Budget (ECU/ha)	Participation (× 1000 ha)	Participation (% of farms)
Belgium	123.0	63.0	5
Denmark	88.5	210.0	10
Germany	142.0	3 000.0	50
Spain	30.6	4 073.8	15
France	51.3	6 343.9	20
Ireland	66.6	1 036.3	20
Italy	74.4	1 484.9	10
Luxembourg	160.5	16.4	15
Netherlands	144.7	67.4	5
Austria	105.0	3 194.0	90
Portugal	83.2	871.7	20
United Kingdom	?	?	?
European Union	97.2		

Source: De Putter (1995), p. 143.

with. Consequently a great number of difficulties may arise concerning its design, implementation and future monitoring.

Lack of scientific and technical information is observed at various levels. A limited number of reports is available about the different agricultural systems and the coexistence of fauna and flora of high conservation value. In Spain the most studied agro-ecosystems are the *dehesas* and steppes. Even in these cases, lack of available, reliable and up-to-date data has been reported. A similar problem has been reported about one of the most important bird areas in Spain, the Mediterranean steppes (Suarez, 1994). Varela-Ortega and Sumpsi (1995) conclude that more studies and detailed research is needed on the global behaviour of each particular ecosystem. Also the contribution of the different agricultural practices to nature conservation should be identified and evaluated.

The agri-environmental regulation is designed to achieve environmental objectives, along with other parts of the CAP (e.g. market and price policies and structural measures such as forestry and rural development). Birdlife International (1994) mentioned the poor integration with other CAP policies (commodity regimes, set-aside, rural development programmes and forestry programmes) to be one of the greatest problems facing Council Regulation (EEC) 2078/92. The potential to achieve the objectives of this regulation depends on the integration with other policies. For example, afforestation programmes which derive from Council Regulation (EEC) 2080/92 will have to be tuned with the proposed agri-environmental measures of Council Regulation (EEC) 2078/92. The environmental objectives under the agri-environmental measures might not be fully achieved in case measures are taken without sufficient coordination with other measures. In general there is insufficient monitoring towards the achievement of EU environmental policy. This might be partly due to the programmes which are developed by Member States. There are also examples (in Extremadura, Spain, see Palomo Molano, 1994) of the development and irrigation plans to be cofinanced by the EU structural funds and even by the cohesion fund contravening the new agri-environmental objectives. Such events point to the necessity of an integrated approach to a nature conservation policy.

4.6   Concluding remarks

The objective of the chapter has been to analyse the effects of the CAP on the environment of the European Union, and to make an inventory of environmental measures in agricultural policies. Focus has been on the reform of the arable crops regime and of the beef regime.

1. There is increasing concern in Europe about the deterioration of the environment. The Treaty of the European Union (Article 130R) calls for the integration of the environment into other community policies. Environmental conditions are increasingly required in agricultural policy. Some measures have been implemented already. However, large differences remain between Member States and in many respects it is too early to judge their implications for the environment and landscape.
2. Both agricultural production and environmental impacts depend on highly location-specific environmental conditions. Reality is much too complex to allow generalizations about the environmental impacts of agricultural policies. Therefore, in assessing the environmental impact of the CAP, the greatest possible attention should be given to local/regional differences of environmental consequences of policy instruments identified per product.
3. Environmental issues are better recognized in the CAP than they were in the past. Environmental requirements presently are included in Council Regulations on products like arable crops, beef and sheep. Environmental clauses in agricultural policy presently allow Member States to put conditions for direct (compensatory) payments. Environmental requirements in market and price policies are included in the Arable Crop Scheme (Regulation (EEC) 1765/92), formulated as management conditions on land which is set aside. Such environmental conditions are presently also added to several livestock schemes, including the Council Regulation on beef market organization.

4. Empirical evidence shows a decline in consumption of agrochemicals to grow cereals during the past decade. The 1992 reform of the cereal regime may be one of the factors which contributed to that trend. Its impact on the environment and landscape comes from changes in price support and from the set-aside regulation. Lower prices may induce farmers to reduce their use of fertilizers, plant protection products and (in certain regions where it is scarce) water. However, farmers may change their cropping plan towards products which require more intensive production methods and higher dosages of agrochemicals (e.g. fruit, vegetables, potatoes). Lower prices have complex implications for the agricultural system and environmental benefits on the one hand may be offset by increased costs. Differences between Member States are largely due to different farming systems and biophysical conditions.

5. A reference area was introduced as part of the reform of the arable crop regime, such that the area which is eligible for the arable payments scheme is limited to the area of arable crops and temporary grass used by 31 December, 1991. This condition has a positive effect on the environment as it prevents farmers from reverting extensive grassland to arable crops. Also, conditions have been formulated in several Member States concerning the management of land which is put aside. Set-aside policies allow for conservation of nature and maintenance of landscape.

6. The set-aside scheme can be applied on a rotational and a non-rotational basis. Farm specific features, like soil productivity and cropping plan, affect the farmer's decision whether to opt for one form or the other. Of both options, the non-rotational form appears to have a more favourable impact on the environment and landscape. A greater diversity of plant species is likely to develop, and this will subsequently support a greater variety of fauna. The management rules on the treatment of land which is put aside are, however, crucial to the environmental impact of both forms of the set-aside scheme.

7. Extensification of livestock production in response to the reform of the beef regime has been limited so far. Experiences in Member States with the scheme indicate the relative unattractiveness of the premium to the farmer and the ineffectiveness of the measure to reduce livestock density. Also, the reduction of livestock prices did not reduce stocking density during the past couple of years because different trends were observed outside agriculture (e.g. monetary changes in some national currencies).

8. The effectiveness of the Accompanying Measures largely depends on market regimes. The response by farmers deciding whether to participate in programmes under these measures depends partly on incentives provided by alternative policies. If the level of support for arable crops were lower compared to present levels, then one could theoretically also achieve the objectives of Regulation 2078/92 at lower costs. The arable support

arrangements introduced in 1992 prevented farmers from counting arable land taken out of agricultural production under agri-environment schemes towards their set-aside requirement under Regulation 1765/92. This was a factor in discouraging arable farmers from participating in some agri-environment schemes. Following the amendment to Regulation 1765/92 in June 1995, arable land taken out of production under agri-environment schemes can be counted against farmers' set-aside requirements, subject to it complying with the normal eligibility rules.

References

Ansell, D.J. and S.A. Vincent (1994), *An evaluation of set-aside management in the European Union with special reference to Denmark, France, Germany and the UK*, Reading, UK: Centre for Agricultural Strategy, CAS Paper 30.

Beaufoy, G., D. Baldock, J. Clark *et al.* (1994), *The nature of farming. Low intensity farming systems of nine European countries*, London, UK: Institute for European Environmental Policy (IEEP).

Birdlife International (1994), *Implementation of EU agri-environment regulation 2078*, Brussels: Birdlife International European Agriculture Task Force.

Brouwer, F.M. and S. van Berkum (1996), *CAP and environment in the European Union: Analysis of the effects of the CAP on the environment and an assessment of existing environmental conditions in policy*, Wageningen, Netherlands: Wageningen Pers.

Commission of the European Communities (CEC) (1991), *Development and future of the Common Agricultural Policy*, Brussels, Belgium: Commission of the European Communities COM(91)100, 1 February.

Commission of the European Communities (CEC) (1992), *Towards sustainability: a European Community programme of policy and action in relation to the environment and sustainable development*, Brussels, Belgium: Commission of the European Communities.

Commission of the European Communities (CEC) (1993), *The agricultural situation in the Community 1992*, Brussels, Belgium: Commission of the European Communities.

Faasen, R. (1995), 'Agricultural pesticide use ... a threat to the European environment?' *European Water Pollution Control*, **5**(2), 34–40.

Hawke, N. and N. Kovaleva (1994), 'Environmental protection under the new set-aside scheme', *The ALA Bulletin*, December, pp. 50–53.

Ministry of Agriculture, Fisheries and Food (MAFF) (1994), *CAP reform: arable area payments 1994/95*, London, UK: MAFF.

OECD (1997a), *Environmental benefits from Agriculture: Issues and Policies, The Helsinki Seminar*, Paris, France: Organization for Economic Cooperation and Development.

OECD (1997b), *The Environmental Effects of Land Diversions Schemes*. Paris, France: Organization for Economic Cooperation and Development.

Palomo Molano, J. (1994), 'Agricultura y Medio Ambiente en Extremadura', *Agricultura*, **738**, 44–5.

Putter, J. de (1995), *The greening of Europe's agricultural policy: the 'agri-environmental regulation' of the MacSharry reform*, The Hague, Netherlands: Ministry of Agriculture, Nature Management and Fisheries.

Suarez, F. (1994), *La protección de las estepas mediterráneas. Directrices generales para la propuesta de una estrategia de conservación*, Report by Department for the Environment.

Tracy, M., (1989), *Government and agriculture in Western Europe, 1880–1988*, London, UK: Harvester-Wheatsheaf.

Varela-Ortega, C. and J.M. Sumpsi (1995), *The CAP and the environment in Spain*, Contributed paper to the project CAP and Environment in the European Union.

Williamson, J. (1993), 'CAP reform set-aside: environmental friend or foe?', in USDA/ERS, *International agriculture and trade reports. Europe*, Washington, US: Department of Agriculture/Economic Research Service, RS-93-5, Situation and outlook series.

5 Consistency between environmental and competitiveness objectives of agricultural policies: economics of price support, set-aside, direct payments and other Common Agricultural Policy instruments

Alain Carpentier, Hervé Guyomard and Chantal Le Mouël

5.1 Introduction

For a long time, the basic instrument of the Common Agricultural Policy (CAP) has been market price support. The use of this instrument has over time become increasingly costly in terms of budget, complicated administration, distortion of resource use, detrimental environmental effects and international trade tensions. The 1992 CAP reform has changed the direction of the CAP in partially shifting the burden of support from the consumers to the taxpayers with the objective of reducing the negative effects mentioned above. Furthermore, the CAP reform was essential in paving the way for a GATT (General Agreement on Tariffs and Trade) settlement on agriculture in the Uruguay Round (see, e.g., Guyomard *et al.*, 1994; Sumner, 1994).

The emphasis on grains and other arable crops (i.e., oilseeds and protein crops) of the 1992 CAP reform makes sense in the light of their importance in land use, livestock–crop interactions via the feed sector as well as international agricultural trade and relationships. The new instrumentation of support in the arable crop sector should improve the economic incentives from price signals. Both the set-aside programme and the move away from price support towards direct payments to producers should result in some decline in production, at least relative to what would otherwise have been the case. Compensatory payments based on historical area and yields are, at least theoretically, decoupled from yields. Nevertheless, as noted by Moschini and Sckokai (1994) or Harvey (1995), they cannot be considered fully decoupled. Even if the Uruguay Round Agreement (URA) considers CAP direct aids as 'decoupled' transfers that can be included in the so-called blue box, they remain tied to the obligation of producing certain crops, they require setting aside some land and they are based on current acreage declaration. In addition, compensatory payments may influence production decisions via acreage allocation demands (Guyomard *et al.*, 1996; Oude Lansink and Peerlings, 1996).

Even if farm programmes are not the only factors affecting agricultural management decisions, it is now well recognized that they have significant impacts on agricultural land use, output supply and input demand, commodity prices, producer incomes and fixed or quasi-fixed output rents. The effects of farm programmes on the agricultural sector and on the economy as a whole are continually being analysed. There is, in particular, a growing literature on the effects of farm programmes, and more generally of agricultural activities, on environment. This surge in interest stems from the recognition that agriculture is, in some cases, a primary source of environmental pollution and degradation.

As noted by Kuch and Reichelderfer (1992), agricultural policies can affect environmental quality by influencing management decisions which result in two sorts of fundamental processes, i.e., changes at the extensive margin of production (the amount of land used in agricultural production) and changes in the intensity of land use (the amount of non-land inputs used per hectare). In the European Union (EU), it is widely recognized that pre-reform CAP instruments have resulted in 'excessive' use of fertilizers and pesticides detrimental to the environment, these inputs often being applied at rates that could not be justified economically without considerations of present and future farm support programmes. Mahé and Rainelli (1987) clearly showed how the scarcity of the land factor resulted in an increase in both the price of land and the intensification level, here simply defined as the ratio of chemical inputs on land quantity. They also showed that the pre-reform price support mechanism increased these two movements and that it was only a second best policy for supporting farm labour income since a major part of the support was dissipated in the land rent. Furthermore, this policy also led to environmental negative effects at the extensive margin since production moved onto marginal lands, and ecologically sensitive as well as vulnerable zones were converted to agricultural production. The pre-reform CAP has thus probably contributed to socially inefficient chemical input use, not only by an excessive use to achieve higher yields and to maximize government programme payments on agricultural lands, but also by a use to expand production onto marginal lands or to support production in regions poorly suited to a particular crop.

The purpose of this chapter is threefold. We first propose a simplified analytical framework of crop producer behaviour allowing us to analyse the effects of changes in key agricultural policy instruments and/or exogenous variables at both the intensive and extensive margin of production. The model is mono-product and considers land as a fixed, but allocable factor of production. This fixed amount of land is allocated between two enterprises, the first one corresponding to an 'intensive' technology which implies high levels of chemical input use and the second one corresponding to an 'extensive' technology which uses low levels of fertilizers and pesticides per hectare. Following Lichtenberg (1985, 1989) and Just *et al.* (1991), we explicitly consider land quality as an argument of production and behavioural functions and we analyse the producer problem on a quality class by class basis[1]. Comparative statics are used to examine the potential effects of changes in key policy parameters and exogenous variables.

The second objective of the chapter is to analyse to what extent the 1992 CAP reform may be viewed as a first response to the problem of chemical input inefficiency in the EU crop sector and induced non-point source pollution. In that context, we first analyse the potential impact of the new CAP arrangements in the crop sector, i.e., lower support prices, per hectare compensatory payments and set aside, on the intensity of land use. We show that yields and farming intensity are likely to decrease due to support price cuts, but that the set-aside programme may offset a large part of this effect. In the same way, comparative static results are used to analyse the various parameters which may influence conversion of land from the intensive technology to the extensive technology, i.e., to analyse changes at the extensive margin of production. We show that output support price cuts are likely to favour land conversion from the intensive technology to the extensive technology, but again that the set-aside programme and 'induced' input price decreases may offset conversion incentives.

Finally, we extend the analysis by including negative social costs arising from 'excessive' chemical input use. In that context, we analyse the effects of environmental policies (pollution emission taxes as well as input or output taxes) on producer behaviour at the intensive margin of production, i.e., for a given land quality. We then show that uniform taxes on pollution emissions, input or output, undifferentiated according to land quality, are not optimal policy instruments.

The chapter is organized as follows. The analytical framework is presented in Section 5.2. Comparative static results and implications for policy design are discussed in Section 5.3. Section 5.4 extends the analysis by considering negative social costs resulting from intensive production techniques and focuses on the relationship between environmental input or output taxes and land quality. Section 5.5 concludes.

5.2 Analytical framework

5.2.1 Notations and assumptions
Consider a mono-product farm with a fixed land stock sufficiently large so that the acreage L is heterogeneous in quality. Following Lichtenberg (1985, 1989) and Antle and Just (1991), let q be a scalar measure of land quality, normalized

---

1   The alternative to considering the problem on a quality class by class basis is to allow decreasing marginal returns to land (see, e.g., Chambers and Just, 1989; Coyle, 1993).

to lie between zero and one, and $G(q)$ represent total acreage of quality no less than q. Accordingly, $g(q) = dG(q)/dq = G'_q(q)$ is the amount of acreage having quality q. Each available technology is described by a well-behaved neo-classical production function which exhibits constant returns to scale in land. Denote the per hectare production function $y = f(x,q,u)$ where x is a vector of variable inputs used to produce the considered crop when the uth technology is employed. The parameter u lies between u^- and u^+ and the greater u is, the more intensive the technology is. Each per hectare production function satisfies the following assumptions:

a1) $f'_{x_i}(.) > 0$

a2) $f(.)$ is strictly concave in (x,u)

a3) $f'_q(.) > 0$

a4) $f''_{x_i x_j}(.) \geq 0$ for $i \neq j$

a5) $f''_{u x_i}(.) \geq 0$ with a strict inequality for at least one input

a6) $f''_{uq}(.) > 0$

a7) $f''_{q x_i}(.) \geq 0$ with a strict inequality for at least one input

Assumptions a1), a2) and a3) are standard. Assumptions a1) and a2) mean that variable inputs display a positive and decreasing marginal productivity, while assumption a3) indicates that yields are an increasing function of land quality, *ceteris paribus*. In practice, the parameter q corresponds to a scalar measure of agronomic quality of a site with respect to crop production. This quality depends on soil properties (slope, structure, composition, water flows, ...), climate features (rainfall, temperature, photosynthesis, ...) as well as interactions between soil properties and climate features. Assumptions a4) to a7) are less obvious and require some explanations. Each of these assumptions closely relies on technical ground.

Assumption a7) indicates that land quality is assumed to increase the marginal productivity of variable inputs. The parameter q is an indicator of the ability of a site to provide water, nutrients and pesticides in sufficient quantities to the plant as well as adequate temperature and sunshine. Assumption a7) follows immediately. Furthermore, as regards to the provision of water, nutrients and pesticides to the plant, one may underline that 'good' soil properties (mainly slope, composition and structure) contribute to limiting the amount of variable inputs which are likely to be wasted. In that context, one can reasonably expect that the marginal productivity of a variable input increases with land quality. The relationship between land quality and input use largely determines the 'environmental' properties of a land area with respect to crop production. In fact, assumption a7) suggests that the higher the land quality is, the more applied inputs remain available to the crop and the less they may be harmful to non-targeted sites such as water resources.

Assumption a5) means that intensifying the technology increases the marginal productivity of variable inputs. As regards fertilizers and pesticides, this relationship actually lies at the root of intensive cropping technology properties (Meynard, 1991). The main characteristic of intensive cropping technologies is to promote high-yielding conditions in order to achieve high yields. It results that intensive practices rely on the use of high-yielding varieties, large seed density, and early sowing. Such practices contribute to making variable input applications more efficient, even if the relationship between intensive cropping patterns and variable input use is not exactly of the same nature according to the considered input. In the case of fertilizers, the nature of the relationship is obvious. Early sowing of highly productive seeds contributes to increase of the growth potential of cultivated crops, i.e., their nutrient assimilation. As a result, the more intensive the cropping practices are, the higher the marginal productivity of fertilizers. In the case of pesticides, the nature of the relationship between intensive cropping patterns and input use is quite different. On the one hand, due to selection choices, highly productive plants are generally more vulnerable to pests and diseases. More precisely, high-yielding plants use a large part of their 'energy' to grow, which results in detrimental effects on their resistance to pests and diseases. On the other hand, long growing seasons and large seed densities increase the likelihood of severe pests and disease damages. It follows that intensive cropping techniques increase the vulnerability of crops to severe pests and disease damage so that they call for effective crop protection. In that context, the more intensive the cropping techniques are, the more productive the pesticides are (Harper and Zilberman, 1989; Meynard, 1991).

Assumption a6) indicates that land quality is assumed to increase the marginal productivity of intensive cropping patterns. This assumption clearly suggests that intensive cropping practices may not be viewed as substitutes for land quality. In other words, considering that intensive cropping patterns are used to enable the crop to achieve its maximum productive potential, land quality must be viewed as one of the various factors allowing this achievement. As an example, long growing seasons benefit the crop growth as long as the soil remains in a good state (with respect to humidity and structure) and sunshine is sufficient during the complete growing period.

In a similar way, assumption a4) also suggests some kind of complementarity among inputs. It states that an increase in the use of one variable input induces an increase in the marginal productivity of the others. In other words, variable inputs 'cooperate' in output production (Rader, 1968). The main idea supported by this assumption is that each input has a well-defined non-substitutable role in the production process. The latter may be divided into several complementary sub-processes (soil preparation, crop nutrition, crop protection, harvest, etc.) and each of these sub-processes is associated with specific inputs. For example, fertilizer application is aimed at feeding the crop, whereas pesticide application relates to crop protection. Crop nutrition and crop protection may then be viewed as two distinct aspects of the global production process. In addition, it is interesting to note that additional arguments for fertilizer and pesticide cooperation are provided by the fact that fertilizer application increases the likelihood of pests and disease damage, such as fungi and weed damage.

Finally, it is important to note that a negative marginal productivity resulting from technology intensification is not ruled out *a priori* (in other words, it is not assumed that $f'_u(.) \geq 0$). Such a case may occur when highly intensive cropping practices are used on low quality land and/or with low input use.

At this stage, three remarks are in order. First, extensive cropping techniques may be warranted when high input use is prohibited (due to the economic context or legal constraints) and/or when land quality is low. Second, the 'success' of the cropping technology intensification process appears heavily dependent on the availability of land of high quality on the one hand and on the use of inputs such as fertilizers and pesticides on the other hand. This dependence is theoretically formalized by assumptions a4) to a7) which state that variable inputs x, land quality q and technology u 'cooperate' in output production. Third, a function $f(x,q,u)$ which satisfies assumptions a4) to a7) is said to be supermodular in (x,q,u) (Topkis, 1978; Milgrom and Roberts, 1990; Milgrom and Shannon, 1994). In that case, one shows that the derived demand of each variable input is: a) non-increasing in variable input prices (i.e., variable inputs are never gross substitutes), b) non-decreasing in output price, c) non-decreasing in technology intensification level u, and d) non-decreasing in land quality q.[2] In order to simplify the presentation, we now assume that x corresponds to a scalar since in the multi-input case, each of these inputs responds in a similar way to a change in an exogenous variable. Under this additional hypothesis, assumptions a1) to a7) may be written as:

$$A1) f'_x(.) > 0 \; ; \; A2) f''_{xx}(.) < 0 \; ; \; A3) f'_q(.) > 0 \; ; \; A4) f''_{ux}(.) > 0 \; ; \; A5) f''_{uq}(.) > 0 \text{ and}$$
$$A6) f''_{qx}(.) > 0$$

5.2.2 Characterization of optima and land allocation patterns

For simplicity, consider the problem of allocating the total acreage L between two technology combinations corresponding to intensification levels u^- and u^+, respectively. Let $l_{u^-}(q)$ be the proportion of land of quality q used with the extensive technology u^-. Following Lichtenberg (1985, 1989), the decision problem of the profit-maximizing producer is then to choose $l_{u^-}(q)$ for each land quality q, i.e.,

---

2   The two last results follow from a direct application of theorem 10 in Milgrom and Shannon (1994).

$$\max \int_0^1 \left[\pi(p,w,q,u^-) \cdot l_{u^-}(q) + \pi(p,w,q,u^+) \cdot (1 - l_{u^-}(q)) \right] \cdot g(q) dq \quad (5.1)$$

where p is the output price, w is the variable input price, and $\pi(p,w,q,u)$ is the per hectare profit function defined by:

$$\pi(p,w,q,u) = \max_{y,x}(pf(x,q,u) - wx)$$
$$= py^*(p,w,q,u) - wx^*(p,w,q,u) \; ; \; u = u^-,u^+ \quad (5.2)$$

Programme (5.1) shows that the optimal land allocation is to devote all land of quality q to the extensive technology u^- when $\pi(p,w,q,u^-) > \pi(p,w,q,u^+)$ and, inversely, to devote all land of quality q to the intensive technology u^+ when $\pi(p,w,q,u^+) > \pi(p,w,q,u^-)$. Before characterizing the various patterns of land allocation, we first show the two following propositions.

Proposition 1. $x^*(p,w,q,u^-) \leq x^*(p,w,q,u^+)$.
Proof. We assume an interior solution for $x^*(p,w,q,u^-)$ and $x^*(p,w,q,u^+)$ in programme (5.2). First-order conditions imply that the following equality is verified at the optimum:

$$f_x'(x^*(p,w,q,u^-),q,u^-) = f_x'(x^*(p,w,q,u^+),q,u^+) = w/p \quad (5.3)$$

From A4), we have:

$$f_x'(x^*(p,w,q,u^-),q,u^+) > f_x'(x^*(p,w,q,u^-),q,u^-)$$

Using (5.3), we then have:

$$f_x'(x^*(p,w,q,u^-),q,u^+) > f_x'(x^*(p,w,q,u^+),q,u^+) = w/p$$

Hence,

$$x^*(p,w,q,u^+) > x^*(p,w,q,u^-).$$

QED.

Proposition 2. The implicit function $H(p,w,q,u^-,u^+)$ is defined by the difference $\pi(p,w,q,u^-) - \pi(p,w,q,u^+)$. We then have $dH(p,w,q,u^-,u^+)/dq < 0$.
Proof. Differentiating the function $H(p,w,q,u^-,u^+)$ with respect to land quality q, one obtains:

$$dH(p,w,q,u^-,u^+)/dq = p \cdot [f_q'(x^*(p,w,q,u^-),q,u^-) - f_q'(x^*(p,w,q,u^+),q,u^+)]$$

From A5), we have:

$$f_q'(x^*(p,w,q,u^-), q,u^-) < f_q'(x^*(p,w,q,u^-),q,u^+)$$

From proposition 1, we have:

$$f_q'(x^*(p,w,q,u^-), q,u^-) < f_q'(x^*(p,w,q,u^+),q,u^+)$$

Hence,

$$dH(p,w,q,u^-,u^+)/dq < 0.$$

QED.

Proposition 1 shows that the per hectare variable input demand is an increasing function of the intensification parameter u. Proposition 2 indicates that the per hectare profit function associated with the extensive technology intersects the unit profit function obtained with the intensive technology from above.

Let the critical land quality $\tilde{q}$ be defined by:

$$H(p,w,\tilde{q},u^-,u^+) = \pi(p,w,\tilde{q},u^-) - \pi(p,w,\tilde{q},u^+) = 0$$

Using the two previous propositions and the definition of the critical land quality $\tilde{q}$, it is now possible to characterize the patterns of land allocation as follows:

i)   When the critical land quality $\tilde{q}$ is greater than one, $\pi(p,w,1,u^-) > \pi(p,w,1,u^+)$ and all the land stock is allocated to the extensive technology (which is more profitable than the intensive technology on all land qualities in that case).

ii) When the critical land quality $\tilde{q}$ is lower than zero, $\pi(p,w,0,u^-) < \pi(p,w,0,u^+)$ and all the land stock is allocated to the intensive technology (which is more profitable than the extensive technology on all land qualities in that case).

iii) When the critical land quality $\tilde{q}$ lies between zero and one, all land of quality less than $\tilde{q}$ is allocated to the extensive technology and all land of quality greater than $\tilde{q}$ is allocated to the intensive technology. Acreages allocated to the extensive and intensive technology are given by, respectively:

$$L_{u^-} = \int_0^{\tilde{q}} g(q)dq = G(\tilde{q}) \qquad (5.4a)$$

$$L_{u^+} = L - L_{u^-} = \int_{\tilde{q}}^1 g(q)dq = G(1) - G(\tilde{q}) \qquad (5.4b)$$

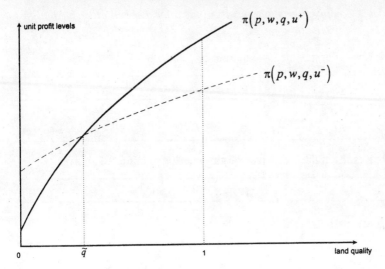

Figure 5.1 Land allocation mechanism on a class by class basis: the case of an interior solution

This land allocation mechanism on a class by class basis is depicted graphically in Figure 5.1 in the case of an interior solution. The critical land quality $\tilde{q}$ corresponds to the point where the extensive per hectare profit function $\pi(p,w,q,u^-)$ intersects the intensive per hectare profit function $\pi(p,w,q,u^+)$ from above. Accordingly, land of quality lower (respectively higher) than $\tilde{q}$ is allocated to the extensive (respectively intensive) technology.

5.3   Comparative static results and implications for policy design

Comparative statics may now be used to examine the potential effects of changes in key policy instruments of the CAP (i.e., output support price, set aside and per hectare compensatory payments) and/or in other exogenous variables (i.e., variable input prices). Results are summarized in Table 5.1. They are used to analyse the potential impact of the 1992 CAP reform on both the intensity of land use and the land allocation decision.

5.3.1 Comparative static results

5.3.1.1   Policy changes and adjustments at the intensive margin of production

Adjustments at the intensive margin of production are first addressed (Table 5.1, panel a). The first row gives the impact of changes in policy instruments on the per hectare variable input use while the second row gives the corresponding impact on yields. These results are obvious and are directly linked to unit production and profit function properties. The per hectare demand for the

Table 5.1   Comparative static results at the intensive and extensive margins of production

Panel a. Results at the intensive margin

α	w	p	θ	a	q	u
$dx^*(p,w,q,u)/d\alpha$	$-$	$+$	0	0	$+$	$+$
$dy^*(p,w,q,u)/d\alpha$	$-$	$+$	0	0	$+$	$+$

Panel b. Results at the extensive margin (interior solution, i.e., $\tilde{q} \in [0,1]$)

α	w	p	θ	a
$d\tilde{q}/d\alpha$	$+$	$-$	0	0
$dL_{u^-}/d\alpha$	$+$	$-$	$-$	0

variable input is an increasing function of the output price p and a decreasing function of its own price w. It does not depend on the set-aside rate θ and per hectare compensatory payments a. The per hectare output supply is an increasing function of the output price and a decreasing function of the variable input price. It does not depend on the set-aside rate and per hectare compensatory payments.

Comparative static results show, in particular, that compensatory payments of the CAP reform which are based on historical area and yields are decoupled at the intensive margin of production and hence, do not influence per hectare input use and yields for a given technology choice. They also show that the CAP reform should result in some decline in per hectare input use and yields, at least relative to what would otherwise have been the case. They finally show that the output–input price ratio is the main variable which influences input use and yields at the intensive margin of production.

5.3.1.2   Policy changes and adjustments at the extensive margin of production

The discussion now focuses on impacts at the extensive margin (Table 5.1, panel b). The first row gives the impact of changes in policy instruments on the critical land quality while the second row gives the corresponding impact on acreage allocated to the extensive technology. We first consider the case of an interior solution, then the case of a corner solution.

The interior solution case   The producer simultaneously uses the extensive technology u^- on his low quality land (i.e., of quality lower than $\tilde{q}$) and the intensive technology u^+ on his high quality land (i.e., of quality greater than $\tilde{q}$). Consider the impact of a change in the variable input price. Differentiating the acreage equation (5.4a) with respect to the variable input price, one obtains:

$$dL_{u^-} / dw = (\partial G(\tilde{q})/\partial q).(d\tilde{q} / dw) \tag{5.5}$$

Since $\partial G(\tilde{q})/\partial q$ is positive, the sign of dL_{u^-}/dw is the same as the sign of $d\tilde{q}/dw$. We then consider the implicit function $H(p,w,q,u^-,u^+)$ evaluated at the critical land quality $\tilde{q}$. By definition, $H(p,w,\tilde{q},u^-,u^+) = 0$. Differentiating the latter with respect to w, one obtains:

$$\frac{dH\left(p,w,\tilde{q},u^-,u^+\right)}{dw} = \frac{\partial \pi\left(p,w,\tilde{q},u^-\right)}{\partial w} + \frac{\partial \pi\left(p,w,\tilde{q},u^-\right)}{\partial q}.\frac{d\tilde{q}}{dw}$$

$$- \frac{\partial \pi\left(p,w,\tilde{q},u^+\right)}{\partial w} - \frac{\partial \pi\left(p,w,\tilde{q},u^+\right)}{\partial q}.\frac{d\tilde{q}}{dw}$$

$$= -\left[x^*\left(p,w,\tilde{q},u^-\right) - x^*\left(p,w,\tilde{q},u^+\right)\right]$$

$$+ \left[\frac{\partial \pi\left(p,w,\tilde{q},u^-\right)}{\partial q} - \frac{\partial \pi\left(p,w,\tilde{q},u^+\right)}{\partial q}\right].\frac{d\tilde{q}}{dw}$$

$$= 0$$

Hence,

$$\frac{d\tilde{q}}{dw} = \frac{x^*\left(p,w,\tilde{q},u^-\right) - x^*\left(p,w,\tilde{q},u^+\right)}{\pi'_q\left(p,w,\tilde{q},u^-\right) - \pi'_q\left(p,w,\tilde{q},u^+\right)} \tag{5.6}$$

Proposition 1 implies that the numerator in (5.6) is negative while proposition 2 implies that the denominator in (5.6) is strictly negative. Hence,

$$d\tilde{q}/dw > 0 \text{ and } dL_{u^-}/dw > 0 \tag{5.7}$$

By a similar reasoning, one shows:

$$\frac{d\tilde{q}}{dp} = \frac{-y^*\left(p,w,\tilde{q},u^-\right) + y^*\left(p,w,\tilde{q},u^+\right)}{\pi'_q\left(p,w,\tilde{q},u^-\right) - \pi'_q\left(p,w,\tilde{q},u^+\right)} \tag{5.8}$$

Hence,

$$d\tilde{q}/dp < 0 \text{ and } dL_{u^-} / dp < 0 \tag{5.9}$$

An intuitive interpretation of the two previous results is the following. An increase in the price of the variable input gives an incentive to cut back on its use and to substitute other less costly factors. One mechanism for doing so is to convert more land to the extensive technology u^- which, by definition, uses the variable input less intensively. Such an incentive to convert more land to the extensive technology suggests that the critical land quality $\tilde{q}$ increases from, say, $\tilde{q}_0$ to $\tilde{q}_{1+}$ and all land of quality lying between $\tilde{q}_0$ and $\tilde{q}_{1+}$ is now allocated to the extensive technology which is more profitable than the intensive technology on these land quality classes. By a similar reasoning, an increase in the output price gives the producer an incentive to convert more land to the intensive technology. The critical land quality decreases from, say, $\tilde{q}_0$ to $\tilde{q}_{1-}$ and all land of quality lying between $\tilde{q}_{1-}$ to $\tilde{q}_0$ is now devoted to the intensive technology. One can thus conclude that a decrease in the output–input price ratio induces a decrease in the variable input use through adjustments at both the intensive and the extensive margin of production.

Consider now the impact of a (fixed, i.e., non rotational) set-aside policy. Assumptions about production technologies in both the intensive and extensive case imply that the producer will optimally choose to first set aside the lowest land qualities.[3] It results that the lower bound of the land quality interval is now $q$inf, which is strictly greater than zero and is implicitly defined by:

$$\int_{q\mathrm{inf}}^{1} g(q)dq = (1-\theta).\int_{0}^{1} g(q)dq = (1-\theta).G(q) \qquad (5.10)$$

where θ is the land set-aside rate.

If $q$inf is lower than $\tilde{q}$, the producer will set aside extensively used land only. If $q$inf is greater than $\tilde{q}$, the new allocation corresponds to a corner solution where all cultivated land is devoted to the intensive technology since its quality lies between $q$inf $> \tilde{q}$ and 1.

Finally, consider the impact of CAP reform compensatory payments. Since they do not influence either land quality bounds or the critical land quality, they have no impact on land allocation at least in this mono-product simplified framework. In other words, compensatory payments of the CAP reform are not only decoupled at the intensive margin of production, but also at the extensive margin of production.

At this stage, the following remarks are in order. The analytical framework developed in this section considers only one product and assumes that the total area L allocated to this product is constant. In the context of the CAP, one may consider that the product is an aggregate of cereals and oilseeds (hereafter CO

---

3   This result is simply due to the fact that $\pi(p,w,q,u)$ is an increasing function of land quality q.

crops) and that L corresponds to the fixed eligible base area. The fact that compensatory payments are found to be decoupled applies only if L can be assumed to be constant, i.e., if it is profitable to devote the predetermined area L to CO crops in the new CAP regime.[4] Nevertheless, without compensatory payments, it is likely that the area in CO crops would decrease compared to the area of sugar beets, potatoes and/or fodder crops (Oude Lansink and Peerlings, 1996). Accordingly, even in the framework of a mono-product technology, compensatory payments cannot be considered fully decoupled since they remain tied to the obligation of producing CO crops. In addition, compensatory payments would also influence production decisions for the various CO crops (wheat, maize, barley, other coarse grains, sunflower, rapeseed, soya and protein crops) via CO crop-specific acreage allocation demands under the binding constraint of a fixed base area. Cahill (1993) and Guyomard et al. (1996) show that, because compensatory payments are very different for the various CO crops,[5] they do influence land allocation decisions and hence, output supplies and variable input use. Nevertheless, it is interesting to note that Guyomard et al. find empirically that the compensatory payments package is, to a large extent, neutral in so far as its effects on yields and supplies, and variable input use, would be only very small. The neutrality is due to the fact that effects of compensatory payments are nearly offset by cross effects of compensatory payments on substitutable CO crops.

The corner solution case   We now consider the case of a corner solution for the land allocation problem, more precisely the case where $\tilde{q}$ is initially lower than zero.[6] In the initial situation, all the available area is devoted to the intensive technology u^+. Comparative static results on critical land quality $\tilde{q}$ are the same as those derived in the case of an interior solution, i.e., $d\tilde{q}/dw > 0$, $d\tilde{q}/dp < 0$, $d\tilde{q}/d\theta = 0$, and $d\tilde{q}/da = 0$.

Consider first a variable input price increase. In that case, the critical land quality increases from, say, $\tilde{q}_0$ to $\tilde{q}_{1+}$. If the new critical land quality $\tilde{q}_{1+}$ remains lower than zero, the input price increase has no impact at the extensive margin of production. But if the new critical land quality $\tilde{q}_{1+}$ becomes greater than zero, some land of low quality, i.e., of quality lying between 0 and $\tilde{q}_{1+}$, is now devoted to the extensive technology.

An increase in the output price induces a decrease in the critical land quality and hence has no impact at the extensive margin of production. However, in the

---

4   On this point, see Roberts et al. (1996) who show that participation in the programme should be very high (nearly 100%) in England if CAP reform parameters (i.e., output levels, set-aside rate and per hectare compensatory payments) remain at current (i.e., 1993) levels.
5   Compensatory payments are much higher for oilseeds than for grains.
6   Comparative static results obtained in this corner solution case can easily be transposed to the corner solution case corresponding to a situation where $\tilde{q}$ is initially greater than 1.

case of an output price cut, as the critical land quality increases, some land of low quality may be converted to the extensive technology.

Finally, the requirement of setting aside a fixed proportion of the available area L has no impact at the extensive margin of production since it enlarges the gap between the critical land quality (which remains unchanged at $\tilde{q}_0 < 0$) and the lowest quality of cultivated land ($qinf > 0$).

5.3.1.3   Policy changes and total impact on input use, output supply and yields Total impacts of policy variable changes on input use, output supply and yields may now be addressed by simultaneously considering changes at the intensive margin and changes at the extensive margin. For simplicity, we consider an interior solution only.[7]

By definition, the total demand function for the variable input is given by:

$$X^* = \int_0^1 x^*\big(p,w,q,u^*(q)\big) \cdot g(q)dq$$

$$= \int_0^{\tilde{q}} x^*\big(p,w,q,u^-\big) \cdot g(q)dq + \int_{\tilde{q}}^1 x^*\big(p,w,q,u^+\big) \cdot g(q)dq \qquad (5.11)$$

Differentiating equation (5.11) with respect to w, one obtains:

$$\frac{dX^*}{dw} = \int_0^{\tilde{q}} \frac{dx^*\big(p,w,q,u^-\big)}{dw} \cdot g(q)dq$$

$$+ \int_{\tilde{q}}^1 \frac{dx^*\big(p,w,q,u^+\big)}{dw} \cdot g(q)dq + \frac{d\tilde{q}}{dw} \cdot g(\tilde{q}) \cdot \Big[x^*\big(.,u^-\big) - x^*\big(.,u^+\big)\Big] \qquad (5.12)$$

The first and second right-hand side terms of (5.12) capture the impact of the variable input price change at the intensive margin of production. They are negative by convexity in prices of the two unit profit functions $\pi(p,w,q,u^-)$ and $\pi(p,w,q,u^+)$. The third right-hand side term of (5.12) measures the impact of the price change at the extensive margin of production. This term is also negative since $d\tilde{q}/dw > 0$ and $x^*(p,w,q,u^-) < x^*(p,w,q,u^+)$. It results that the total demand function for the variable input is decreasing in its own price (i.e., $dX^*/dw < 0$).

---

7   Extending the results to corner solutions is straightforward.

By a similar reasoning, one easily shows that the total demand function for the variable input is increasing in the output price (i.e., $dX^*/dp > 0$), and that the total supply function of the output is a decreasing function of the input price and an increasing function of the output price.

5.3.2 Implications for policy design: the 1992 CAP reform and the extensification issue

It is now widely recognized that the pre-reform CAP, through high and stable output–input price ratios, provided strong incentives for European producers to both increase the intensity of land use and expand intensive production techniques onto marginal lands. In theory, by reducing output–input price ratios, the 1992 CAP reform should induce EU crop producers to reduce variable input use at the intensive margin of production. However, three factors may offset the positive effect of the reform on land use intensity. First, the policy price cut does not necessarily mean an equivalent decrease in market price, as it can be observed from the first three years of CAP reform application. Second, a downward adjustment of chemical prices may partly offset a part of the output price cut. Third, and perhaps more importantly in the long run, price elasticities of yields and input use may be low around the pre-reform 'equilibrium' point. As a result, the effects of price changes are likely to be small. Many empirical studies suggest that price elasticities are rather low in the short run when primary factors (i.e., labour, land and capital) are fixed. They are higher (in absolute value) in the long run when primary factors may adjust to new economic conditions. However, per hectare compensatory payments of the CAP cannot be considered fully decoupled, mainly because they remain tied to the obligation of producing certain crops, i.e., cereals and oilseeds, and they are paid on a fixed eligible base area. It results that land and labour should not substantially adjust (at least at an aggregate level) in response to policy changes introduced in May 1992. Relevant price elasticities are thus constrained or short-run elasticities. Accordingly, the effects of support price cuts on variable input use and yields should be limited at the intensive margin of production, even in the long term.

One can reasonably assume that the pre-reform situation corresponds to a corner solution where the critical land quality $\tilde{q}$ was 'sufficiently' low so that most producers allocate all their available land to the intensive technology. According to comparative static results presented above, the output support price cut decided in May 1992 should increase the critical land quality $\tilde{q}$ and hence, induce (some) producers to convert some low quality land to the extensive technology. But again, the three factors mentioned above (i.e., the imperfect transmission of policy price changes to market prices, the downward adjustment of market prices of chemicals and the low values of price elasticities due to the quasi-fixity of primary factors) are expected to offset the potential positive effect of the reform at the extensive margin of production. Furthermore, even if the critical land quality increases sufficiently so that producers decide to devote a part of their available land to the extensive technology, it is also these low quality land classes that farmers will decide to set aside first.

The previous discussion suggests that one important policy parameter which could affect the level of demand for fertilizers and crop protection chemicals is the reduction in the arable cropping area due to the set-aside requirement. At this stage, it is thus particularly important to highlight the rationale of the set-aside programme and, more generally, the rationale of the new instrumentation of the CAP. The logic of the reform is clear and may be described as follows. Support prices for grains were substantially cut down. The objective of this support price cut was to induce an increase in the domestic demand, and especially in its feed component, thanks to an improved price competitiveness of interior cereals with respect to imported feed ingredients (i.e., protein cakes and substitutes of grains). The support price cut, which is compensated by 'fixed' direct payments per hectare, should induce producers both to reduce variable input use at the intensive margin and to adopt less intensive production techniques which should reduce growth rates in yields in the medium term. In the short term, an improved balance for grains is obtained by a set-aside programme.

The decision to decrease EU support prices for grains should provide substantial gains, essentially in terms of lower user prices for both final consumption and derived demand. The closer the EU prices are to world prices, the greater these gains are. One of the main limits of the 1992 CAP reform is that it fixes the minimum institutional price at a higher level than the world price, which alters the price competitiveness of European grains with respect to third world countries and implies the continuous use of subsidies to export to foreign markets. Furthermore, the first years of CAP reform application have clearly shown that market prices may be substantially higher than these minimum institutional prices. If the EU does not fulfil its GATT commitment in terms of subsidized export volume reduction, the easiest way to operate would obviously be to increase the set-aside rate, which means that the negative effects of this regulatory instrument would be aggravated, i.e., increased costs, decreased competitiveness on the international scene, and fewer incentives to farming more extensively. An alternative way to operate would be to set the domestic price at the world price level, which would allow the EU to export without restitutions (GATT commitments would no longer apply in that case), to increase its competitiveness not only on world markets but also on the domestic scene with respect to substitutes, and to abandon the requirement for land to be set aside. Removing this requirement would allow farmers to operate at minimum total cost and would induce them to use less intensive farming. In the context of the current instrumentation of the CAP, a first step in that direction would be to introduce a double market for grains in which land actually set aside would be cultivated with more extensive techniques (i.e., with low per hectare chemical input levels) and would be remunerated at world price levels.

The new CAP mechanisms introduced in May 1992 were primarily designed and implemented to solve the problems of surplus production for grains, not the ill-defined environmental problems that modern farming may create. One weak feature of the reform is the lack of integration between the environmental stewardship role of agriculture on the one hand, and the food production and trade roles of agricultural activities on the other hand. The analysis developed above implicitly assumes that agricultural pollution problems in the EU, such as nitrate contamination of groundwater supplies, eutrophication of surface water supplies as well as marine waters and smell, mainly arise from the increased use of chemical inputs (and animal waste disposal). Given the link between agricultural pollution and the increasingly intensive agricultural production, the solution advocated by economists, and also by CAP reform promoters, in order to reduce agricultural pollution is to return to lower-intensity farming by reducing the use of agricultural chemicals and by shifting to less intensive land uses. The CAP reform should, at least theoretically, induce a movement towards lower intensive farming. Nevertheless, many factors may offset this positive trend: the imperfect transmission of institutional price changes to market prices, the downward adjustment of market prices of chemicals, the quasi-fixity of primary factors and the low values of price elasticities, the current set-aside programme which implies that it is more profitable to set aside low quality land first and so on. With few exceptions, the use of chemicals at high levels will remain profitable. Our current system of agriculture has developed because of these chemicals and is likely to remain very dependent upon them. Because most of the pollution costs are external to agricultural production, society cannot expect the agricultural problem to be drastically reduced without direct intervention, even if the CAP reform is, but only indirectly, a first step in the right direction.

The following section shows how tax instruments on polluting emissions, output or input may be used to reduce variable input use. The first sub-section compares the (producer) profit efficiency of these three tax instruments in achieving a given reduction in input use per hectare. The second sub-section focuses on the land quality heterogeneity issue.

5.4   Environmental and agricultural policy interactions

The model of section 5.2 can be extended to incorporate the production of a 'bad' output such as pollution by introducing a pollution generation function. This function is defined by $z = z(x,q,u)$ where z are polluting emissions which are generated by variable input use. These polluting emissions are influenced, directly and indirectly via input use, by land quality q and technology choice u. They do not directly depend on output level y.

Consider the producer problem for a given land quality q and a given technology u. Without any environmental regulation, he solves programme (5.2) without taking into account negative environmental externalities arising from input use. Private optimal solutions are denoted $x^*(p,w,q,u)$ and $y^*(p,w,q,u)$. The level of polluting emissions is then $z^*(x^*(p,w,q,u),q,u) \equiv z^*(p,w,q,u)$.

Clearly, this emission level $z^*(p,w,q,u)$ differs from the socially optimal emission level which is obtained by solving the first-order conditions of the following programme:

$$\max_{x,y}(pf(x,q,u) - wx - vz(x,q,u)) \tag{5.13}$$

where v is the (constant) social unit value of emissions.

Socially optimal solutions of programme (5.13) are denoted $x^{**}(p,w,q,u,v)$, $y^{**}(p,w,q,u,v)$ and $z^{**}(p,w,q,u,v)$.

The situation is depicted graphically in Figure 5.2. For a given land quality q and a given technology u, the private optimum corresponds to point P where private marginal cost (i.e., w) and private marginal revenue (i.e., $pf_x'(x,q,u)$) curves intersect. At point P, the marginal product of input x is equal to its private real price, i.e., $f_x'(x^*,q,u) = w/p$, and the producer profit is equal to area abc. The social optimum corresponds to point S where social marginal cost (i.e., $w + vz_x'(x,q,u)$) and private marginal revenue curves intersect. At point S, the marginal product of input x is equal to its social real price, i.e., $f_x'(x^{**},q,u) = [w + vz_x'(x^{**},q,u)]/p$, and the producer profit is equal to area $aa'b'c'$. One easily verifies that x^{**} is lower

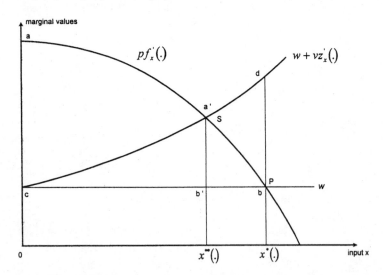

Figure 5.2   Characterization of private and social optima for a given land quality

than x^*, and that z^{**} is also lower than z^* since the pollution generation function is an increasing function of variable input use. The social welfare loss on land quality q corresponds to area $a'bd$ and is given by:

$$swl(q) = \int_{x^{**}}^{x^*} \left[w + vz_x'(x,q,u) - pf_x'(x,q,u) \right] dx = \int_{x^{**}}^{x^*} \left[SCm(x,q,u) - Rm(x,q,u) \right] dx$$

(5.14)

where $SCm(.)$ denotes the social marginal cost function and $Rm(.)$ is the private marginal revenue function.

Government intervention is required to internalize the negative social costs resulting from excessive variable input use. The government may directly regulate input use by an appropriate quota or indirectly by levying a tax on emissions z, input use x and/or output level y.

5.4.1 Impact of environmental policies at the intensive margin of production

A socially optimal input use at the intensive margin of production can be induced through a pollution tax. With a pollution emission tax t_z, the profit-maximizing level of input use on land quality q cultivated with technology u is implicitly defined by (Antle and Just, 1991):

$$pf_x'(x,q,u) - w - t_z z_x'(x,q,u) = 0 \qquad (5.15)$$

The appropriate tax t_3^{**} which induces the producer to equate the value of the marginal product with the social marginal cost of production, i.e., which leads the producer to use the social welfare-maximizing quantity of the variable input at the intensive margin of production, is simply equal to the unit value v of emissions.

A pollution tax is generally not practical. Because emissions are difficult to observe and costly to monitor, input taxes may be a useful alternative to an effluent charge in the case of non-point source pollutants. Imposing a per unit tax t_x on the variable input x that causes pollution should also reduce emissions. In that case, the profit-maximizing level of input use at the intensive margin is implicitly defined by $pf_x'(x,q,u) - w - t_x = 0$ and the social welfare-maximizing input level is obtained by fixing t_x to its optimal value, i.e., $t_x^{**} = vz_x'(x^{**},q,u) \equiv vz_x'(p,w,q,u,v)$. In a similar way, the social welfare-maximizing output tax t_y^{**} is equal to $vz_x'(p,w,q,u,v)/f_x'(x(p,w,q,u,v),q,u)$.

The previous analysis shows that socially optimal taxes, t_z^{**} on polluting emissions z, t_x^{**} on polluting input x and t_y^{**} on output y, all make the producer choose the social welfare-maximizing input use level $x^{**}(p,w,q,u,v)$, for a given land quality q and a given production technology u. These three taxes do not have the same impact on producer unit profit. Since the tax on pollution emissions has clearly the lowest negative impact on unit profit, it is more interesting to compare the profit efficiency of input and output taxes. Unit profit functions when input (respectively output) is optimally taxed may be written as, respectively:

$$\pi(p,w + t_x^{**},q,u) = pf(x^{**},q,u) - (w + t_x^{**})x^{**} \qquad (5.16a)$$

$$\pi(p - t_y^{**},w,q,u) = (p - t_y^{**})f(x^{**},q,u) - wx^{**} \qquad (5.16b)$$

We define the implicit function $D(.)$ as the difference $\pi(p,w + t_x^{**},q,u) - \pi(p - t_y^{**},w,q,u)$. From equations (5.16a) and (5.16b), one obtains:

$$D(.) = \pi(p,w + t_x^{**},q,u) - \pi(p - t_y^{**},w,q,u) = - t_x^{**}x^{**} + t_y^{**}f(x^{**},q,u) \qquad (5.17)$$

This implicit function $D(.)$ equals zero when $t_y^{**}/t_x^{**} = x^{**}/f(x^{**},q,u)$. Substituting optimal taxes by their respective expressions, this condition may equivalently be written as:

$$D(.) = 0 \Leftrightarrow f(x^{**},q,u) = x^{**}.f_x'(x^{**},q,u) \Leftrightarrow y^{**}/x^{**} = f_x'(x^{**},q,u) \quad (5.18)$$

Equation (5.18) shows that input and output optimal taxes will have the same negative effect on producer unit profit if the socially optimal input level x^{**} corresponds to the point where the average productivity of the variable input equals its marginal productivity. Accordingly, if the average productivity of the variable input is greater (respectively lower) than its marginal productivity, then $D(.) > 0$ (respectively $D(.) < 0$) and the unit profit evaluated with an input tax at optimal level t_x^{**} will be greater (respectively lower) than the unit profit evaluated with an output tax at optimal level t_y^{**} It is likely that we are rather in the first regime which corresponds to a situation of decreasing average yields. Accordingly, an optimal tax on input is likely to be superior, from a producer profit point of view, to an optimal output tax, for a given land quality q and a given production technology u.

5.4.2   *Optimal taxation policy and the land quality heterogeneity issue*
The different results presented in section 5.4.1 are defined for a given land quality and a given production technology. They clearly show that socially optimal taxes on pollution emissions, the polluting input or the output directly depend on the land quality index. When land quality heterogeneity is taken into account, the

optimal taxation policy corresponds to a system of differentiated taxes according to land quality.

This sub-section focuses on the relationship between land quality and pollution emissions. For a given land quality, one can reasonably assume that pollution emissions are an increasing function of chemical input use. Nevertheless, this does not necessarily mean that farmers who use high input levels on good quality lands generate more damage to the environment than farmers who use lower input levels on lower quality lands. In other words, the relationship between pollution emissions and land quality may be positive or negative.

From the definition of the pollution generation function, we have (assuming that u is constant):

$$\frac{dz(x^*)}{dq} = \frac{\partial z}{\partial x} \cdot \frac{dx^*}{dq} + \frac{dz(x^*)}{dq} \qquad (5.19)$$

Assumptions A1), A2), A3) and A6) imply that dx^*/dq is positive. Since the pollution generation function is assumed to be an increasing function of variable input use, the first right-hand side term of (5.19) is positive. This first term measures the positive impact on emissions of an increased use of the variable input induced by a higher land quality. The second right-hand side term of (5.19) is indeterminate in sign. It measures the impact on emissions of an increased land quality, other things being equal and in particular for a given variable input level. In the particular case where z does not directly depend on q, this second term equals zero and the total impact of land quality on polluting emissions reduces to the first positive term. In the general case, one can reasonably assume that the second term in (5.19) is negative since q reflects the ability of the soil to provide nutrients to the plant. According to this definition, an increase in land quality leads to a decrease in pollution emissions, other things being equal. If this negative effect more than offsets the first positive effect in (5.19), the relationship between polluting emissions and land quality is negative.

Clearly, there is an important need for empirical studies in order to sign the effect of land quality on polluting emissions on the basis of observed data. In the case where a negative relationship would be confirmed, the main policy implication would be that an optimal input tax scheme should be decreasing in land quality. A second-best uniform tax scheme would penalize in excess farmers who use high input levels on high quality lands. Their costs would be increased 'more than necessary' with respect to the restoration of a social optimum, and the competitiveness of the EU crop sector would be reduced 'more than necessary'.

5.5 Concluding comments

The May 1992 CAP reform mechanisms were first designed to solve the problems of production surplus in the EU (for grains in particular), and not the ill-defined environmental problems that modern farming may create. The new instrumentation of the CAP in the crop sector should, at least theoretically, induce a movement towards lower-intensity farming at both the intensive and the extensive margin of production. Nevertheless, several factors may offset this positive trend (for example, the imperfect transmission of policy price changes to market prices, the downward adjustment of market prices of chemical inputs and the low values of price elasticities). It results that the movement towards lower-intensity farming should be limited in practice. The CAP reform has also proposed a number of specific but very limited environmental measures which offer compensation for producers for farming less intensively or in ways considered compatible with environmental objectives. All these measures are a first step in the right direction. Nevertheless, it is important to note that the decisions adopted in May 1992 (and the new propositions presented in Spring 1997 by the European Commission for a 'reform of the reform') are not very ambitious as regards the reorientation of European agriculture towards meeting the long-run objectives of competitiveness, resource conservation and sustainable development.

It is likely that the sensitivity of the European public opinion to environmental problems will manage to impose cross-compliance conditions to make compensatory payments contingent on nature friendly practices. Proper environmental standards should be targeted by means of specific incentives for positive externalities or disincentives on negative externalities, without directly hindering a more efficient allocation of resources. As an example, land set-aside should be encouraged on the basis of conservation objectives and not in order to manage supply control for reasons of complacency towards foreign competitors. In that context, the last section of this paper shows that researches aiming at improving the design of environmental policies should consider closely the relationship between input use, intensification, pollution emission and land quality.

Agricultural and environmental policies can be complementary or in conflict depending on the characteristics of the problem and the types of policy instruments (Antle and Just, 1991). The conflict in policy objectives should obviously be addressed through efforts to integrate agricultural and environmental programmes. The issue of integration of environmental objectives into sectoral policy has to be considered in the more general context of the re-instrumentation of agricultural policies (that is, the shift from market price support towards more decoupled forms of assistance to farmers) and the level of policy responsibilities.

References

Antle J.M. and R.E. Just (1991), 'Effects of commodity program structure on resource use and the environment', in N. Bockstael and R.E. Just (eds), *Commodity and Resource Policy in Agricultural Systems*, New York: Springer-Verlag.

Cahill S. (1993), 'CAP reform: How Decoupled are the Compensatory Payments?', working paper, Economic Analysis Division, Policy Branch, Agriculture Canada.

Chambers R.G. and R.E. Just, (1989), 'Estimating multi-output technologies', *American Journal of Agricultural Economics*, **71**(4), 980–95.

Coyle B. (1993), 'On modelling systems of crop acreage demands', *Journal of Agricultural and Resource Economics*, **18**(1), 57–69.

Guyomard H., L.-P. Mahé, T. Roe and S. Tarditi (1994), 'The CAP reform and EC–US relations: the GATT as a cap on the CAP', in G. Anania, C.A. Carter and A.F. McCalla (eds), *Agricultural Trade Conflicts and GATT: New Dimensions in US–European Agricultural Trade Relations*, Boulder, Colorado: Westview Press.

Guyomard H., M. Baudry and A. Carpentier (1996), 'Estimating crop supply response in the presence of farm programmes: application to the Common Agricultural Policy', *European Review of Agricultural Economics*, **23**(4), 401–20.

Harper J.K. and D. Zilberman (1989), 'Pest externalities from agricultural inputs', *American Journal of Agricultural Economics*, **71**(3), 692–702.

Harvey D. (1995), 'European Union cereals policy: an evolutionary interpretation', *Australian Journal of Agricultural Economics*, **39**(3), 193–217.

Just R.E., E. Lichtenberg and D. Zilberman (1991), 'Effects of the feed grain and wheat programs on irrigation and groundwater depletion in Nebraska', in N. Bockstael and R.E. Just (eds), *Commodity and Resource Policies in Agricultural Systems*, New York: Springer-Verlag.

Kuch P. and K. Reichelderfer (1992), 'The environment implications of agricultural support programs: A United States perspective', in T. Becker, R. Gray and A. Schmitz (eds), *Improving Agricultural Trade Performance Under The GATT*, Wissenschaftsverlag Vauk Kiel KG.

Lichtenberg E. (1985), 'The role of land quality in agricultural diversification', Ph.D. thesis, University of California, Berkeley.

Lichtenberg E. (1989), 'Land quality, irrigation development, and cropping patterns in the northern high plains', *American Journal of Agricultural Economics*, **71**(1), 187–94.

Mahé L.-P. and P. Rainelli (1987), 'Impact des pratiques et des politiques agricoles sur l'environnement', *Cahiers d'Economie et de Sociologie Rurales*, **4**, 9–31.

Meynard J.M. (1991), 'Pesticides et itinéraires techniques', in P. Byé, C. Descoins and A. Deshayes (eds), *Phytosanitaires, Protection des plantes, Biopesticides*, INRA, Versailles.

Milgrom P. and J. Roberts (1990), 'The economics of modern manufacturing: technology, strategy and organisation', *American Economic Review*, **80**(3), 511–28.

Milgrom P. and C. Shannon (1994), 'Monotone comparative statics', *Econometrica*, **62**(1), 157–80.

Moschini G. and P. Sckokai (1994), 'Efficiency of decoupled farm programs under distortionary taxation', *American Journal of Agricultural Economics*, **76**(3), 362–70.

Oude Lansink A. and J. Peerlings (1996), 'Modelling the new EU cereals and oilseeds regime in the Netherlands', *European Review of Agricultural Economics*, **23**(2), 161–78.

Rader T., (1968), 'Normally factor inputs are never gross substitutes', *Journal of Political Economy*, **76**(1), 38–43.

Roberts D., J. Froud and R.W. Fraser (1996), 'Participation in set aside: what determines the opting in price?', *Journal of Agricultural Economics*, **47**(1), 89–98.

Sumner D. A. (1994), 'Agricultural trade relations between the United States and the European Community: recent events and current policy', in G. Anania, C.A. Carter and A.F. McCalla (eds), *Agricultural Trade Conflicts and GATT: New Dimensions in US–European Agricultural Trade Relations*, Boulder, Colorado: Westview Press.

Topkis D. M. (1978), 'Minimizing a submodular function on a lattice', *Operation research*, **26**(2), 305–21.

6 EU agriculture and the economics of vertically-related markets

Steve McCorriston and Ian M. Sheldon

Introduction

In general, agricultural, trade and environmental policy analysis falls into three categories. The first, and perhaps most common, uses a partial equilibrium framework focusing solely on the agricultural sector. The typical scenario here is to evaluate changes in consumer and producer surplus following a given change in government policy, assuming that the demand curve facing farmers is the consumers demand curve and that the price that consumers pay is (approximately) equivalent to the price producers receive for their output. Much of the research on CAP and GATT reform would fall into this category.[1] A second is the general equilibrium approach that links agriculture with other sectors of the economy. Recently, there have been several applications of computable general equilibrium models to agricultural, trade and environmental policy analysis, the results of which show that policy reform directed at the agricultural sector will affect other sectors of the economy even if these other sectors are only indirectly associated with agriculture via factor markets (see, for example, Hertel, 1996). The third category is to tie agriculture directly with its immediate downstream sectors: by doing so this approach unlinks the direct correspondence between producers and consumers that characterizes the standard partial equilibrium approach by introducing a farm–retail spread. This follows largely the framework introduced by Gardner (1975) and characterizes the downstream sector as involving one or more processing/retailing stages such that the consumer demand curve is not equivalent to the demand for farm products, the difference being due to the size of the farm–retail margin. This framework, which has been commonly used to evaluate the effects of research and development, will apportion changes in surplus to various parts of this food-chain.[2] It is essentially this category of policy analysis which we focus on in this chapter. However, a feature that is common to these multi-market models (as distinct from general equilibrium models), is that each of the downstream sectors are assumed to be perfectly competitive. As we will argue in this chapter, while this approach to policy analysis acknowledges the importance of sectors downstream of the farm sector, it

1 For example, Roningen and Dixit (1990), OECD (1987) and Tyers and Anderson (1992).
2 See Alston (1991) for a review.

fails to incorporate salient features of the food processing and retailing industries.[3]

In this regard, among recent developments in the agricultural economics literature have been attempts to evaluate the degree of competition in downstream food markets. Although there has been much research on the food sector in the spirit of the structure–conduct–performance paradigm (see Connor *et al.*, 1985), this recent research draws upon the so-called new empirical industrial organization (NEIO) literature, the essence of which is to focus on the degree of competition (i.e. firm behaviour) rather than to focus solely on firm numbers.[4] However, this NEIO approach to understanding downstream markets has yet to become a common feature of agricultural, trade and environmental policy analysis.[5]

In principle, the industrial organization of downstream markets can impinge on the analysis of policy reform in three ways. First, it can influence how the benefits and costs of policy changes are evaluated and how their welfare changes are distributed. The second relates to the sectors at which policy is targeted. In the context of vertically-related oligopolistic markets, the stage of production at which the policy is initially targeted will influence the welfare outcome. For example, the welfare impact of an export subsidy targeted at the processed product will likely differ from a similar policy targeted at the raw agricultural products. Similarly, in the context of the current debate on the environmental/trade nexus relating to equalizing environmental standards, raising an industry's abatement costs will not be equivalent to a corresponding import tariff if that industry's structure is oligopolistic. The third theme where industrial organization is relevant is that when markets are oligopolistic, governments may use policies strategically to influence the competitiveness of their domestic industries in world markets. Again, the effect and the desirability of such policies will depend on the oligopolistic nature of the industry which is likely to be targeted. It is in this context that this chapter addresses the vertically-related nature of food markets associated with European agriculture. Principally, the chapter will address the way in which policy evaluation may be influenced by the vertically-related nature of EU food markets. Since this is a recent area of research (at least for us!), only some of the potential applications of the framework are presented here.

The focus of this chapter is therefore two-fold. The first is to outline salient characteristics of the European food sector and some recent developments that have occurred in this sector in recent years. The second is to discuss how the

---

3 An exception is the work of Holloway (1991) who incorporates imperfect competition into a multi-market framework. Note also that – although there are a few exceptions – perfect competition is commonly assumed in computable general equilibrium models.

4 See Perloff (1992) for an overview of the NEIO to agricultural and food markets.

5 Of course, one could also extend the analysis to sectors upstream from agriculture, which are also imperfectly competitive. See McCorriston and Sheldon (1989) for an analysis of environmental policy accounting for the oligopolistic nature of the UK fertiliser market.

evaluation of agricultural, trade and environmental policy reform may be sensitive to the assumptions made about the structural characteristics of downstream markets. The organization of the chapter reflects its dual purpose. The first part provides a cursory overview of salient features of the European food sector focusing on market structure at the processing and retailing stages, linkages between sectors, and recent trends including merger activity and foreign direct investment. The second part focuses on research issues that arise and presents some empirical results from recent research we have undertaken that attempts to evaluate the outcome of policy reform while accounting for imperfect competition.

6.1   The European food sector

6.1.1 The food sector and economic activity

The share of the agricultural sector in total economic activity is relatively low. For example, in the UK, agriculture contributes around 1.5 per cent to GDP with comparable shares across the rest of the EU except for the lesser developed regions of Ireland, Greece, Spain and Portugal. However, if one takes the food sector as a whole, its contribution to GDP is considerably higher. For example, in the UK, the food retailing, processing and agricultural sectors together account for 9 per cent of GDP suggesting that the food sector is more important than the sole focus on the agricultural sector belies.

A further indication of the importance of the food sector can be assessed by focusing on industrial activity only. In this regard, the European food sector is a leading contributor to industrial output in the EU. Indeed, as Table 6.1 shows, in 1994, the food sector was *the* most important sector by value of output which was in excess of that produced by the chemical industry, the motor vehicle industry and electrical engineering. The food sector is also a major employer, employing over 2.3 million in 1994, again well in excess of many important industrial sectors in the EU. The importance of extra-EU trade, however, is relatively lower, probably due to the relatively high degree of protectionism offered to agriculture and the food industries in the EU.

Although many studies focus on the trade effects of agricultural and environmental policy reform, an often-ignored point is that trade in processed food products dominates total world trade in food/agricultural products. The relevant data is given in Table 6.2. In 1972, trade in manufactured foods accounted for 58 per cent of total trade in food/agricultural products; by 1990, the share of manufactured foods in total food/agricultural trade had risen to 64 per cent, while, in value terms, trade in manufactured foods have increased by over 670 per cent over the same period. The EU countries are among the leading exporters of processed food products with France and the Netherlands together accounting for around 20 per cent of total world trade in manufactured foods.

Table 6.1   Industrial sectors in the EU (1994)

Sector	Production (mn ECU)	Employment	Extra-EU exports (mn ECU)	Extra-EU imports (mn ECU)
Food, Drink Tobacco	472 239.5	2 330 732.7	33 783.1	24 162.9
Chemicals and man-made fibres	309 657.5	1 584 460.6	67 203.1	41 034.5
Chemical Industry	298 027.6	1 539 606.9	65 867.7	39 405.7
Motor vehicles and parts	276 346.0	1 613 547.6	45 635.6	23 948.8
Electrical Engineering	262 324.2	2 334 034.8	58 841.6	62 355.0

Source: *Panorama of EU Industry 1995–96* (EC Commission)

Table 6.2   World trade in food/agricultural products, 1972–90

	Total world trade in food/agricultural products (US$ bn)	Total trade in processed food products (US$ bn)	
1973	65.41	38.02	
1990	323.94	205.96	
		Of which:	
		France	9.8%
		Netherlands	8.9%
		Germany	6.7%
		UK	4.3%
		Bel-Lux	4.1%
		Denmark	3.9%
		Italy	3.5%

Source: ERS/USDA

6.1.2 Structure of the food processing sector

A major feature of the food processing sector in many countries is the dominance of a relatively small number of firms in each of the sub-sectors of food manufacturing activity. This is highlighted in Table 6.3 for four EU countries: France, Germany, Italy and the UK. Although the four-firm concentration ratios

Table 6.3   Four-firm seller concentration ratios, European food processing industries

Industry	France	Germany	Italy	UK
Bread	4.5	7.0	4.0	58.0
Canned vegetables	40.0	N/A	80.0	81.0
Flour	29.0	38.0	6.7	78.0
Processed meat	23.0	22.0	11.0	N/A
Salt	98.0	93.0	80.0	99.5
Sugar	81.0	60.0	72.0	94.0
Baby foods	88.0	83.0	88.0	80.0
Beer	82.0	25.0	55.0	59.0
Biscuits	62.0	49.0	46.0	62.0
Mineral water	77.0	27.0	55.0	73.0
Pet foods	86.0	93.0	N/A	83.0
Soft drinks	70.0	57.0	84.0	48.0
Soup	91.0	84.0	N/A	75.0
Sugar confectionary	51.0	39.0	29.0	38.0

Source: Sutton (1991)

(CR4) vary between sub-sector and by country, nevertheless, the general picture is one of relatively high concentration across the EU food processing sector.

The CR4 figures shown in Table 6.3 can perhaps obscure the fact that the degree of concentration is higher than these statistics suggest. Table 6.4 reports the market shares for the leading two or three firms in the UK food processing sector. Particularly notable here is the sugar, chocolate confectionary, savoury snacks, instant coffee, breakfast cereals, and canned soup sectors where the dominant two or three firms account for over 70 per cent of sales in that industry.

6.1.3   Structure of the food retailing sector

Similar to the food processing sector, food retailing also shows signs of market dominance by a small number of retail outlets. Relative to the food manufacturing sector, the degree of dominance is more variable across EU countries though the degree of concentration is still considerable. For example, in France and Belgium the CR5 is around 40 per cent. In the Netherlands, the CR5 is 33 per cent while in Spain it is lower than 20 per cent. However, in the UK, the degree of concentration is relatively high with a CR5 of 68 per cent. The relevant data is shown in Table 6.5.

Table 6.4   Market shares of leading 2–3 firms in the UK food processing sector

Market	Market share of leading number of firms (in brackets)	Market	Market share of leading number of firms (in brackets)
Bread	60 (2)	Breakfast cereals	73 (3)
Flour	50 (2)	Biscuits	52 (3)
Packaged cakes	59 (2)	Canned fish	63 (2)
Margarine	60 (2)	Yogurt	47 (3)
Ice cream	52 (2)	Sugar	98 (2)
Chocolate confectionary	80 (3)	Sugar confectionary	45 (3)
Preserves	33 (2)	Potato crisps	63 (3)
Savoury snacks	77 (3)	Baked beans	55 (3)
Canned tomato	43 (2)	Instant coffee	79 (3)
Tea	68 (3)	Canned soup	74 (2)
Baby food	63 (3)		

Source: Burns and Henson (1995)

Table 6.5   Market shares in the UK food retailing sector, 1994

Firm	Market share (%)
Sainsbury	21.2
Tesco	19.7
Argyll	9.1
Asda	11.5
Gateway	6.5
Total 5	68.0

Source: Burns and Henson (1995)

In sum, taken together, the data suggests that the European food sector can be characterized as one of successive stages (agriculture, food processing, food retailing) with the latter two stages being characterized by varying degrees of dominance by a small number of firms at each stage and in sub-sectors of activity. However, in characterizing the industrial organization of the food sector, it is also important to consider linkages between these successive stages.

6.1.4 Linkages between successive stages

The simplest way of thinking about linkages between the food retailing and manufacturing sectors focuses on arm's length transactions. In this case, it is assumed that the food manufacturers produce a certain quantity of output (which depends of course on the nature of competition at that stage) and sell the good on the market for whatever price it gets. The food retailing firms, at the other side of this transaction, take the manufacturing price as given, the amount they demand also being dependent on the nature of competition, in this case at the retailing stage. The key point here is that while competition matters, it matters only at each horizontal stage, that is, there is no bargaining *between* the manufacturing and retailing stages over what the appropriate price for the product (input) should be. Although it makes modelling of the 'food chain' simpler, this notion of arm's length pricing can be criticized insofar as it is an inappropriate characterization of competition between the two stages. The somewhat crude alternative to arm's length pricing is to assume bilateral bargaining between each stage. This appears to be particularly relevant in the UK case where the leading food retailers are seen to exert their influence on the food manufacturing sector. Indeed, there appears to be important circumstantial evidence of this (for example, the Monopolies and Mergers Commission 1981). Thus the alternative to arm's length pricing assumption would appear to be a model of bilateral oligopoly.

The reasons why this rejection of arm's length pricing is crude are twofold. First, from a modelling perspective, it is often difficult to derive a bilateral oligopoly model that could be usefully applied to the food sector. Second, the mechanism of this bilateral market power is typically more subtle than the rejection of arm's length pricing would suggest. Specifically, vertical market power is likely to be reflected more in the nature of the contracts between the food retailing and manufacturing sectors both in terms and conditions of the various contracts and in the specification of the products that food manufacturers provide to the retailers.

Vertical contracts that deviate from arm's length pricing can be characterized as non-linear contracts or vertical restraints. 'Vertical restraints' captures a multitude of practices, including: discounts in a variety of forms (for example, overriders, aggregate rebates); slotting allowances (for example, provision of retail equipment such as freezers); and tying, where the manufacturer sells a bundle of the goods at a lower price than it would cost if buying each good separately. These practices are common between the food retailers and manufacturers and are often viewed with suspicion by competition authorities as the number of referrals to the UK's Monopolies and Mergers Commission would testify.[6] It is in the nature of these contracts that the balance of power between retailers and manufacturers is reflected. For example, in motivating his analysis of alternative vertical restraints Shaffer (1991) argues that it is the scarcity of shelf space relative to the large number of new products that manufacturers

6   McCorriston and Sheldon (1997) present an overview of the literature on vertical restraints and the cases investigated by the US and UK competition authorities with reference to the food sector.

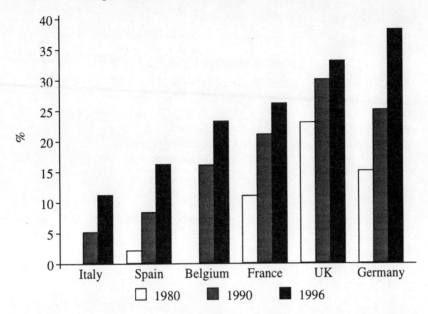

Figure 6.1   Retailer's own-label trends in Europe – % share of the retail market

provide that tilts the balance of power in favour of the food retailers.[7] In this regard, it is notable that following the investigation of vertical restraints in the UK food industry, the UK's Monopolies and Mergers Commission also concluded that the balance of power lay with the food retailing sector. The growing dominance of retailers in influencing the terms of bilateral contracts has also been highlighted in a recent report to the Office of Fair Trading, the UK government's department responsible for competition matters (see Dobson and Waterson, 1996).

Another way in which retailers influence the food manufacturing sector is in regard to the specification of products to be produced. This has given rise to the phenomenon of 'own-label' products sold by the food retailers. While these products were originally thought of as low-quality alternatives to the branded products, the quality of these products is now perceived, at least, to match that of the branded products. As Figure 6.1 shows, market share for own-label products is increasing in EU countries with the highest market penetration being in the UK and the lowest in Italy.

One problem with these aggregate figures is that the obscure market shares across sub-sectors. As Table 6.6 shows for the UK, the share of own-label

---

7   Interestingly, Shaffer (1991) notes that the number of new food products available in the US increased from 2600 per year in 1978 to 10 200 per year in 1987.

Table 6.6   Own-brand market share in the UK, 1993

Product	1993	Product	1993
Meat products	68.2%	Chilled foods	57.9%
Dried fruit and vegetables	56.9%	Pasta and rice	47.3%
Frozen foods	36.7%	Table sauces and dressings	36.1%
Sweet and savoury spreads	34.6%	Canned food	33.0%
Dairy products	31.2%	Bakery and cereals	28.8%
Snacks	18.9%	Seasonings and sweeteners	18.2%

Source: Burns and Henson (1995)

products can vary considerably between food markets with the highest degree of own-label market penetration occurring in the processed meat and chilled foods markets.

In sum, the nature of the interaction between the food processing and retailing sectors is an important feature of the EU food sector and arguably more subtle than those (implicitly) suggesting a bilateral bargaining framework.

6.1.5 Merger activity in the EU food sector

So far, the discussion has provided a rather static overview of the EU food sector. But, as we have already shown with the increased penetration of own-label products, the characteristics of the food sector can change over a relatively short period of time. This has been the case with firm numbers and ownership as reflected in mergers and acquisitions in the EU food sector. Table 6.7 provides the necessary evidence. As the table shows, merger activity in the EU food sector increased substantially over the 1980s: in 1983–84, there were 11 recorded mergers in the EU food sector; by 1989–90, the number of mergers had increased to 102. Indeed, merger activity in the EU food sector has been second only to the chemical sector relative to mergers occurring in the EU as a whole. From an economic perspective, mergers are a double-edged sword. On the one hand, they reduce the number of competing firms in the relevant stage of the food chain. Insofar as this influences vertical market competition, this serves to reduce the competitive nature of the food chain as a whole. On the other hand, mergers arguably provide efficiency benefits which, by reaping economies of scale, provide output at a lower unit cost. Interestingly, Salinger (1990) suggests that post-merger performance is typically poorer than firms' pre-merger performance. The deterioration of company performance following acquisition and merger has also been highlighted in a recent study of UK firms (see Dickerson, Gibson and Tsakalotos, 1997). It would be an interesting exercise to consider whether this would be true of mergers in the EU food sector.

Table 6.7   *Acquisitions of majority holdings (including mergers), European Community food and drink sector*

Year	National	Community	International	Total food sector	Total all sectors
83/84	7	2	2	11	155
84/85	20	1	1	22	208
85/86	25	7	2	34	227
86/87	39	11	2	52	303
87/88	25	18	8	51	383
88/89	35	27	14	76	492
89/90	41	44	17	102	622
90/91	29	26	16	71	455
91/92	32	23	6	61	383

Source: EC Commission, Annual Report on Competition Policy, various issues.

6.1.6 Foreign-direct investment

Somewhat related to merger activity in the EU food sector has been the increase in foreign-direct investment. Of note is that foreign-direct investment has increased dramatically since the mid-1980s, particularly between EU countries. Table 6.8 presents the relevant statistics for foreign-direct investment in the food sector.

Table 6.8   *Foreign-direct investment in the EU food sector (mn ECU)*

	1984	1985	1986	1987	1988	1989	1990	1991
Total EU outward Extra-EU investment[1]	–534	402	–841	–2305	–4211	–6374	612	–832
Total EU inward Extra-EU investment[2]	294	732	4	1191	3337	–1037	–1565	–313
Intra-EU investment (by receiving branch)[2]	47	188	149	392	2042	1945	1389	3422

Notes
1   A negative figure represents net investment; a positive figure represents net disinvestment.
2   A positive figure represents net investment; a negative figure represents net disinvestment.

Source: Eurostat (various)

In many respects, a preferable way to gauge the importance of foreign investment in the domestic economy is to measure the proportion of domestic production accounted for by foreign firms. Figure 6.2 shows the proportion of the value of UK food output that is accounted for by foreign-owned firms. Over the period 1982 to 1991, foreign-owned firms share of output increased from 14 per cent in 1982 to around 23 per cent in 1991 with a notable increase in foreign-owned firms' share occurring since 1989.

The growth of foreign-direct investment and the increase in merger activity are both likely to be related to the liberalization of capital markets in the late 1980s and the creation of the Single European Market after 1992. Whatever the cause, the evidence nevertheless suggests that substantial changes have occurred in the EU food sector since the mid-1980s.

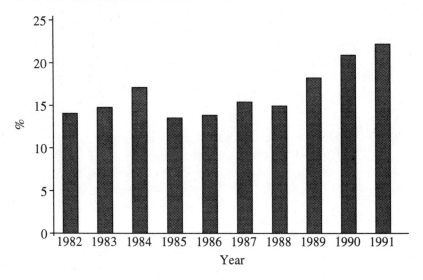

Source: Giulietti, McCorriston and Osborne (1998).

Figure 6.2   Proportion of UK production shipped by foreign-owned firms

6.2   Implications for policy analysis

The discussion above suggests a considerable agenda for agricultural economics research. Much of this research would be usefully focused on the industrial organization of the food sector: for example, identifying the degree of competition in specific markets following recent developments in the NEIO literature; the post-merger performance of firms in the food manufacturing sector; and the cause and effect of foreign direct investment, to name only a few.[8] However, given

8   Giulietti, McCorriston and Osborne (1998) have investigated the causes of foreign direct investment in the UK food sector over the 1980s.

that much of agricultural economic analysis is focused on identifying the effects of policy reform, it would appear imperative to capture the characteristics of the food retail and processing sectors in applied work. Some recent attempts to do so are reported below.

Policy analysis with imperfect competition has been a recent growth area in the general economics literature. However, the adaptation of the NEIO literature for policy analysis in agricultural economics is relatively scarce.[9] Here we discuss what factors are likely to be included in a model that encapsulates salient features of a vertically-related food market with imperfect competition at each successive stage. The focus here is on how industrial organization affects policy evaluation rather than the use of these policies strategically. Subsequent sections report some empirical results and discuss wider environmental and regulation issues that may be influenced by the nature of market structure.

6.2.1 Model outline

The essential features of the model include several stages of production/value-added, imperfect competition at each stage, and product differentiation at the retail stage. Since the way in which these models are typically solved is to start at the final stage and proceed upstream we will follow this procedure here. For convenience we will assume arm's length pricing, though deviations from this will be reported below.

At the retail stage, the direct demand function facing firms is dependent on the price of the good (P) and the extent of substitutability with other goods (σ_p):

$$Q^D = f(P, \sigma_p) \tag{6.1}$$

Given this demand function, firms maximize profits depending on how they perceive their competitors to respond, the level of output produced by each firm therefore being determined by firm behaviour (V_F^D) and firm numbers (n_F^D). These factors therefore determine the slope of the perceived marginal revenue function at the retail stage.

The perceived marginal revenue curve is the demand curve facing the processing sector and is summarized below:

$$Q^U = f(Q^D(\cdot), n_F^D, V_F^D) \tag{6.2}$$

Given this demand curve, therefore, firms at the processing stage maximize profits depending on how they perceive their competitors will respond. As with the retail stage, the level of output for individual firms will be dependent

---

9   Recent exceptions include Suzuki, Lenz and Forker (1993) and Giraud-Héraud *et al.* (1995).

on firm behaviour V_F^u and the number of firms (n_F^u) at the food manufacturing stage. Note, however, that the processors' perceived marginal revenue curve will also depend on the nature of competition at the retail stage and the degree of product differentiation, both of which are encapsulated by $Q^D(\cdot)$

As above, the perceived marginal curve gives rise to the demand curve for agricultural output as given by:

$$Q^A = f(Q^u(.), n_F^u, V_F^u) \qquad (6.3)$$

Note that the demand curve for agricultural output now reflects imperfect competition *throughout* the food chain. The level of demand for agricultural output and hence the farm-gate price is influenced by firm behaviour *both* at the processing and at the retailing stages, firm number at *both* stages and the degree of product differentiation at the retail stage. Obviously the number of successively oligopolistic stages will depend on the degree of processing that the raw material requires before reaching the final consumer.[10]

What does this framework imply for policy analysis? Two key results emerge. First, the incidence of price reforms (i.e. how much is finally passed-through to consumers) is *endogenously* determined by the nature of competition and firm behaviour throughout the food chain.[11] Also, as firm numbers change (for example, by merger), this will also affect the degree of price transmission. Second, the distribution of welfare changes will also be endogenously determined. Essentially, as the food chain (or any stage) becomes less competitive, the greater the increase in firms' profits and the lower the change in consumer surplus following price reform. The above framework has been developed and calibrated with data from specific industries to provide analysis of actual policy reform scenarios. The results of these are outlined briefly below.[12]

6.2.2 Agricultural price reform and the UK processed cheese sector

Table 6.9 summarises results from a recent study of agricultural price reform applied to the UK cheese market (McCorriston and Sheldon, 1996). Cheese is manufactured by using milk from the dairy sector, prior to being sold through retail outlets. As the data presented in Table 6.5 suggests, the UK food retail sector is dominated by four firms. The UK cheese processing sector is also

10   A further factor that influences the food processing sector's demand for the raw agricultural product is the extent of substitutability between farm products and other inputs in the firms' costs functions. In large part, this is the focus of the multi-market models discussed above. For a recent attempt to deal with input substitutability while allowing for imperfect competition in the food sector see McCorriston, Morgan and Rayner (1998).

11   As is known from the public finance literature, the functional form of the demand curve can also influence the degree of tax incidence. See Seade (1980).

12   This model is calibrated in a manner similar to computable general equilibrium models. See McCorriston and Sheldon (1996) for further details.

Table 6.9   Welfare effects of policy reform with successive oligopoly

Market structure	Change in consumer surplus (£m) (1)	(1) as percentage of standard model s results (2)	Change in profits (£m) (3)		(3) as percentage of initial profit (4)
Standard model (perfect competition)	141.58	–	–		–
Two-stages			Stage 2	27.08	9.6
Actual behaviour	122.17	0.86	Stage 1	10.72	10.1
Two-stages			Stage 2	27.63	9.8
Cournot behaviour	56.26	0.40	Stage 1	64.99	61.8
Two-stages			Stage 2	43.85	15.6
Monopoly	34.83	0.25	Stage 1	66.14	62.9

Source: McCorriston and Sheldon (1996)

concentrated, though less so than the retail sector, with two firms accounting for around 40 per cent of total production. In the simulation exercise, it was assumed that the guaranteed price for milk was reduced by 30 per cent. Note also that initially the calibrated model reflects actual firm behaviour. In subsequent simulations, we varied the number of vertical stages and the degree of competition at each stage.[13]

With standard analysis (i.e. consumers and producers face the same price and perfect competition), a 30 per cent cut in guaranteed prices for milk would increase consumer surplus by £142 m. However, accounting for actual behaviour in successive processing and retailing stages, consumer surplus would have increased by £122 m., 14 per cent less than the standard case. The change in consumer welfare is dissipated to firms in the form of increased profits following reform, firms profits at both stages increasing by approximately 10 per cent in each case.

As the market becomes less competitive, consumers gain less from reform and firms gain proportionately more. With Cournot behaviour at both the processing and retailing stages, following the same 30 per cent cut in dairy prices, consumer surplus would increase by only £56 m. (60 per cent less than that suggested by the standard competitive model). With monopoly at each stage, consumer surplus would increase by only 25 per cent of the standard model's results. In both cases, firm's profits correspondingly increase by greater amounts following policy reform with both Cournot and monopoly behaviour, though firm's profits at the processing stage increase by more than at the retail stage.

13   Here we only report the results relating to firm behaviour. Results relating to the number of successive stages can be found in McCorriston and Sheldon (1996).

6.2.3 Alternative vertical contracts

As discussed above, a potentially important feature of vertically-related markets is the nature of the linkages between successive stages. In a different vertically-related market set-up, McCorriston (1995) explores the effect of alternative contracts on price incidence following reforms of the EU banana sector.[14] This sector involves multinationals who own several successive stages or who are supplied exclusively by producers/distributors from specific countries. With Cournot behaviour at each successive stage, three alternative contractual arrangements were explored. These were arm's length pricing, supply contracts and vertical integration. The results from this exercise are reported in Table 6.10.

Table 6.10   Price incidence following EU banana market reforms

	Change in retail prices (%)
Standard perfectly competitive approach	−22
Successive Cournot with arm's length pricing	−6
Successive Cournot with supply contracts	−2
Vertically integrated markets	−16

Source: McCorriston (1995)

The results show that the nature of the vertical contracts can have an important influence on consumer price changes and, by extension, the related welfare effects. Following the liberalization of the EU banana regime, banana prices would have been expected to fall by 22 per cent given the assumptions of the standard competitive model. With a successively oligopolistic model, with Cournot behaviour at each stage, assuming arm's length pricing, retail prices are estimated to fall by only 6 per cent. With supply contracts, prices would fall by only 2 per cent. The reason for this is that supply contracts have the effect of market foreclosure in upstream stages, that is, they make the chain of markets less competitive since upstream suppliers cannot compete directly in the subsequent downstream market. However, when successive stages become vertically integrated, price incidence increases to 16 per cent. In this case, the chain of successive markets now becomes a single stage thus eradicating the

14   For a general discussion of the EU banana market reforms see Read (1994). McCorriston and Sheldon (1996) also calibrate a successive oligopoly model to the UK banana market.

double-marginalization problem that characterizes successively-oligopolistic markets.

6.2.4 Further issues

In the preceding discussion on the impact market structure may have on policy outcomes, the focus has been on agricultural price and trade policy reform. However, the industrial organization of markets will also impact on environmental and other regulatory issues that affect the 'food chain'. To the extent that environment policy involves the use of tax (or tax equivalent) instruments, then the principles behind preceding analysis of changes to downstream firms' costs (due to price support or trade policy) will carry through to applications with environmental concerns. However, there are wider issues affecting the food sector in which market structure characteristics may have an impact. We address two of them here: the use of standards to improve environmental quality or food safety, and the impact of industrialization of agriculture via vertical coordination on environmental and sustainability issues. It should be noted that our discussion here is tentative and as such can be read as suggestions for future research on the potential effects of industrial organization in downstream markets on wider food sector issues.

As suggested above, the use of tax policy to influence firm behaviour is one instrument for addressing environmental and regulatory concerns; but it is not the only instrument. The use of minimum standards to improve the quality of final or intermediate goods by regulatory authorities constitutes an alternative approach. Examples where minimum standards may be imposed include food quality, the bio-degradability of products or packaging, and labelling among others. Of interest is how the effect of such non-price regulatory measures may be affected by the nature of competition in the markets in which they are imposed.

The theoretical approach to addressing these issues differs from the one we have outlined above. In the model outlined in section 6.2.1, it was assumed that firms would choose output to maximize profits (though we could easily have considered the strategic variable to be price). However, in oligopolistic settings where quality matters, firms choose quality (and subsequently price) to maximize profits so that, in a duopolistic market for example, one firm produces a lower quality good while the other produces the higher quality good. This character-ization of the market and firm behaviour allows us to consider the potential impact of minimum quality standards to address environmental or food safety concerns.

Ronnen (1991) has explored this issue with interesting results. Specifically, if the minimum quality standard imposed is higher than that of the (initially) lower quality good, all consumers can benefit. The reason for this is due to the way in which the imposition of the minimum standard narrows the quality differential between the lower and higher quality good such that price competition between the two goods intensifies. While in the Ronnen (ibid.) model quality depends on fixed (sunk) costs, more recently Crampes and Hollander (1995) have considered the case where quality standards depend on variable costs (for example, packaging, labelling, and so on). In a duopolistic setting, Crampes and Hollander show that consumers may or may not benefit from the imposition of the minimum quality standard; the outcome depends on how the firm producing the higher-quality good responds to the imposition of the minimum standard. The source of difference between the Ronnen approach and that of Crampes and Hollander lies in the nature of cost structure that is influenced by the quality choice. In the Ronnen model, quality depends on fixed costs, such that improving quality has an indirect effect on market prices which subsequently influences the post-minimum standard outcome. However, in the Crampes and Hollander approach, since quality depends on variable costs, varying quality has a direct effect on prices. While the difference between the two approaches is relatively subtle, nevertheless it is important for determining the likely outcome from policy that focuses on standards rather than taxes.

Irrespective of the detailed assumptions and results of these two papers, the framework is an interesting one for considering environmental and regulatory issues as they are imposed in the food sector. As in the analyses of price support, trade policy or tax equivalent environmental policy reforms, the characteristics of market structure can influence who gains and by how much from these alternative policy instruments.

A further issue that arises in considering the industrial organization of vertically-related markets relates to the characteristics of coordination between successive stages. Of particular note is that in recent years the food chain in both the EU and US has been undergoing a process of industrialization especially in the animal sector which is increasingly characterized by large-scale production. A striking feature of industrialization has been the switch from open market transactions to vertical coordination through some form of contract or through vertical integration between stages. This shift toward closer vertical coordination has been driven both by changes in the specification technology of production and also by the requirements of processors for more precisely defined products to meet changing consumer demands (Drabenstott, 1994).

In terms of vertical market structure, it was argued that successive oligopoly in the food system may reduce the transmission of changes in farm-gate prices to food consumers because of the distortion caused by double-marginalization. Changes in vertical coordination in the food system, however, may be beneficial in terms of the distribution of the benefits of farm policy reform. It is well-known in industrial organization that vertical integration will remove the problem of double-marginalization. In addition, if processors were exercising monopsony power over farmers prior to vertical integration, close coordination is predicted to result in reduction of the monopsony distortion (Perry, 1978, Azzam, 1996).

This in turn results in an increase in the level of agricultural input being processed.

There may, however, be welfare losses from increased vertical coordination. In particular, there are concerns with the environmental 'nuisance' of large-scale animal production, and the external cost it may impose on society (Ervin and Smith, 1994). Hence, the benefits of increased vertical integration due to the removal of one market distortion, double-marginalization, have to be traded off against the losses due to the introduction of another distortion, environmental externalities. The direct impact of these externalities and the extent to which they are induced by the structure of downstream industries is an important avenue for future research.

6.3   Conclusion

This chapter has focused on the industrial organization of downstream food markets, paying particular attention to the EU food sector. This sector is characterized by successive stages of production/distribution with imperfect competition being a feature of each stage. Linkages between these stages also have features that distinguish them from simple arm's length (or spot market) pricing. Furthermore, the EU food sector has undergone substantive changes over the last decade *vis-à-vis* the growth of own-label products, the number of mergers that have occurred and the growth of foreign direct investment. However, while more research needs to be undertaken to investigate further the underlying features of the EU food sector, we have argued in this chapter that industrial organization should also be incorporated into policy analysis. As the examples presented here show, the presence of successively-oligopolistic markets and the contractual arrangements between each successive stage can have an important bearing on the welfare outcome following policy reform. In this regard, developing models that more accurately characterize the features of the specific food market under consideration, will offer greater insight into the outcomes of, and indeed the motivation for, agricultural, trade and environmental policy reform.

References

Alston, J.M. (1991), 'Research benefits in a multimarket setting: a review', *Review of Marketing and Agricultural Economics*, **59**, 23–52.

Azzam, A. (1996), 'Testing the monopsony-inefficiency incentive for background integration', *Americal Journal of Agricultural Economics*, **78**, 585–90.

Burns, J. and S. Henson (1995), *The Food Manufacturing and Retail Food Distribution System of the Future: Convergence Towards the UK Model?* Paper presented at conference 'Food Retailer–Manufacturer Competitive Relationships in the EU and USA', University of Reading, July.

Connor, J.M., R.T. Rogers, B.W. Marion and W.F. Mueller (1985), *The Food Manufacturing Industries*, Lexington MA: Lexington Books.

Crampes, C. and A. Hollander (1995), 'Duopoly and quality standards', *European Economic Review*, **39**, 71–82.

Dickerson, A.P., H.D. Gibson and E. Tsakalotos (1997), 'Impact of acquisitions on company performance: evidence from a large panel of UK Firms', *Oxford Economic Papers*, **49**, 344–61.

Dobson, P.W. and M. Waterson (1996), *Vertical Restraints and Competition Policy*, Report for the Office of Fair Trading.

Drabenstott, M. (1994), 'Industrialization: Steady current or tidal wave', *Choices*, Fourth Quarter, pp. 4–8.

EC Commission, *Annual Report on Competition Policy*, Luxembourg, Various.

EC Commission (1996) *Panorama of EU Industries 1995–96*, Luxembourg.

Ervin, D.E. and K.R. Smith (1994), 'Agricultural industrialization and environmental quality', *Choices*, Fourth Quarter, p. 7.

Eurostat (1994) *Direct Investment in the European Community, 1984–1991*, Luxembourg.

Gardner, B.L. (1975), 'The farm-retail price spread in a competitive food industry', *American Journal of Agricultural Economics*, **57**, 399–409.

Giraud-Héraud, E., C. Le Mouël and V. Réquillart (1995), 'Competition and collusion in the world coffee market', *European Review of Agricultural Economics*, **23**, 336–53.

Giulietti, M., S. McCorriston and P. Osborne (1998), 'Foreign direct investment in the UK food processing sector', mimeo, University of Exeter.

Hertel, T.W. (1996), *Global Trade Analysis Using the GTAP Model*, Cambridge: Cambridge University Press.

Holloway, G.J. (1991), 'The farm-retail spread in an imperfect competition food industry', *American Journal of Agricultural Economics*, **73**, 979–89.

McCorriston, S., C.W. Morgan and A.J. Rayner (1998), 'Processing Technology, Market Power and Price Transmission', *Journal of Agricultural Economics*, **49**, 185–201.

McCorriston, S. (1995), *Policy Reform with Downstream Vertical Contracts*, paper presented at American Association of Agricultural Economics conference, Indianapolis, USA, August.

McCorriston, S. and I.M. Sheldon (1989), 'Welfare implications of nitrogen limitation policies', *Journal of Agricultural Economics*, **40**, 143–51.

McCorriston, S. and I.M. Sheldon (1996), 'Trade reform in vertically-related markets', *Oxford Economic Papers*, **48**, 664–72.

McCorriston, S. and I.M. Sheldon (1996), *Agricultural Price Reform with Successive Oligopoly*, Mimeo, University of Exeter.

McCorriston, S. and I.M. Sheldon (1997), 'The economics of vertical restraints and its relevance to competition policy in the food marketing system', *Agribusiness: An International Journal*, **13**, 237–52.

Monopolies and Mergers Commission (1981), *Discounts to Retailers*, HC311, London: HMSO.

OECD (1987), *National Policies and Agricultural Trade,* OECD, Paris.

Perloff, J.M. (1992), 'Econometric Analysis of Imperfect Competition and Implications for Trade Research', in I.M. Sheldon and D.R. Henderson (eds), *Industrial Organization and International Trade: Methodological Foundations for International Food and Agricultural Market Research*, Organization and Performance of World Food Systems: NC-194, Research Monograph Number 1.

Perry, M.K. (1978), 'Vertical integration: the monopsony case', *American Economic Review*, **68**, 561–76.

Read, R.A. (1994), 'The EC internal banana market: the issues and the dilemma', *The World Economy*, **17**, 219–35.

Roningen, V.O. and P.M. Dixit (1990), 'Assessing the implications of freer agricultural trade', *Food Policy*, **1**, 67–76.

Ronnen, U. (1991), 'Minimum Quality standards, fixed costs, and competition', *Rand Journal of Economics*, **22**, 290–504.

Salinger, M. (1990), 'The concentration–margins relationship reconsidered', *Brookings Papers on Economic Activity: Microeconomics*, pp. 287–335.

Seade, J. (1980), 'Profitable costs increases and the shifting of taxation', *University of Warwick Economic Research Paper*, No. 26.

Shaffer, G. (1991), 'Slotting allowances and resale price maintenance: a comparison of facilitating practices', *Rand Journal of Economics*, **22**, 120–35.

Sutton, J. (1991), *Sunk Costs and Market Structure*, Cambridge, MA: MIT Press.

Suzuki, N., J.E. Lenz and O.D. Forker (1993), 'A conjectural variations model of reduced Japanese milk price supports', *American Journal of Agricultural Economics*, **75**, 210–18.

Tyers, R. and K. Anderson (1992), *Disarray in World Food Markets – A Quantitative Assessment*, Cambridge: Cambridge University Press.

PART III

7 Are support measures and external effects of agriculture linked together? Conceptual notes and empirical evidence from the Austrian agricultural sector

Franz Sinabell

7.1 Introduction

Virtually every government in industrial countries intervenes in agricultural markets. Besides arguing for a 'fair' level of income, comparable to that outside the agricultural sector, numerous other reasons for agricultural support have been brought forward. According to Winters (1987, p. 291) agricultural policies have been put into effect in industrialized countries in order to

1. promote agricultural efficiency and the optimal utilization of production factors;
2. provide a local supply for domestic food processors;
3. ensure 'reasonable' prices for consumers;
4. ease the farm sector's speed and costs of adjustment to external factors;
5. pay due regard to the social structure of agriculture;

From a welfare economics point of view, many of these goals can be reached most effectively by subsidizing the factor labour in the vulnerable sector (Bhagwati and Srinivasan, 1969). However, governments tried to reach these goals with various kinds of policies like minimum prices above the level of world prices or tariffs and quota on trade, which implied substantial welfare losses for society. In addition to the fact that some of these instruments are in direct conflict with many of the national goals of economic policy, they caused trade conflicts which have been settled temporarily within the Agreement on Agriculture during the Uruguay Round (see for example, Schwar, 1995).

One method of government intervention in agricultural markets which only recently entered the discussion in high income countries, is to compensate farmers for the provision of public goods, to reduce negative external effects linked to agricultural production and to promote sustainable agricultural policies (see for example, Hofreither and Vogel, 1995). Since most of the older policy aims are still on the agenda (this is at least true for Austria; Puwein, 1994) policy makers are confronted with the problem of reaching a larger number of goals with a more restricted set of instruments.

The question of the liberalization of trade in agricultural commodities coming into conflict with the principles of sustainable development is difficult to resolve. Trade models lead to the conclusion that there will be positive welfare effects and increased economic growth. Growth, however, might stimulate the depletion of natural resources (a number of contrasting arguments are brought forward by Daly, 1994 and Bhagwati, 1994). Therefore many authors propose a structured discussion in order to reach agreements where environmental and trade concerns are dealt with in an integrated way (for example, Esty, 1994, Steininger, 1994, Gardner, 1995).

This study wants to contribute to such a discussion by examining whether indicators that are used to measure the openness of the agricultural sector to foreign trade and the external effects of agricultural production can be analysed within a uniform conceptual framework. The analysis shows that this is in fact possible, if environmental costs and benefits of production can be valued in monetary terms. As such evaluation results are not available it is proposed to use environmental indicators as proxies for social damages.

Empirical estimates based on data from Austria indicate that product-specific regional transfers to the agricultural sector are interrelated with indicators of environmental damage. Such a relationship cannot be found with respect to positively valued services of agriculture: the distribution of transfers shows quite a different pattern of the environmental benefits from countryside stewardship practices. We suppose that such evidence gives policy makers valuable information on how to allocate support to regions where positively valued environmental services of farmers are provided and on how to modify existing support schemes in regions where environmental damage can be observed.

7.2   Indicators of sustainability and protection coefficients

Liberalizing agricultural markets will eventually lead to a reduction of input subsidies and to agricultural commodity prices which are close to world market prices. Both these consequences are seen as essential for a tight integration of agricultural and environmental policies (OECD, 1993). The argumentation is based on the assumption that production stimulating policies like price support schemes potentially lead to detrimental environmental effects. Maier and Steenblick explain this position as follows:

> Over the long run, moving agriculture onto a sustainable path and maintaining it there will require a mix of persuasion, financial incentives and disincentives, and other instruments as appropriate. In order to get the mix right, governments will have to work closely with farmers and farming associations, providing access to education and training and creating the right conditions for the adoption of more environmentally friendly production methods and technology. The maximum effectiveness of such

policies can be achieved only if the distortions in production caused by agricultural subsidies are reduced. (Maier and Steenblik, 1995)

The protection coefficient PSE[1] is used to indicate the level of such distortions caused by agricultural subsidies, whereas a similar measure, the AMS (Aggregate Measure of Support), is used to measure compliance with the Agreement on Agriculture made in the Uruguay Round. However, there is no similar 'measure of sustainability' for agriculture.

Several indicators were proposed, for example, the diversity of crops planted in a given area (Lyson and Welsh, 1993), or a whole set of indicators including the use of fertilizer and pesticides, the number of hedges in a given area and the acreage of fallowed parcels of land (see Nehrer, 1992). Alternatively various environmental and sociological indicators were considered simultaneously (Dumanski *et al.*, 1990; Piorr, 1996). PSE values which are based on a normative concept refer to transfers and social cost associated with discretionary policies whereas indicators of sustainability as those mentioned are mainly referring to 'optimal' situations that are determined by natural science parameters.

Welfare economics offers the well established concept of external effects allowing measures of protection as well as indicators of sustainability to be integrated under one framework if deviations from the path of sustainability can be measured in monetary terms. Given that such valuations exist, the question arises of whether or not PSE values actually are consistent with the concept of external effects. Another question concerns whether PSE values in combination with environmental indicators can be used to indicate which direction policy changes should take.

7.3   Protection coefficients and external effects
In theory the market price of a change in agricultural output should reflect the social opportunity cost. In practice market prices are frequently different, mainly due to market imperfections, the most important of which is, in agriculture, government intervention (Saunders, 1996). The most frequently used indicator to measure market imperfection is the Nominal Protection Coefficient (NPC) which is calculated by dividing the domestic price by the world market price of a given commodity. An NPC > 1 indicates that the domestic market of such a commodity is distorted.

An approach to measuring the social cost of agricultural output is to estimate the Effective Rate of Protection (ERP) based on the concept of effective

---

1   Gross Total PSE (Producer Subsidy Equivalent) is defined as total assistance transferred to producers by means of *market price support* (net of *levies on output*), direct payments, and *other support*, but before deducting of the *feed adjustment*, to arrive at the *net total* PSE, where *feed adjustment* is the sum of the additional costs of animal feed to livestock producers as a result of *market price support on feeds for which* PSEs are calculated and taxes on feeds and processed feedstuffs (OECD, 1995, p. 288).

protection developed by Corden (1966). By using the difference between value added at domestic prices and the value added at world prices and expressing it as a percentage of the value added at world prices, the ERP of a given commodity will not systematically overestimate the social opportunity cost as is the case with the NPC if inputs are protected as well and therefore could be put to alternative uses (see Tsakok, 1990).

Several assumptions which underlie the concept of effective protection may be seen as problematical. ERPs assume that the trading status of a country would be unchanged given no support, that changes in domestic supply will not influence world market prices, and that there are fixed input/output coefficients. It is further assumed that there are no significant impacts on exchange rates, no transportation costs, no external effects of production, that there is homogeneity of production, and full employment of production factors.

All these assumptions also underlie the methodology of PSE that was proposed by Josling (1973) to measure the income transfer to producers in a protected sector. The PSE, further developed by the OECD, has been modified in a way to 'measure the value of the monetary transfers to agricultural production from consumers of agricultural products and from taxpayers resulting from a given set of agricultural policies, in a given year' (OECD, 1995, p. 193). Although according to this definition it seems that the PSE measures transfers only, it is covering social costs as well (the relative shares depend on market conditions and on the set of policies).

Several authors deal in depth with this measure (among them Christen, 1990; Tsakok, 1990; O'Connor *et al.*, 1991) showing that policy measures with quite different effects on trade or production may have similar PSE values (Schwartz and Parker, 1988, Cahill and Legg, 1990), or investigating the influence the underlying assumptions have on the ranking of countries (Masters, 1993; Bureau and Kalaitzandonakes, 1995). Guyomard and Mahe (1994) show the effects that production quota in combination with price support measures have on that indicator. None of these authors took account of the presence of external effects, however. In the next paragraphs a graphical model is used to show how this indicator is affected if external effects are no longer negligible.

PSE in its most simple form (the product specific *market price support* element of the PSE) is equivalent to the Subsidy Equivalent (SE). The SE is calculated by multiplying the quantity of a good produced in a country where there is a tariff on imports by the difference between domestic and world market prices. All the information required to calculate the value of SE for a given period can be observed quite easily in markets (see Vousden, 1990, 32pp. for an extensive treatment).

In Figure 7.1 the situation of a market where domestic producers are protected by a tariff is depicted. World market price is p_w, the price for domestic producers

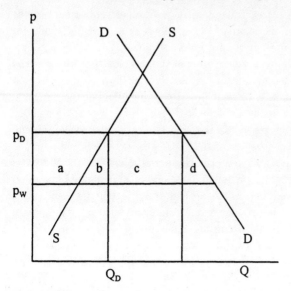

Figure 7.1   Subsidy equivalent and consumer tax equivalent in a partial equilibrium

after introducing a tariff is p_D. D and S are demand and supply, respectively. The Subsidy Equivalent (SE) is equal to area $a + b$. This area represents the transfer from consumers to producers (a) and includes the social costs (b) which arise because of the production loss (resulting from allocating resources to produce too much of the commodity in question). Summing up, the Subsidy Equivalent is composed of both transfers and social costs (SE $= a + b$).

Now consider a situation where a *positive external effect* is linked to the production of this commodity. If the external effect has the property of a pure public good and is directly linked to the production of the commodity in question, the government might find it appropriate to subsidize this agricultural activity.[2] In such a situation the SE only measures the total amount of transfers, no social costs are included this time if the compensation scheme is implemented in an efficient way.[3]

Exporters abroad may notice that production is subsidized (local farmers get a higher price than p_w) and can observe the increased production volumes. They

2   This could be the case if cows or sheep are necessary to prevent alpine grassland from reverting to scrub and there are hikers and tourists enjoying these landscape amenities. The optimal quantity of a public good is determined by the condition that the sum of the individual willingness to pay for the public good has to exceed the total cost of providing it (see Varian, 1992 p. 414 for a formal treatment).
3   The efficiency of such a policy crucially depends on the design of the compensation scheme.

might argue that they lose market shares due to policy intervention because the protection coefficient SE is positive. If the only way to match demand for landscape amenities with their supply is to subsidize agricultural products technically coupled with them, other forms of support clearly would not lead to that goal. Direct payments to farmers that are decoupled from production could be used for consumption only, without any stimulating effect on the provision of the public good. Therefore, the implementation of a programme to internalize environmental benefits may imply that the SE becomes positive whereas social costs are zero.

The basic relationship between a protection coefficient like the SE and a *negative externality* can be demonstrated in the graphical model in Figure 7.2. In this case the country has a protective agricultural policy in place and raises the domestic producer price p_D above the reference price p_w. This policy increases the production volume according to the supply function S to the level of Q_S. In such a situation the *subsidy equivalent* is the sum of the areas a to f: The loss of welfare resulting from this protectionist policy (Dead Weight Loss DWL_p) is illustrated by the triangles b and f.

Now suppose that environmental damage (a negative external effect) is associated with the production of this commodity. Since too much of this particular commodity is produced internalizing the social costs would require production to be shifted to S'. If the environmental costs are not internalized the

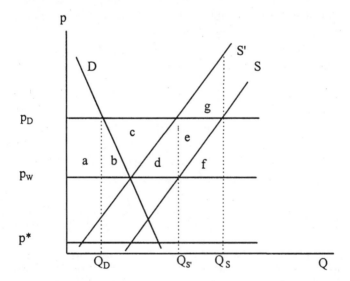

Figure 7.2   Liberalizing a market in presence of production-related negative external effects

social costs due to negative external effects (DWL_E) are given by the area $d + e + g$. The total loss of welfare therefore is given by the sum of welfare losses via protectionist policies ($DWL_P = b + f$) and welfare losses via negative externalities ($DWL_E = d + e + g$).

Following the argument of Maier and Steenblik (1995) an abolition of the tariff could already lead to a dramatic reduction of social cost. The only source of inefficiencies remaining would be the environmental costs (d). If the environmental damage is proportional to output, a tax on production could reduce DWL_E to zero (for the producers this is equivalent to the lower price p^*). In such a situation farmers on the local market might argue that they are discriminated against in comparison to foreign competitors because the SE has become negative as a consequence of the environmental tax. As in the situation where government internalizes a positive externality, again the SE is different from zero, whereas social costs are zero.

Table 7.1 gives a systematic overview of the effects of policy interventions if external effects of production are present:

1. the prices are: p_W (world market price), p_C (domestic consumer price), p_P (domestic producer price), p^* the 'optimal price' reflecting marginal social opportunity costs;
2. effects can be measured with several indicators: DWL, public budget, and SE;
3. effects can be neutral (0), increase the value of an indicator (+), or decrease its value (–);
4. damages of external effects can be covered by the taxpayer (budget: +), can be paid for by future generations, or by firms/consumers (current budget: 0);
5. positive external effects can be paid for by the public (budget: +), or can be internalized on the basis of private contracts (budget: 0).

The interpretation of the various prices in Table 7.I is as follows: In a situation where social opportunity cost are reflected on markets ($p_P = p^*$) by definition no external effects occur. This is probably most frequently the case and underlies one of the core assumptions of measures like the SE.

If prices observed on markets (e.g. p_P) are lower than p^*, however, a positive external effect is associated with the production of a given commodity. In such a case the market price is too low to induce producers to provide the optimal amount (this is equivalent to an implicit tax on production). If market prices are above the 'optimal' price ($p_P > p^*$) producers get a hidden subsidy because negative external effects are not internalized and thus a more than optimal production takes place.

Table 7.1　*Effects of policy intervention in the presence of external effects of production*[4]

Reference situation		No external effect	Positive external effect No measure taken	Negative external effect
Effect	Prices	$p_w = p_c = p_P = p^*$	$(p_w = p_c = p_P) < p^*$	$(p_w = P_c = p_P) > p^*$
	DWL	0	+	+
	Budget	0	+ or 0	– or O
	SE	0	0	0
Measure		Subsidy	Subsidy (private compensation)	Tax (private compensation)
Effect	Prices	$(p_w = p_c = p^*) < p_P$	$(p_w = p_c) < (p_P = p^*)$	$(p_P = p^*) < (p_w = P_c)$
	DWL	+	0	0
	Budget	–	– or (0)	+ or (0)
	SE	+	+ or (0)	– or (0)
Measure			Tariff	Import subsidy
Effect	Prices	$(p_w = p^* =) < (p_P = p_c)$	$p_w < (p_P = p_c = p^*)$	$(p_P = p^* = p_c) < p_w$
	DWL	+	+	+
	Budget	+	+	–
	SE	+	+	–

In Table 7.1 various situations are summarized: If a government is subsidizing production in a situation where there are no external effects SE is positive, taxpayers lose money (budget '–') and social costs arise (DWL '+'). If tariffs (or in the short run equivalent measures like quotas or non-tariff barriers to trade) are introduced as a measure to internalize positive external effects, still social costs occur (DWL '+').

The first best policy in such a situation is to pay for the provision of the public good directly (see panel 'subsidy') which would involve the SE to become positive (SE '+'). Only in cases where private compensation for such services is taking place is the SE zero. In a situation where negative external effects are present, the first best policy to internalize social costs is to collect a Pigouvian tax or to establish institutions that make polluters liable. Where a tax is imposed, social costs vanish (DWL = 0), and the measure of protection becomes negative (SE = '–') indicating that production is taxed. Only in cases where polluters directly compensate people harmed by their activity does the SE become zero.

4　It is assumed that no spillover effects on neighbour countries occur. Figures in brackets refer to a situation where private compensations are used to internalize environmental costs or benefits.

In situations where no external effects exist, the SE is a useful indicator for social costs associated with market distortions. The major advantage is that it can be calculated quite simply based on market observations (SE and DWL have the same sign whatever policy is implemented). The interpretation becomes ambiguous if externalities are associated with production. Since the OECD definition of the PSE does not account for external effects and is calculated in a similar way to the SE, a positive product-specific PSE can be interpreted in two ways: (a) social costs arise due to market distortions induced by government intervention, or (b) the government takes action to stimulate the production of public goods which are in short supply. A negative value can be interpreted: (a) the government is distorting markets at the cost of producers, or (b) the government is correcting market distortion by internalizing social costs. To avoid such ambiguities it is necessary not to ignore external effects and to account for environmental taxes and compensations for the provision of public goods in a consistent way.

7.4   Social cost and benefits of Austrian agricultural production

The total PSE of Austrian agriculture was 37.4 billion ATS (Austrian Schillings) in 1994 (about 2.7 billion ECU) with a percentage PSE of 62 per cent and a producer NAC (Nominal Assistance Coefficient) of 2.52 (OECD, 1995). These figures indicate that considerable transfers associated with social costs were the consequence of intervening in agricultural markets. Estimates of the social cost due to agricultural policies exist only for the bread grains market for the period before Austria's accession to the EU (see Hofreither *et al.*, 1995). This study shows the puzzling fact that the welfare gains of down- and upstream industries were higher than that of grain producers.

In Austria both positive, as well as negative external effects due to agricultural production can be observed (see Sinabell, 1995 for a recent survey). Hofreither and Sinabell (1994) argue that liberalizing agricultural markets in Austria which implies lower producer prices will have positive effects for environmental quality if this policy is combined with programmes under which farmers are paid for environmental services based on cost-benefit criteria.

Negative effects are mainly the result of an intensive use of farm chemicals which leads to a loss of plant species and other organisms; a further effect is the pollution of groundwater. Recent monitoring data shows that current threshold values are being exceeded on an area equivalent to 40 per cent of arable land (BMLF and BMJUF, 1996). But no monetary estimates of the damages exist, so the social costs due to external effects are unknown.

Therefore, the question of how PSE values are related to the social costs of agriculture cannot be resolved. However, environmental indicators can serve as a proxy if they are highly correlated with social cost. This is certainly true for nitrate content in groundwater. The additional costs for water providers who have to blend water from different sources or have to invest in purification facilities are estimated to amount to two billion ATS, 150 million ECU, for the period from 1993 to 2000 (Gerhold, 1993).

Most important among positive externalities of the Austrian agriculture are countryside stewardship goods. In several regions where a beautiful landscape is a major input for the tourist business, private cooperation exists between hoteliers and farmers providing these services (see Hackl and Pruckner, 1997 for a recent analysis). Several studies were carried out in which estimates of the value of positive external effects were made (Pruckner and Hofreither, 1992, Baaske *et al.*, 1991 and 1995, Pevetz *et al.*, 1990, and Pruckner, 1993). Reliable estimates of the monetized value of countryside stewardship services of Austrian agriculture were made by Pruckner and Hofreither (1992) and Pruckner (1993) who asked tourists from abroad for their willingness to pay for agricultural landscape. So far there is no reliable estimate of Austrian citizens' willingness to pay for similar public goods. Results from Sweden (Drake, 1992) suggest that it may be quite remarkable in areas where landowners switch from agricultural to forest production.

7.4.1 Transfers to producers on a regional level

The model depicted in Figure 7.2 suggests a relationship between a protection coefficient and environmental costs where border protection measures exacerbate negative externalities. As shown in this figure, the SE is proportionally related to both elements of total welfare loss ($DWL_E + DWL_P$) if negative external effects occur. If these effects are actually linked with production one would expect to observe high damage where product specific transfers are high. Nitrate content in groundwater can serve as a proxy for environmental damage since water with a nitrate content exceeding 50 mg NO_3/l may not be sold to consumers. In polluted regions water providers are required to make additional investments which are not paid for by the polluters.

To test such relationships required that the PSE figures for Austria had to be broken down to community level in order to construct a 'Regional Transfer Indicator' (RTI). A deviation from the PSE methodology is given by the fact that agricultural land was used in the denominator to allocate transfers not directly related to a single product because most of the data was available on a regional level (the OECD uses production volumes of commodities instead). Levies on fertilizers were not subtracted as the OECD methodology requires, but were assumed to be collected to internalize some of the costs associated with nutrient emission.[5] This deviation from the PSE methodology is necessary to reach

5   This assumption may be questioned by the fact that the money collected by this levy was used for export subsidies of grains. The distributional consequences of this tax were that grain producers gained on cost of all other producers using mineral fertilizer as input. This input levy was abolished in 1994.

consistency with the results derived in the previous chapter. No payments based on cost–benefit criteria were made for the production of specific countryside stewardship goods during this period. Therefore, payments from countryside stewardship schemes were treated like direct payments.

In calculating the RTI the first step was to break down the market price support element of the PSE on local crop and livestock production quantities (the 'general services' element was allocated according to production volumes). The next step was to partition the 'other support', and 'direct payments' elements to the relevant acreage basis. Thus several indicators were calculated which captured different elements of support, for example *Crop-RTI* captures *market price support* and *other support* which is directly related to plant production whereas the *Neutral-RTI* captures *direct payments*.

7.4.2 Regional transfers and environmental effects

Anderson and Strutt (1994) showed in a cross country analysis that PSE values are significantly correlated with the amount of fertilizer used. They argue that liberalizing trade which will reduce PSE values in several countries will likely lead to a reduced input of farm chemicals with positive environmental effects.

Experiences from the policy change which took place in New Zealand confirm these arguments. During the period from 1979 to 1994 the percentage PSE dropped from 18 per cent to 3 per cent in New Zealand (OECD, 1995). Lifting trade barriers and reducing support of the farm sector not only strengthened competitiveness and helped to save consumers' and taxpayers' money but also led to positive effects for the natural environment (Reynolds *et al.*, 1993). These empirical findings back model results of Tobey and Reinert (1991) who conclude that agricultural policy reform encourages a reduction of farm inputs.

In the following section empirical data from Austria will be used to test two hypotheses. The first one is that we would expect higher environmental damage in regions where price support measures lead to an increase in the use of farm inputs compared to regions where support to farmers is dominated by direct payments. This analysis goes one step further than the work of Anderson and Strutt (1994). They used an indicator of potential emission (fertilizer input), here an indicator of the damage (nitrate content of groundwater) is used. The second hypothesis is that we would expect that government compensates farmers for the production of landscape amenities and therefore direct transfers to farmers should be higher in regions where such amenities can be observed.

7.4.2.1 Regional transfers and environmental pollution in Austria

To be able to test the first hypothesis a very detailed model would be required that captures the major linkages between farm production, policy intervention and the physical effects on the natural environment (such a model was developed by Vatn *et al.* 1996). A simpler approach was chosen for this study because such a sophisticated model does not exist in Austria.

Hofreither and Rauchenberger (1995) and Hofreither and Pardeller (1996) developed econometric models that can be used to analyse the effects of land use changes on the nitrate content of Austrian groundwater. In their cross-section analysis they used natural environment parameters, land use data and input intensity data as explanatory variables (about 1100 observations are included in the data set, however not for all the variables).

Data and structure of one of their models were taken and regional transfer indicators were chosen as explanatory variables instead of land use variables. Given the lack of data for important parameters it is practically impossible to establish a theoretically sound and empirically valid model to describe the complex relationships between the variables. Therefore we confined ourselves to testing the hypothesis of a statistically significant correlation between nitrate pollution of Austrian groundwater and the various RTI-variables in a cross-section analysis. This attempt can be seen as a first step to test if a causal connection between support and environmental damage exists.

The econometric analysis shows that the model in which the transfer indicator *Crop-RTI* was used as an explanatory variable yields almost the same results as the model by Hofreither and Pardeller (see model 2 and model 3 in the Appendix). As expected, the result indicates that those regions are more likely to be polluted where high transfers stimulate crop production. The variable capturing direct payments (*Neutral-RTI* in model 4) has a negative sign which implies that direct payments probably do not contribute to groundwater pollution. All these results hold for quite different forms of regression equations and sub-samples.

The results have to be interpreted with great care, however. The models estimated are too simple to describe the complex interaction between diverse farming practices and heterogeneous soil, groundwater, and climatic conditions. Since correlations among variables do not imply causal relationships further research is required to test the validity of the results presented here. The inclusion of other potential polluters besides agriculture could be a starting point. Such efforts are hindered by the lack of site specific variables that would allow more complex models to be tested, however.

7.4.2.2 Regional transfers and landscape amenities in Austria   In the following paragraphs the interrelationship between transfers to farmers and landscape amenities in Austria will be investigated. Compensations are made for various services, among them the protection of semi-natural habitats, the maintenance of landscape elements, and the preservation of typical cultural landscapes. The lack of data does not enable us to test whether such payments are in fact necessary to compensate farmers for providing public goods or if they are a form of hidden income support. Therefore this issue will be dealt with only briefly.

In Figure 7.3 the regional distribution of three indicators among the Austrian *Länder* (provinces) is depicted:

1. tWTP is the aggregated Willingness To Pay for agricultural landscape by tourists from abroad (about 0.75 billion ATS = 0.056 billion ECU; see Pruckner, 1993);
2. tRTI (total Regional Transfer Indicator) is the aggregated total transfer to farmers (the annual average of the 1990–93 period is 41 billion ATS = 3 billion ECU);
3. APEA 96 are the payments from the Austrian Programme for Environment and Agriculture under regulation EC 2078/92 from those schemes that are

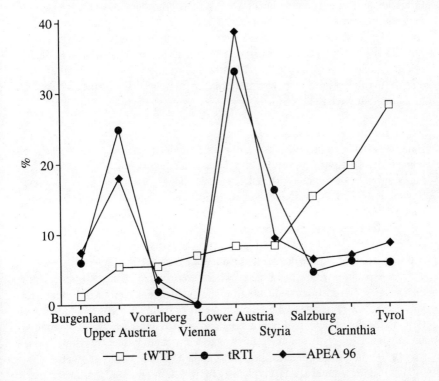

Figure 7.3   Regional shares of the aggregates of total willingness to pay (tWTP), regional transfers to the agricultural sector (tRTI) and the payments under the Austrian Programme for Environment and Agriculture (APEA 96)

intended to stimulate the production of landscape amenities (payments under these schemes amounted to 1 billion ATS from a total of 8 billion ATS for the whole APEA programme; BMLF, 1997).

Figure 7.3 shows that farmers in *Länder* where tourists value the agricultural landscape most highly (Salzburg, Carinthia, Tyrol) get relatively low support. With respect to the tRTI indicating the total level of support before the EU accession this is plausible because these *Länder* are relatively smaller. With respect to payments under the APEA 96 schemes designed to stimulate landscape amenities, the graph shows that the designers of the programme obviously had some parameters in mind other than the value tourists attach to agricultural landscapes.

This very different distribution among the regional aggregates of the willingness to pay and payments under the APEA programme lead Hackl and Pruckner (1997) to the conclusion that there is considerable room for policy makers to improve the link between demand and supply of environmental services. Another interesting aspect is that the payments under the environmental programme in 1996 show the same distribution as the transfers that were made before Austria became an EU-Member State. It rather seems that the environmental programme was designed to match perfectly the pattern of transfers that were made before 1995.

7.5   Summary and conclusions

External effects can be observed and contribute to the net of social costs and benefits linked with agricultural production. Social costs due to market intervention by governments stimulated the development of protection measures, however, one of their underlying assumptions is that external effects are negligible. Governments in high income countries have responded to externalities by regulating agricultural emission and paying farmers who provide environmental services. Given that protection measures do not account for external effects there is a danger that their value cannot be interpreted correctly. This is especially relevant in cases where environmental taxes intended to internalize social costs are deducted from the total value of a protection measure. It is also relevant in cases where governments or local authorities compensate farmers for the provision of public goods in an efficient way. These payments should not be interpreted in the same way as transfers to farmers resulting from, say, tariffs, but as the price for goods not traded on commodity markets.

The Producer Subsidy Equivalent (PSE) is defined as an 'indicator that measures the value of the monetary transfers to agricultural producers resulting from agricultural policies in a given year' (OECD, 1996, p. 227). In this broad definition the PSE does not account for external costs or benefits. It would not be useful to change the methodology to overcome this shortcoming because one of the advantages of this indicator – to observe policy changes over time – could be impaired. However, the informational content of the PSE calculation could be improved, if environmental taxes and compensations for the provision of public goods were accounted for in a separate measure. This may become more important in future when the volume of such transfers and taxes is likely to increase. A necessary precondition is to define guidelines for programmes that in fact compensate producers for providing public goods. Strict guidelines are necessary in order to be able to differentiate them from programmes that support farmers in other ways.

The empirical sections of the paper focused on social costs associated with agricultural policies. Referring to a partial equilibrium model it was shown that transfer indicators like the PSE are in relation to the social costs due to external effects of production. Empirically it was shown that transfers to Austrian plant producers have a significant correlation with nitrate content in groundwater (the database is from the pre-accession period to the EU). Although data did not allow for testing a causal relationships between a measure of regional transfers and environmental damages, the results of this study indicate that the way agricultural policies were designed in Austria still have an influence on the level of groundwater pollution. In addition, there is some evidence supporting the view that nitrate contamination would not be increased if a change was made from transfers stimulating production to transfers not linked to output.

Referring to positive externalities of Austrian agriculture it was shown that programmes designed to pay farmers for countryside stewardship services do not match the distribution of the aggregate willingness to pay for these services. Modifying existing schemes would allow the supply of landscape amenities to be more closely linked with their demand.

Appendix

Table A7.1   *Estimated parameters of nitrate pollution of groundwater (regression results for regions with more than 400 mm precipitation between October and March)*

	Model 1		Model 2		Model 3		Model 4	
Observations	424		401		432		432	
Variables	coeff.	t-value	coeff.	t-value	coeff.	t-value	coeff.	t-value
Intercept	27.24	10.46	5.03	3.54	6.21	4.48	12.26	11.69
N-balance	0.06	4.87						
Share maize			0.15	3.82				
Share grassland			−0.42	−6.56				
Precipitation	−0.02	−4.39	−0.46	−2.01	−0.73	−3.38	−1.23	−6.85
Redox			−0.68	−9.21	−0.63	−8.57	−0.61	−7.60
Crop-RTI					0.03	10.22		
Neutral RTI							−0.70	−6.75
Adjusted R^2	0.12		0.42		0.41		0.34	
SE regression	17.29		0.82		0.82		0.90	

Note: Hofreither and Pardeller (1996) provide a detailed model description and explanations to the variables used. Equation 1 is a linear model, whereas the other equations were formulated in log-linear form.

Source: Results for equations 1 and 2 are from Hofreither and Pardeller (1996, Table 2) results for the other two equations are own estimates.

References

Anderson, K. and A. Strutt (1994), *On Measuring The Environmental Impacts of Agricultural Trade Liberalization*, Paper presented at the Symposium 'Agricultural Trade and the Environment: Understanding and Measuring the Critical Linkages', Toronto, 17–18 June.

Baaske, W., J. Millendorfer and M. Riebe (1991), 'Quantitative Bewertung der ökologischen Leistungen einer bäuerlichen Landwirtschaft' (Valuation of ecological services of peasants), unpublished research report, Studiengruppe für internationale Analysen, Laxenburg, Austria.

Baaske, W., R. Sulzbacher and O. Villani (1995), 'Öffentliche Güter – Modelle ihrer Bewertung und Abgeltung am Beispiel der österreichischen Land- und Forstwirtschaft' (Valuation of public goods – Austrian case study), Studie im Auftrag des Bundesministeriums für Land- und Forstwirtschaft, STUDIA Schlierbach, Schlierbach.

Bhagwati, J. (1994), 'Ein Plädoyer für freien Handel' (A defence of free trade), *Spektrum der Wissenschaft*, January pp. 34–9.

Bhagwati, J.N. and T.N. Srinivasan (1969), 'Optimal Intervention to Achieve Non-Economic Objectives', *Review of Economic Studies*, **36**, 27–38.

BMLF and BMJUF (Bundesministerium für Land- und Forstwirtschaft, Bundesministerium für Jugend, Umwelt und Familie) (eds.) (1996), *Wassergüte in Österreich* (Austrian Water Quality Monitoring), Annual Report 1995, Vienna.

BMLF (Bundesministerium für Land- und Forstwirtschaft) (1997), *Grüner Bericht 1996* (The State of Agriculture, 1996), Vienna.

Bureau, J.-C. and N.G. Kalaitzandonakes (1995), 'Measuring Effective Protection as a Superlative Index Number: An Application to European Agriculture', *American Journal of Agricultural Economics*, **77**, 279–90.

Cahill., C. and W. Legg (1990), 'Estimation of Agricultural Assistance using producer and Consumer Subsidy Equivalents (PSEs/CSEs), Theory and Practice', in: OECD *Modelling the Effects of Agricultural Policies 14–45*, Special Issue No. 13, OECD.

Christen, P. (1990), *Die Bedeutung des PSE CSE für die internationale Handelsordnung: dargestellt am Beispiel der Agrarpolitik* (The Significance of PSE and CSE for International Trade: the Example of Agricultural Policy), Grüsch.

Corden, W.M. (1966), 'The Structure of a Tariff System and the Effective Protection Rate', *Journal of Political Economy*, **74**, 221–37.

Daly, H.E. (1994), 'Die Gefahren des freien Handels' (The risks of free trade), *Spektrum der Wissenschaft*, January pp. 40–46.

Drake, L. (1992), 'The non-market value of the Swedish agricultural landscape', *European Review of Agricultural Economics*, **19**, 351–64.

Dumanski, J., C.E. Beus, R.E. Howell, and J. Waud (1990), 'Guidelines for evaluating sustainability of land development projects', *Entwicklung + ländlicher Raum*, 3/90, 3–6.

Esty, D.C. (1994), *Greening the GATT*, Institute for International Economics, Washington.

Gardner B.L. (1995), 'Rationalizing Agricultural Export Subsidies: Comment', *American Journal of Agricultural Economics*, **77**(1), 205–8.

Gerhold, S. (1993), 'Ökologische Gesamtrechnungen: Erhöhte Kosten der Trinkwasseraufbereitung aufgrund von Umweltbelastungen' (Ecological accounting: the cost of drinking water purification), in: *Statistische Nachrichten*, **8**, 635–8.

Guyomard, H. and L.-P. Mahé (1994), Measures of distorting support in the context of production quotas', *European Review of Agricultural Economics*, **21**(1), 5–30.

Hackl, F. and G. Pruckner (1997), 'Towards More Efficient Compensation Programmes for Tourists' Benefits From Agriculture in Europe', *Environmental and Resource Economics*, **10**, 189–205.

Hofreither, M.F. and K. Pardeller (1996), 'Agrarproduktion und Nitratbelastung des Grundwassers' (Agricultural production and nitrate pollution of groundwater), *Die Bodenkultur*, **47**(4), 279–90.

Hofreither M.F., K. Salhofer and F. Sinabell (1995), *Promotion of the Agricultural Sector and Political Power in Austria*, WPR-Diskussionspapier No. 38-W-95.

Hofreither M.F. and S. Vogel (1995), *The Role of Agricultural Externalities in High Income Countries*, Proceedings of the 37th Seminar of the European Association of Agricultural Economists, Kiel: Vauk.

Hofreither, M.F. and F. Sinabell (1994), *Zielsetzungen für eine Nachhaltige Landwirtschaft* (Goals for Sustainable Development of the Agricultural Sector), Report Band 48, Umweltbundesamt, Vienna.

Hofreither, M.F. and F. Rauchenberger (1995), 'Administrative versus ökonomische Einflüsse auf die Nitratbelastung von Grundwasser – Eine ökonometrische Analyse agrarstruktureller Einflußfaktoren' (Administrative versus economic instruments to reduce nitrate pollution of groundwater – an econometric analysis), *WPR-Forschungsbericht* im Auftrag des BMLF (Forschungsprojekt No. 775/93), Vienna.

Josling, T. (1973), *Agricultural Protection. Domestic Policy and International Trade*, 73/LIM/9, C, FAO, Rome.

Lyson, T.A. and R. Welsh (1993), 'The production function, crop diversity, and the debate between conventional and sustainable agriculture', *Rural Sociology*, **58**, 424–39

Maier, L. and R. Steenblik (1995), 'Towards Sustainable Agriculture', *The OECD-Observer*, **196** 36–7.

Masters, W.A. (1993), 'Measuring Protection in Agriculture: the Producer Subsidy Equivalent Revisited', *Oxford Agrarian Studies*, **21**(2), 133–42.

Nehrer, D. (1992), 'Ecological sustainability in agricultural systems: Definition and measurement' *Journal of Stustainable Agriculture*, **7**, 124–31.

O'Connor, H.E., A.J. Rayner, K.A. Ingersent and R. C. HINE (1991), 'Aggregate Measures of Support in the Uruguay-Round: Application to the EC Cereals Sector', *Oxford Agrarian Studies*, **19**(2), 91–103.

OECD (1993), 'Agricultural and Environmental Policy Integration: Recent Progress and New Directions', Paris: OECD.

OECD (1995), 'Agricultural Policies, Markets and Trade in OECD Countries. Monitoring and Outlook 1995', Paris: OECD.

OECD (1996), 'Agricultural Policies, Markets and Trade in OECD Countries. Monitoring and Evaluation 1996', Paris: OECD.

Pevetz, W., O. Hofer and H. Pirringer (1990), 'Quantifizierung von Umweltleistungen der öster-reichischen Landwirtschaft' (A quantitative valuation of environmental contributions of the Austrian agricultural sector), *Schriftenreihe der Bundesanstalt für Agrarwirtschaft*, **60**.

Piorr, H.-P. (1996), *Ecological and socioeconomic consequences of the EU-reform policy after 1996 in North-East Germany*, Paper presented at the Workshop on Mineral Emission from Agriculture in Oslo, 25–28 January.

Pruckner, G. (1993), *Die ökonomische Quantifizierung natürlicher Ressourcen: Eine Berwertung überbetrieblicher Leistungen der österreichischen Land- und Forstwirtschaft* (The economic quantification of natural resources: a valuation of external effects of the Austrian agricultural sector), Dissertation, Department of Economics, Johannes Kepler University, Linz.

Pruckner, G. and M. Hofreither (1992), *Überbetriebliche Effekte der Österreichischen Landwirtschaft* (External effects of Austrian agriculture), Discussion paper No. 6-W-92, Institut für Wirtschaft, Politik und Recht, Universität für Bodenkultur, Vienna.

Puwein, W. (1994), 'Abgeltung der Landschaftspflege – Subvention oder Produktionsentgelt' (Transfers for countryside stewardship – subsidy or fair remuneration), in W. Schneeberger and H.K. Wytrzens (eds), *Naturschutz und Landschaftspflege als agrar- und forstpolitische Herausforderung*, Österreichische Gesellschaft für Agrarökonomie, Vienna, pp. 17–24.

Reynolds, R., W. Moore, M. Arthur-Worsop and M. Storey (1993), *Impacts on the Environment of reduced Agricultural Subsidies. A Case Study of New Zealand*. MAF Policy Technical Paper 93/12, Policy Section, Ministry of Agriculture and Fisheries, Wellington.

Saunders, C. (1996), *Financial, Public Exchequer and Social Value of Changes in Agricultural Output*, Centre for Rural Economy Working Paper Series, Working Paper 20, University of Newcastle-upon-Tyne.

Schwar, P. (1995), 'Die Agrarverhandlungen in der GATT-Uruguay Runde – Eine Kontroverse zwischen Freihandel und selektivem Schutz für die Landwirtschaft' (Agricultural negotiations in the Uruguay Round – a conflict between free trade and agricultural protection), *Austrian Journal of Public and International Law*, **49**(2–4), 183–201.

Schwartz, N.E. and S. Parker (1988), 'Measuring government intervention in agriculture for the GATT negotiation', *American Journal of Agricultural Economics* pp. 1137–45.

Sinabell, F. (1995), *Externe Effekte der österreichischen Landwirtschaft* (External Effects of Austrian Agriculture), in M.F. Hofreither (ed.), ÖIAA-Schriftenreihe, Bd. XLVI. Vienna: Facultas Verlag.

Steininger, K. (1994), 'Reconciling trade and environment: towards a comparative advantage for long-term policy goals', *Ecological Economics*, **9**(1), 23–42.

Tobey, J.A. and K.A. Reinert (1991), 'The effects of domestic agricultural policy reform on environmental quality', *The Journal of Agricultural Economics and Research*, **43**(2), 71–82.

Tsakok, I. (1990), *Agricultural Price Policy*, Ithaca, New York: Cornell University Press.

Varian, H.R. (1992), *Microeconomic Analysis*, New York: W.W. Norton & Company.

Vatn, A., L.R. Bakken, M.A. Bbleken, P. Botterweg, H. Lundeby, E. Romstad, P.K. Roorstad and A. Vold (1996), 'Policies for Reduced Nutrient Losses and Erosion from Norwegian Agriculture. Integrating Economics and Ecology', *Norwegian Journal of Agricultural Sciences*, Suppl. 23.

Vousden, N. (1990), *The economics of trade protection*, Cambridge: Cambridge University Press.

Winters, A.L. (1987), 'The Political Economy of the Agricultural Policy of Industrial Countries', *European Review of Agricultural Economics*, **14**, 285–304.

8 Principles for the provision of public goods from agriculture: modelling moorland conservation in Scotland

Nick Hanley, Hilary Kirkpatrick, David Oglethorpe and Ian Simpson

Acknowledgements: The first sections of this chapter benefited greatly from Hanley's involvement in the Rural Amenities Project, undertaken by the OECD's Rural Development Programme. The empirical section of the chapter is based on work funded by Scottish Natural Heritage. The authors are grateful for this funding, and for research assistance from Louise Scott. We are also grateful to Ian Bateman for helpful comments.

8.1 Introduction

The Polluter Pays Principle (PPP) has become a well-known and widely applied concept in the OECD since its establishment in the early 1970s, when it was put forward as one of the 'Guiding Principles Concerning the International Economic Aspects of Environmental Policies' in 1972 (Seymour, Cox and Lowe, 1992). It was then adopted three years later in 1975 (OECD, 1975). There has been some confusion as to what exactly the principle implies for polluters' responsibilities: for example, whether the principle implies that the polluter must only meet the cost of reducing emissions to socially-mandated levels (under regulation) or indicated levels (under a pollution tax) or whether in addition the polluter should pay for any damage costs associated with this socially-desired level of emissions (Pezzey, 1988). However, the general default position of industrial polluters having to pay the abatement costs associated with bringing their emissions to socially-desired levels is now fairly well accepted in the OECD,[1] rather than what might be called a 'Pay the Polluter' principle. It has also been remarked by many commentators that the agricultural sector has been largely exempted from the application of the Polluter Pays Principle, with farmers frequently being subsidized to reduce emissions from, for example, nitrogenous fertilizers spread on fields in the UK (Parsisson, Hanley and Spash, 1994). Reasons offered for this failure to apply the PPP to farming have included the non-point nature of discharges, stochastic influences on discharges, and the political power of the farm lobby (Baldock, 1992; Tobey and Smets, 1996).

---

1 Although OECD governments also make capital grants available to polluters to reduce abatement costs (and emission levels) over the longer run (Opschoor and Vos, 1989).

The Polluter Pays Principle implies that private agents pay some of the costs associated with the production of negative externalities. An obvious policy question is therefore whether a symmetrically-opposite principle exists for private agents producing positive externalities, which increase the stock of public goods. That government, as the representatives of consumers, can bring about an optimal level of the supply of such public goods (a Lindahl equilibrium) has, of course, been a well-known part of welfare economics for many years. However, a 'Principle' that encapsulates this approach to public good provision has been lacking in name, if not (as we later show with respect to farming) in application.

Before outlining such a principle, however, it is important to note that the difference between negative and positive externalities, and thus the choice of principle, can be argued to be largely politically and culturally determined through the establishment of property rights. Consider a farmer whose farm practices impact negatively on water quality. The farmer brings about a change in these practices which improves water quality, at the cost of lost profits. Should the farmer be compensated for these lost profits? If the farmer is viewed as having taken action to reduce a negative externality (to cut pollution) then the PPP is applicable. But if the farmer is viewed as having generated a positive externality by increasing the supply of the public good 'water quality' then is this still so?

One means of answering this question rests on the concept of a 'reference point' of environmental quality (Bromley and Hodge, 1990; Hodge, 1994). This reference point might be described as that level of environmental quality which society believes *should* exist. If society believes that the reference point for water quality exceeds the current level, then farmers will be conceived of as generating external costs; however, if the current level is now greater than the reference point, then farmers are viewed as generating external benefits.

Alternatively, the decision over whether an action constitutes the reduction of a negative externality or an increase in a positive externality might be based on a 'with and without' comparison. In this instance, this would involve asking if the farmer had not been farming, whether uncompensated *costs* on third parties would exist. If they would not (no water pollution), then the farmer's actions can be claimed to give rise to a negative externality, with any mitigating actions being classed as reducing this negative externality. However, if in the absence of the farmer's actions uncompensated *benefits* to third parties are absent, then the farmer is producing a public good, and actions to increase this should be described as such. An example here might be 'traditional' rural landscapes in England which are dependent on a particular form of farming for their appearance; or habitat such as lowland heath, which is a non-natural habitat requiring a particular low-intensity grazing regime to maintain it.

Whether in either case farmers are compelled without compensation, taxed or subsidized depends on guiding principles such as the Polluter Pays Principle. Such principles might be viewed as 'rule-of-thumb' devices which reflect society's view of fair distributions of income following a change in the level of externality (and are thus moral and/or political in nature), and which avoid resource-consuming arguments over whether to charge, subsidize or compensate in each individual case. Principles, on this basis, are thus both useful and potentially efficient in a world of high transactions costs.

In the rest of this chapter, we consider two candidate principles for the supply of public goods from agriculture, and then describe an empirical analysis which illustrates the use of one of these principles in the conservation of an ecologically-important habitat (heather moorland) in northern Scotland. Some conclusions close the chapter.

8.2 Two possible principles for the supply of external benefits from agriculture

Given the potential usefulness of principles, an obvious question is whether an equivalent to the PPP exists, which could be as widely adopted in the OECD for policies which encourage the generation of external benefits. Two candidate principles are the Beneficiaries Pay Principle (BPP) and the Provider Gets Principle (PGP). The BPP, a well-known principle from public finance, may be extended to the provision of public goods from agriculture or, more generally, from rural land managers (Brown, 1994). The BPP, given the assumption that rural land managers have property rights over their land, implies:

1. that those who benefit from such public goods, such as day trippers to scenic rural areas, or hunters in wetlands, should pay a marginal value-based fee to the providers of such goods. This fee can be on a per trip basis, on an annual basis (access permits), or can be implemented by land purchase or leasing;
2. that these payments compensate the rural providers of public goods for the opportunity costs of public good provision.[2] For example, the payments might compensate farmers for not intensifying production by draining wetlands;
3. that the interaction of marginal willingness to pay (demand) and opportunity cost (supply) will result in an efficient level of public good provision.

However, application of the BPP is complicated by physical, legal and cultural difficulties of excluding non-paying beneficiaries, and by the likely existence of passive-use values for public environmental goods, such as pleasant 'traditional' farm landscapes. If the supply of rural public goods were entirely

2   Note that these opportunity costs are assumed to be positive.

determined by the BPP, then it follows that this level of supply would be too small from an efficiency point of view.

An alternative principle is the 'Provider Gets Principle' (Blochliger, 1994). The Provider Gets Principle (PGP) is orientated more to the supply side of rural public goods than to the demand side. It involves the government identifying an 'appropriate' level of supply for rural public goods, and then directing public funds at the providers of these goods according to the opportunity costs of supply, representing, for example, lost profits to a farmer from not draining wetland. The source of these funds is not considered, but rather the fact that, given the existing property right regimes in many OECD countries, rural land managers often cannot be forced to supply these public goods without compensation for the opportunity costs that this implies.[3] The PGP, unlike the BPP, avoids the problem of identifying beneficiaries, and merely requires that (i) the suppliers of amenities can be identified; (ii) that a means be found of transferring funds to them; (iii) that funding is available to finance these transfers; and (iv) that an appropriate level of amenity supply be identified. This last point might be addressed conceptually on economic efficiency grounds by comparing costs and benefits of alternative levels of supply. However, this is very unlikely to be the only actual (or indeed desirable) criterion on which such decisions are taken, whilst the difficulties of estimating a marginal benefits schedule where non-market environmental effects are involved means that this optimum could not in any case be identified in practice.

In a review of case studies from nine OECD countries,[4] Hanley (1995) found a high level of use of the PGP in the provision of public goods from agriculture in particular, and rural land use in general; but very little use of the BPP. In many countries, government schemes exist which offer farmers payments to supply public, environmental goods. Typically, standard payment rates are offered to farmers who will voluntarily agree to meet a number of carefully-specified environmental objectives, such as reduced herbicide use, stone wall maintenance, or broadleaved-woodland planting. Examples of such schemes include the Environmentally Sensitive Areas scheme and management agreements under the Wildlife and Countryside Act in the UK; the North American Waterfowl Management Plan, funded by both US and Canadian taxpayers; and the National Fund for the Protection of Rural Landscapes in Switzerland. Other, similar schemes exist in Ireland, Sweden, the Netherlands and Austria. Current changes in the Common Agricultural Policy of the European Union involves a switch away from crop price support and towards

---

3 Although the extent to which this is so varies across countries. Denmark, for instance, places many legal obligations on rural land managers to supply public environmental goods without compensation (Hanley, 1995).

4 The countries were the UK, USA, Australia, Canada, Denmark, France, Italy, Japan and Switzerland.

more direct income support (such as the Arable Areas Payment Scheme). Payments for environmental performance are also increasing, under the agri-environment accompanying measures to the MacSharry reforms of 1992, although total spending on such environmental schemes remains a small part of the total CAP budget (total spending on CAP support in the UK was £2536 million in 1994–5; of this, only 4.3 per cent was attributable to agri-environmental measures). Such agri-environmental policy reforms do, however, signal further future use of the PGP in the European Union.

The next section of the chapter reports on an empirical analysis of one possible application of the PGP to habitat conservation in Scotland. We chose to model this policy option since, as noted above, it is in line with other aspects of agri-environmental policy reform in the EU, and as it also fits well with the 'voluntarism' approach which has dominated nature conservation in the UK since the 1940s. This approach seeks to avoid compelling rural landowners to produce environmental improvements (or to avoid environmental damages), but rather to persuade them to do so by offering voluntary payments in line with profits foregone and/or costs incurred. The implicit assumption that rural landowners have property rights to use their land as they see best is also contrary to the idea of financial penalties, such as over-grazing taxes, to mitigate ecologically-inappropriate land use patterns. A voluntary payments scheme is thus a practical policy option.

8.3   Modelling the application of the PGP to moorland conservation in Scotland

From an ecological point of view, heather moorland is an ecosystem of international importance (Ratcliffe and Thompson, 1988). Such landscapes are semi-natural in that whilst flora and fauna developed spontaneously, this development is and has been strongly influenced by man (Gimingham, 1995). Heather moorland is home to birds such as the Hen Harrier (*Circus cyaneus*), Golden Eagle (*Aquila chrysaetos*) , Merlin (*Falco columbarius*) and Short-eared Owl (*Asio flammeus*), all of which are protected under Article 1 of the EU Birds Directive. Another indication of the conservation importance of heather moorlands is that 435 of Scotland's 1039 Sites of Special Scientific Interest contain significant amounts of the habitat (Ward, MacDonald and Matthew, 1995), whilst the UK has in addition agreed to protect heather moorland under the EC Habitats Directive. Heather moorland is also an integral part of traditional Highland scenery, being valued for its landscape quality.

In the 1940s heather moorland covered around 20 per cent of Scotland, but between then and the 1970s there has been an 18 per cent reduction in this area (Tudor *et al.*, 1994). Moorland has been lost as the result of the expansion of coniferous forestry, and reclamation by farmers into grass pastures, whilst much of the remaining area is degraded due to excessive grazing pressure from sheep. Sheep numbers on a national scale have risen substantially since the UK's accession to the Common Agricultural Policy of the EU, due to the policy providing price support for sheep meat and headage payments per ewe. Moorland loss is reversible, but not by the removal of grazing alone. Regeneration would require the removal of all vegetative cover, the scarifying of soil and the subsequent exclusion of stock. This would allow the *potential* regeneration of heather from the seed bank in the soil. Allowing heather moorland degradation thus depletes the natural capital stock, but not in an irreversible way. However, such remedial action would be of high cost and of uncertain success, whilst the recovery of insect and bird species associated with heather moorland might also be problematic.

Heather moorland may be seen as a semi-natural ecosystem which generates external benefits in terms of nature conservation and landscape beauty (although to our knowledge no valuation studies, using techniques such as contingent valuation, have been carried out specifically on heather moorland in the UK). Farmers, through overgrazing, reduce the supply of these external benefits to the public. However, abandoning grazing entirely would also probably reduce conservation benefits below an ecologically optimal level, since totally un-grazed heather may become woody and die, whilst in areas south of Shetland, totally un-grazed land may revert to scrub woodland.[5] In terms of the discussion in section 2, it is therefore not clear whether we should classify a farmer's actions in reducing overgrazing as increasing a positive externality or reducing a negative one. For the purposes of the following discussion however, we shall describe reductions in overgrazing as an action which leads to an increase in the supply of a public good, namely heather moorland of high ecological value.

8.3.1 Heather moorland in Shetland
The empirical work reported in this chapter[6] relates to management of dwarf shrub-dominated vegetation in the Shetland Islands, an archipelago of over 100 islands of which only 15 are inhabited. The archipelago has an approximate land area of 1433 sq km, of which 86 830 ha consists of heather-dominated vegetation and 14 804 ha of heather–grass mosaics. The climate is hyperoceanic, characterized by Dry and Robertson (1982) as being cool to very cold and wet. Windiness is the most distinctive climatic characteristic of Shetland, and gales occur on an average of 58 days per year. The pattern of relief reflects a complex geology with Shetland being divided into two geologically distinct parts by the north–south trending Walls Boundary Fault. The landscape today is almost totally tree-less, although from macrofossil and pollen profile data it is possible to date the

---

5   Although in fact no empirical evidence exists on Shetland to demonstrate the effects of the total removal of grazing pressure.
6   Work on this project was also carried out in the Orkney Islands: see Hanley *et al.* (1995) for a description of this.

emergence of a *Betula* (birch) dominated community from around 10 400 BP. This was succeeded by *Betula-Corylus* with *Calluna* dominated communities on the higher ground (Lewis, 1907, 1911; Erdtman, 1924; Johansen, 1975; Hulme and Durno, 1980). A decline in tree pollen had commenced before Neolithic settlement but accelerated with increased human activity from c. 4800 BP. *Calluna* and other heath and mire species began to increase, almost certainly as a result of natural and human-induced soil nutrient leaching and acidification. About 3000 years ago, heather-dominated communities increased markedly, and the landscape then entered a period of relative stability up until the beginning of commercial (as distinct from subsistence) sheep farming in the late 19th Century.

Since this period, the area of heather moorland in Shetland has declined. The National Countryside Monitoring Scheme estimates a reduction in blanket mire and heather moorland from 1281 km² in the 1940s to 1186 km² in the 1970s. Data also indicate a shift in dwarf shrub dominated vegetation to grassland and an increase of 52.6 km² in semi-improved grassland (NCMS, 1992).

Statutory conservation sites cover 10.7 per cent of Shetland and include 4906 ha of uplands, 16.5 ha of peatland, 34 ha of maritime heath and 3021 ha of serpentine heath. Moorland communities of special interest include *Calluna-Vaccinium mytillus-Sphagnum* heath which is particularly vulnerable to over-grazing, and *Racomitrium* rich *Calluna-Erica cinereria* heath unique to the islands. Shetland's heather moors are also of considerable importance for birds, both at the national and international level. About 95 per cent of the British population of Whimbrel nest there, along with important breeding populations of Merlin and Golden Plover; all of these birds are protected under the 1981 Wildlife and Countryside Act and the EC Birds Directive (Batten *et al.*, 1990).

Agriculture on Shetland is dominated by store lamb production (that is, breeding lambs which are sold on to other farmers outside of Shetland for fattening). Breeding ewe numbers rose from 116 385 in 1982 to 156 299 in 1993. This has meant an increase in the stocking rate from 2.38 ewes/ha of rough grazing land to 3.08 ewes/ha. Whilst a substantial portion of grazing lands are privately owned (63 588 ha in 1993), many crofters also have access to common grazings. These common lands are regulated by a Clerk of the Commons, who maintains a register of maximum permitted stocking rates per crofter. These grazing allocations may be lent or leased to other crofters. Crofters have an incentive to utilize fully their grazing allocations, otherwise they may be transferred to other commoners. Birnie and Hulme (1990) have argued that common grazing land in particular is subject to ecological overgrazing.[7]

7   Note that the individual crofter may choose to stock in excess of the ecological carrying capacity, since the consequence of such an action (a conversion of heather to rough grassland) will increase the number of sheep the crofter can keep, as grass has a higher productivity than heather from a grazing point of view. Overgrazing may thus be privately efficient, even if socially inefficient.

8.3.2 Ecological modelling

Overgrazing may be defined as occurring when sheep (or other ruminants) remove excessive amounts of dry matter from plants, leading to the death of these plants and their possible replacement by other species (we define 'excessive' in the specific context of our empirical work below). The extent to which plants can support grazing depends on the amount of animal uptake (determined primarily by the stocking rate); and on the natural productivity (growth) of the plant. In order to determine how much of Shetland's moorlands are technically overgrazed therefore required the estimation of growth rates for heather. We sampled heather growth rates at 10 sites, which varied in both altitude and windiness (exposure), both of which are negatively related to heather productivity. Annual productivity was measured as the length of that year's long shoots on 100 randomly selected plants on each site. This length varied from 0.8 cm/year to 3.6 cm/year. As expected, productivity was found to decline with increasing exposure; underlying geology also seems to influence growth rates. Overall heather growth rates on Shetland are very low relative to growth rates measured at other UK sites (Bayfield, 1984; Welch, 1984). These site-specific measurements of heather productivity were then generalized to all heather moorland on Shetland using a Geographic Information System (GIS), in which land cover, altitude and exposure classifications were used to categorize land by class of heather productivity (MLURI, 1993a).

In order to determine grazing pressure, data was collected on sheep numbers, vegetation types and fertilizer applications at 19 'grazing units'. These grazing units were selected on a stratified random sample basis, and included both privately-owned and common grazings. Information on soils and climate for each grazing unit was collected from secondary sources. A model developed by the Macauley Land Use Research Institute (MLURI), known as the Hill Grazing Model, was then run using this input data (MLURI, 1993b). The model predicts, for each sample site, the amount of vegetation produced and available to sheep, the annual uptake by sheep, and the value of this uptake as a percentage of production: the 'utilization' rate. Comparing actual versus predicted utilization rates, the model was found to correctly allocate all sites in a sub-sample of five sites where actual values were measured into the appropriate utilization class. Predicted utilization rates vary from 0 per cent to 92 per cent, with a mean value of 22.6 per cent across all heather types.

The final step in the ecological modelling was to predict, for any given site, the reduction in grazing pressure needed to prevent heather degenerating into rough grassland. This was done by comparing (predicted or actual) utilization rates with maximum tolerable utilization rates, previously identified for heather by Grant and Armstrong (1993) as being equal to 40 per cent of annual growth: the Grant and Armstrong results were thus used to define 'excessive' removal of plant dry matter. This exercise revealed that ten of the 19 sample sites were technically overgrazed, and that across the archipelago as a whole 36 per cent of the total heather moorland area was predicted to be technically overgrazed. However, this overgrazing is not uniformly distributed, being concentrated in certain land classes (notably suppressed heather and blanket bog). Overgrazing will result in a succession to grassland communities (*Nardus sp.*) and peat erosion, a decline in moorland bird species, and a loss of moorland plant communities.

8.3.3 Economic modelling

As established earlier in the chapter, the principle of the government paying farmers to produce environmental goods (or not to deplete these goods) is well-established in the OECD. In addition, rural environmental policy in the UK has firmly steered clear of regulation, preferring a voluntary approach backed up by payments to farmers (Lowe *et al.*, 1985). These payments are typically set with some regard to the opportunity costs of conservation to the farmer (such as foregone profits from intensification), plus any direct costs involved in conservation actions (such as the cost of planting amenity woodland). This reflects a legal and cultural position that farmers have the property rights over most rural service flows deriving from their land, so that society must bribe (compensate) them to secure a supply of costly environmental goods. (Typically in the UK, farmers are only restricted, in terms of land use, with regard to development, for instance, housing.)

In the case of Shetland moorland, it was therefore most realistic to model a policy whereby farmers are offered payments to reduce damage to the heather moorland resource, in line with the opportunity costs they face. Two approaches may be found in similar policies in the UK: uniform payment schemes, whereby within some defined area (such as an Environmentally Sensitive Area), uniform payment rates are offered to all farmers fulfilling a certain set of conservation commitments; and payments differentiated on a per-farm basis, such as management agreements to protect Sites of Special Scientific Interest under the Wildlife and Countryside Act. In this research, the latter option was modelled.[8] Uniform payment rates are clearly less efficient than per-farm payment rates, since we expect opportunity costs to vary across farms. However, uniform payment schemes are likely to have lower transactions costs than differentiated payments.

In order to calculate opportunity costs to farmers in Shetland of reducing stocking rates, a Linear Programming (LP) model was constructed and calibrated

---

8   Although since this research was completed, the UK government announced a Moorland Extensification Scheme, which pays a uniform rate of £25 per ewe removed from overgrazed heather. To qualify for the payments, farmers must initially be stocking at over 1.5 ewes/ha., and reduce this to 1 ewe/ha. A minimum 25 per cent heather cover is stipulated for land to enter the scheme.

to represent each of the 13 farms included in the ecological survey reported above. Whilst LP models are subject to some well-known limitations (linearity of constraints, fixed input–output coefficients, risk neutrality), such models do enable both the flexibility of farm systems and the dual value (marginal value product) of fully-utilized resources to be represented, and thus continue to be widely used (Michalek, 1994). Input data came from the Scottish Agricultural Colleges farm management database, a farm survey carried out for this project on Shetland, and Scottish Office Agriculture Environment and Fisheries Department (SOAFD) June census returns. The farm survey revealed low levels of fertilizer application, and a high percentage (mean 43 per cent) of income derived from sources other than farming. This latter finding was expected, since farming on Shetland might more accurately be described as crofting. Ewe numbers in the survey varied from 12 to 2590 per holding, with very little other livestock being kept or other crops produced.

The LP model was tested by comparing predicted stocking rates, ewe numbers and lambs produced with observed levels. These tests showed the model to perform relatively well: Table 8.1 gives details. Each LP model run also predicts farm income (we were not able to collect survey data on individual farm income); the models can thus be used to investigate the estimated reduction in income caused by imposing stocking limits on any farm.

Table 8.1   LP calibration results

Farm	Ewes predicted	Ewes actual	Stocking rate predicted	Stocking rate actual	Farm income predicted (£)
01	831	851	0.061	0.062	4415
02	167	170	0.078	0.079	1797
03	590	598	0.368	0.373	11 592
04	12	12	0.247	0.247	104
05	2584	2606	0.430	0.434	24 496
06	398	400	0.117	0.118	1871
07	2290	2350	0.099	0.102	11 060
08	660	652	0.028	0.027	4724

Notes:
Stocking rate is total livestock units per forage hectare: each ewe counts for 0.15 of a livestock unit. 'Ewes' also allows for small amounts of grazing pressure from suckler cows.
Farm income is defined as Management and Investment Income, before land/property charges.

Using the ecological models described above, 'critical' stocking rates were derived for each farm, representing both privately-owned rough grazing and common grazings to which the farmer had access. These critical rates were defined as rates above which ecological deterioration could be expected to occur, given the land cover type, underlying geology, and climatic factors. By comparing these critical rates with actual rates, it was possible to calculate the necessary reduction in ewe numbers for each farm in the survey. These reductions were then introduced into the LP models as additional constraints facing the farmer, and the consequent reduction in farm income noted. For a risk-neutral farmer, this amount represents the minimum bribe the farmer should expect, given profit maximization and full information, in order to agree to the stocking rate cut. Table 8.2 gives details of these results.

Table 8.2   *Necessary reductions in sheep numbers and associated minimum payments to farmers*

Farm	Absolute reduction in sheep numbers required	% reduction in sheep numbers required	Minimum payment per ewe removed
1	210	29	£12.75
2	152	91	£17.32
3	490	83	£30.31
4	3	25	£8.67
5	150	6	£5.70
6	260	65	£19.18
7	1567	68	£7.73
8	559	94	£21.87

Five of the farms (sites) were classified as not currently overgrazed, thus no reduction in ewe numbers was needed in these cases. Given the assumptions of the LP model, these five farms find it economically-optimal to restrict grazing levels below critical limits. For the remaining farms, necessary reductions can be quite large. For those farms where reductions are needed, these vary substantially both in absolute terms and as a percentage of current sheep numbers. The opportunity costs to farmers (calculated as average costs) of abiding by these limits also varies substantially; these variations reflect opportunities for alternative enterprises on the farm, management skills and physical conditions such as exposure which may affect lambing rates.

Minimum required payment rates might also be expected to vary with the price that farmers receive for their outputs. In this respect, two values seemed important: the headage payment received per ewe, and the price at which lambs

Table 8.3   Changes in the mean minimum payment required (calculated at the mean stocking rate restriction) as support prices change

	Farm income	Farm income after grazing restriction	Minimum payment per ewe removed
Base case [a]	5451	702	£11.20
Headage payment −50%	−5672	−5672	£0.00
Headage payment −25%	−1442	−3002	£3.68
Headage payment +25%	12344	4407	£18.72
Headage payment +50%	19386	8111	£23.54
Lamb prices −50%	−4839	-5076	£0.59
Lamb prices −25%	252	−2187	£5.75
Lamb prices +25%	10666	3591	£14.71
Lamb prices +50%	16210	6481	£20.23

Note: [a] The base case refers to an initial weighted average of all farms in the sample under market and policy conditions at the time of the survey.

can be sold. Table 8.3 reports some sensitivity analysis of the mean minimum payment as these two values are altered. The great dependence of farming in Shetland on support payments is obvious in this table: as headage payments in particular are cut, farm incomes quickly become negative. As the value of support falls, the value of the marginal lamb produced or ewe kept also falls, thus the table shows declining minimum payments would be needed to maintain farm incomes should the value of support fall to these levels. Indeed, in the base situation reported in Table 8.3, the return per ewe with subsidies is less than the subsidy itself, implying a negative free-market return per ewe. Since the LP objective function is one of profit maximization, and more money can be made by doing nothing than by carrying on with ewe production, then the maximal income (a negative value) simply reflects fixed costs. When the headage payment is reduced to 50 per cent of the current level, then no sheep are kept and so no compensation is necessary to remove them!

Finally in this section, it is of interest to note that an alternative to the per-head payments scheme modelled here is the 'Environmentally Sensitive Areas' scheme, which has been in operation in Shetland since 1994. Under this scheme, farmers must draw up conservation plans for their whole farm, to include upper limits on grazing pressure. Entrance to the scheme is voluntary, with those joining receiving area-based payments, of around £21–£45/hectare depending on the conservation plan specified. So far, only 10 per cent of eligible farmers in Shetland have joined the scheme. This may be due to the facts that total payments to any one farm are subject to a rather low ceiling (£4000 per year), and that for those farmers with access to common grazings, *all* holders of such rights on any given common must join the scheme (through the Commons Grazings Committee) at the same time. Joining the ESA scheme may in any case not reduce overgrazing if the stocking rate specified in the farm conservation plan is equal to or greater than the current actual stocking rate.

8.4   Conclusions

This chapter has considered the use of one principle, the Provider Gets Principle (PGP), for the provision of public goods from agriculture. Such principles were argued to be useful 'rules of thumb' for answering questions as to who should pay for what where external costs and benefits are present. The espousal of any one principle in a particular case also represents a moral call by society on who should pay for the cost of environmental improvements: there is no objectively correct principle to choose. Much use of the PGP was, however, found in OECD countries in the context of agri-environmental policy.

The chapter then went on to show how PGP-type payments could be calculated for the conservation of a threatened but valuable habitat in Scotland, using ecological–economic modelling. This revealed the highly non-uniform nature of desired reductions in stocking rates, and in minimum necessary payment rates across farms. The farm-specific payments scheme modelled involves reductions in grazing pressure in a non-uniform way, such that the required reduction in stocking varies spatially according to current overgrazing, itself a function of spatially variable heather growth rates. An extension of the model would be to target areas where the benefits of heather regeneration are higher with greater payments than areas of lower benefit. A single farmer might thus be able to claim varying rates according to where on his farm he targeted grazing restrictions. Our implicit assumption is that one hectare of heather regenerated is equally valuable irrespective of where it occurs: this may not be so if 'islanding' effects are significant, or in landscape quality terms. How such variable quality would be indexed, though, is a difficult problem.

Alternatively, a system could be modelled where a uniform grazing restriction was applied, with uniform or differentiated compensation payments (farmers will face varying costs in meeting such a uniform restriction on grazing). This uniform grazing restriction would need to be set with regard to the most sensitive site (that is, where heather recovery was most problematic): in the Shetland case, this would involve restricting all farms to a maximum of 0.06 ewes/ha. This would obviously, however, over-restrict grazing on all other units, and thus impose a higher overall resource cost. We recognize that such a uniform maximum is excessively restrictive, and would recommend basing it instead on the average ecological limits across *overgrazed* units, which is 0.79 ewes/ha., while dealing with especially-sensitive areas on a case-by-case basis.

Generally, we note that uniform rates are becoming increasingly common in the UK in agri-environmental schemes, and offer savings in transactions costs. They also minimize scope for strategic behaviour on the part of farmers, contrary to the farm-specific negotiations that precede management agreement payments under the Wildlife and Countryside Act to protect Sites of Special Scientific Interest (Spash and Simpson, 1994). In our case, a uniform rate could be that calculated for the weighted average or base farm in Table 8.3: namely £11 per ewe removed. However, an adequate reduction in grazing pressure would only be forthcoming if instead the uniform rate were set with regard to the farm with the *highest* opportunity costs of reducing sheep numbers; this gives the much higher figure of £30.31 (sample farm 3, in Table 8.2). This compares fairly closely with the £25 per ewe payment recently announced by the UK government in the new Moorland Extensification Scheme (MAFF, 1995).[9]

It is also possible to calculate the aggregate costs of a differentiated payment rates scheme, and to compare these to the case of uniform payments, for farms in the sample. This shows the maximum that it would be worth spending on additional transactions costs for the more efficient differentiated scheme. For the sample farms as an aggregate, a uniform rate would have to be set with regard to the highest marginal cost farm, that is at £30.31. This would imply a total cost for the eight farms currently overgrazing of £103 691 per annum. This compares with a total cost of £50 600 per annum under differentiated payments. Thus, up to this 51 per cent saving in compensation payments could be expended in additional transactions costs, and still generate a saving over the uniform payment scheme. We are, however, unable to generalize these calculations to all farms in Shetland with our current data set.

We also note that overgrazing on Shetland is exacerbated by the high level of financial support paid by the European Union to farmers through the CAP (recall that Table 8.3 shows the minimum payment as increasing in the level of support payments); in this case, government subsidies create environmental damage. It might be argued that a simpler way of reducing overgrazing would be to cut support payments or eliminate them entirely; however, this is extremely unlikely to happen to a sufficient degree in the short to medium term, since farmers have what Bromley and Hodge (1990) would term 'presumptive entitlements' to support payments as a result of past policies. An alternative would be to make eligibility for support payments dependent on ecological good practice, as a form of cross-compliance. However, whilst the Hill Livestock Compensatory Allowance scheme regulations do contain a clause stating that payments may be withheld if farmers are found guilty of overgrazing, Agriculture

9 Since the start of the Moorland Extensification Scheme in Scotland in 1995, only 11 farmers have entered the scheme nationally. This low sign-up rate may be due to the low level of payments on a national scale, and overlaps with the Environmentally Sensitive Areas scheme (farmers may not sign up for both schemes).

Department officials made it clear that this clause has never actually been enforced, whilst the term 'overgrazing' therein is set with regard to agricultural, rather than ecological, principles (SOAEFD, 1996).

It is also important to note that if overgrazing is characterized as a negative externality, then according to the discussion in Section 2 the payments scheme analysed in this chapter is actually an example of applying a 'Pay the Polluter' principle, rather than an application of the 'Provider Gets Principle'. What is more, if those farmers who are currently overgrazing to the greatest extent receive the highest payments for reducing grazing, relative to those who were previously grazing in an ecologically-responsible manner, then this implies rewarding 'bad actors' whilst penalizing the ecologically responsible.[10]

Finally, we have not been able to address here whether, in economic terms, such a support scheme would be worthwhile on narrow economic efficiency (cost-benefit analysis) grounds, since no estimates exist for the non-market conservation value of heather moorland on Shetland. This implies that it is impossible to say on grounds of economic efficiency whether more or less heather moorland should be protected, or how much more or less. Ecologists, however, are clear that heather moorland, as an important but diminishing habitat, is in need of protection, using schemes such as the voluntary payments scheme analysed in this chapter.

References

Baldock, D. (1992), 'The polluter pays principle and its relevance to agricultural polices in the EC', *Sociologia Ruralis*, **32**(1) , 49–65.

Batten, L., C. Bibby, P. Clement, G. Elliott, and R. Porter (1990), *The Red Data Birds of Britain*, London: T & A Poyser.

Bayfield, N.G. (1984), 'The dynamics of heather stripes in the Cairngorm Mountains', *Journal of Ecology*, **72**, 515–27.

Birnie, R.V. and P.D. Hulme (1990), 'Overgrazing of peatland vegetation on Shetland', *Scottish Geographic Magazine*, **106**, 12–17.

Blochliger, H.-J. (1994), 'Main results of the study' in *The Contribution of Amenities to Rural Development*, Paris: OECD.

Bromley, D. and I. Hodge, (1990), 'Private property rights and presumptive policy entitlements: reconsidering the premises of rural policy', *European Review of Agricultural Economics*, **17**(2), 197–214.

Brown, G. (1994), 'Rural amenities and the Beneficiaries Pay Principle', in *The Contribution of Amenities to Rural Development*, Paris: OECD.

Dry, F.T. and J.S. Robertson (1982), 'Orkney and Shetland', Aberdeen: Macaulay Land Use Research Institute.

Erdtman, G. (1924), 'Studies on the micropaleontology of postglacial deposits in northern Scotland with special reference to the history of woodlands' *Journal of the Linnean Society, Botany*, **46**, 451–504.

Gimingham, C.H. (1995), 'Heaths and moorland: an overview of ecolgical change', in D. Thompson, A. Hesher and M. Usher (eds), *Heaths and Moorlands: Cultural Landscapes*, Edinburgh: HMSO.

Grant, S.A. and H.M. Armstrong (1993), 'Grazing ecology and the conservation of heather moorland', *Biodiversity and Conservation* **2**, 79–94.

10   We are grateful to one of the referees for pointing this out.

Hanley, N. (1995), 'Rural amenities and rural development: empirical evidence', Synthesis report to the Rural Development Programme, Paris: OECD.

Hanley, N., H. Kirkpatrick, D. Oglethorpe and I. Simpson (1995), 'Ecological economic modelling of the conservation of threatened habitats: heather moorland in Orkney', Discussion papers in Ecological Economics 95/4, University of Stirling.

Hodge, I. (1994), 'Rural amenity: property rights and policy mechanisms', in *The Contribution of Amenities to Rural Development*, Paris: OECD.

Hulme, P. and S. Durno (1980), 'A contribution on the phytogeography of Shetland', *New Phytologist*, **84**, 165–9.

Johansen, J. (1975) 'Pollen diagrams from the Shetland and Faroe Islands', *New Phytologist*, **75**, 369–87.

Lewis, F.J. (1907) 'The plant remains of the Scottish peat mosses: Part III: the Scottish Highlands and Shetland Isles', *Transactions of the Royal Society of Edinburgh*, **46**, 33–70.

Lewis, F.J. (1911), 'The plant remains of the Scottish Highlands and Shetland Isles', *Transactions of the Royal Society of Edinburgh*, **47**, 793–833.

Lowe, P., G. Cox, M. MacEwen, T. O'Riordan and M. Winter (1985), *Countryside Conflicts*, Aldershot: Gower.

MAFF (Ministry of Agriculture, Fisheries and Food) (1995), 'Earl Howe Launches New Moorland Scheme', Press release 122/95: Whitehall, London: MAFF.

Michalek, J. (1994), 'Models for an evaluation of the effects of changed policies on pesticide use', in J. Michalek and C. Henning-Hanf (eds), *The Economic Consequences of a Drastic Reduction in Pesticide*, Kiel: Wissenschaftsverlag VK.

MLURI (1993a), *The Land Cover of Scotland 1988: Final Report*, Aberdeen: Macaulay Land Use Research Institute.

MLURI (1993b), *Hill Grazing Management Model, Version 1*, Aberdeen: Macaulay Land Use Research Institute.

NCMS (National Countryside Monitoring Scheme) (1992), *Northern Isles*, Perth: Scottish Natural Heritage.

OECD (1975), *The polluter pays principle: definition, analysis, implementation*, Paris: OECD.

Opschoor, H. and J. Vos (1989), *Economic Instruments for Environmental Protection*. Paris: OECD.

Parsisson, D., N. Hanley and C. Spash (1994), 'The polluter pays? The case of nitrates in water', Discussion papers in Ecological Economics 94/9, University of Stirling.

Pezzey, J. (1988), 'Market mechanisms of pollution control: polluter pays, economic and practical aspects', in R. Kerry Turner (ed.), *Sustainable Environmental Management*, London: Belhaven.

Ratcliffe, D.A. and D.B. Thompson (1988), 'The British uplands: their ecological character and international significance' in M. Usher and D.B. Thompson (eds), *Ecological Change in the Uplands*, Oxford: Blackwells.

Seymour, S., G. Cox and P. Lowe (1992), 'Nitrates in water: the politics of the polluter pays principle', *Sociologia Ruralis*, **32**(1), 82–103.

SOAEFD (1996), Explanatory notes: Sheep Annual Premium scheme and Hill Livestock Compensatory Allowances, Edinburgh: Scottish Office Agriculture, Environment and Fisheries Department.

Spash, C. and I. Simpson (1994), 'Utilitarian and rights-based approaches for protecting Sites of Special Scientific Interest', *Journal of Agricultural Economics*, **45**(1), 15–26.

Tobey, J. and H. Smets (1996), 'The Polluter Pays Principle in the context of agriculture and the environment', *World Economy*, **19**(1), 63–87.

Tudor, G.J., E.C. Mackay, and F.M. Underwood (1994), *The National Countryside Monitoring Scheme: the Changing Face of Scotland*, Perth: Scottish Natural Heritage.

Ward, S., A. MacDonald and E. Matthew (1995), 'Scottish heaths and moors: how should conservation be undertaken', in D. Thompson, A. Hester and M. Usher (eds), *Heaths and Moorlands: Cultural Landscapes*, London: HMSO.

Welch, D. (1984), 'Studies in the grazing of heather moorland in North-East Scotland', *Journal of Applied Ecology*, **21**, 197–207.

9 The impact of the Uruguay Round on the agro-food sector and the rural environment in Italy

Margaret Loseby

9.1 Introduction

In a recent OECD publication it was stated that 'With respect to the specific terms of the Agreement on Agriculture itself, it is difficult, without a case-by-case, country-by-country analysis, to draw general conclusions concerning the magnitude or direction of effects' (OECD, 1995a).

Unfortunately, for Italy, as for other countries, such a country study does not yet exist, so for the moment, the only solution appears to be an informed crystal ball approach, and this particular version is oriented somewhere between the extremes of the gloomy fears of some farmers' and processors' associations on the one hand, and the cheerful confidence in the merits of free trade expressed in some GATT and GATT-related documents.

But although at present conjectures are inevitable, in the future the task of asssessing the impact of the Agreement on Agriculture will not be more straightforward. This is because it will be extremely difficult to extricate and define the effects of this Agreement from those of the Uruguay Round as a whole (not to mention from those of other policy influences yet to come) on the macroeconomic environment into which the agro-food sector is necessarily integrated.

The scheme which has been followed in this chapter, then, is to illustrate the fears expressed by operators as to the consequences foreseen for the Italian agro-food sector as a result of the Agreement on Agriculture. The validity of these fears will be assessed firstly with reference to relevant macroeconomic indicators and subsequently in the light of microeconomic research which has brought evidence of a qualitative nature, less easily quantifiable in statistical terms, but not for this reason irrelevant.

9.2 Fears

The fears expressed concerning the effects of the Uruguay Round on Italian agriculture are inextricably linked with those relating to the effects of the reform of the Common Agricultural Policy on the European Union. To quote an authoritative observer

..the coincidence between the reform of the Common Agricultural Policy and the Uruguay Round agreement has a very specific significance, i.e. that of having converted a laborious internal agreement within the Community into an international commitment guaranteed by ... the World Trade Organisation. (Colombo, 1995)

However that may be, these fears are essentially two: that of loss of income on the part of farmers, due to the commitment to decrease price support; and that of an inability to meet new conditions of competition which will follow from changes in the system of protection and the reduction in subsidies for agricultural exports.

As regards the first, Italian farmers are sceptical about the income effects of the system of payments introduced by the MacSharry reform in order to compensate for loss of income deriving from price reductions. Not surprisingly, perhaps, considering that 'usually reliable' sources in Brussels contemplate the fading out of these payments; that it is unlikely that they will be substituted by national support to agricultural incomes in view of the sorry state of public finances; and considering that in any case, a notable proportion of Italian agricultural production (fruit and vegetables 23 per cent, and vineyards 9 per cent, by value in 1994, to mention the most prominent) are excluded from compensatory payments, even though it will, as cereals and livestock, be subject to lower levels of protection following the Agreement.

As regards the second fear, inability to meet new competitive conditions, it is often asserted that the structure of land holdings in Italy, dominated as it is by small and fragmented holdings, inhibits the adoption of cost-saving techniques. Moreover, it is inappropriate for responding to the changing nature of demand for agricultural products, where modern retailing together with processing industries play such an important role and require large quantities of constant quality produce, delivered to a strict time schedule. Apart from these aspects, food retailing, both in Italy and in the principal export markets for Italian products, is increasingly dominated by multinational firms which can readily switch their sources of supply between different nations, and, by implication, away from Italy.

Let us therefore investigate more thoroughly the basis for these fears.

9.3 Loss of income

That farmers should fear for a loss of income as a consequence of a reduction in public support to the sector is not surprising if one considers that in the average of the period 1990–92 this has been estimated as equivalent to 37.9 per cent of the value of final output (INEA 1995f).

That proportion, however, includes items which will not necessarily be eliminated by acceptance of the Agreement. The sensitive items are payments by the Intervention Board (12.87 per cent) and production subsidies (14.73 per cent). The dimensions of these two items give an idea of the reduction in support to be expected as a result of the Agreement, even though some of the payments included will be allowed to continue.

Payments by the Intervention Board are analysed in Table 9.1 as a proportion of the value of final output of the crops absorbing the greater part of AIMA (the Italian Intervention Board) payments over the long period (1983–92) and the more recent period (1990–92).

Table 9.1   The ratio between market support and value of output for the most strongly supported sectors

Sector	% of total agr. output, 1994	% AIMA payments: total output	
		1983–92	1990–92
Oilseed	3.2[a]	79.0	112.8
Olives	4.5	61.2	74.9
Fruit & Veg.	22.9	7.2	5.7
Dairy	11.2	5.4	6.8
Livestock	39.4	8.3	9.9
Sugar	n.a.	18.0	42.1
Vines	9.1	20.8	13.5
Tobacco	n.a.	109.4	121.4
Cereals	10.6	15.5	19.8

Notes: Calendar year payments from AIMA do not always correspond with year of production
[a] Industrial crops

Source: Calculated on data from INEA 1994b and INEA 1995a

Clearly, the fears of producers of tobacco and oilseeds appear to be justified: support has amounted to a very large proportion of the value of final output. Nevertheless, these products represent a very small part of the value of total agricultural production. On the other hand, it can clearly be seen that agricultural activities which contribute a large proportion of the value of total output, such as fruit and vegetables and livestock, enjoy a relatively limited degree of price support. Nevertheless, it cannot be excluded that where operating margins are low, as is often the case, even this low level of support may be considered essential for survival.

Table 9.2 shows the proportion of value added due to production subsidies by Region. The subsidies considered include compensatory payments associated with the MacSharry reform together with other subsidies existing prior to the reform, but exclude price support, aid to investment and to the agro-food industry. These subsidies are likely to be phased out in due time.

Table 9.2   *Ratio between agricultural production subsidies and Regional*
            value added (%)

	1990	1993	1994
Piemonte	7.0	10.1	11.1
Valle d'Aosta	27.8	40.5	30.8
Liguria	3.9	6.2	5.2
Lombardia	4.7	6.6	8.3
Trentino Alto-Adige	7.7	10.2	7.1
Veneto	8.9	13.3	12.3
Friuli-Venezia Giulia	8.3	16.5	15.6
Emilia Romagna	7.6	9.6	8.6
Toscana	15.4	14.5	15.2
Umbria	21.7	25.8	24.4
Marche	10.8	15.9	14.9
Lazio	9.4	13.2	12.9
Abruzzo	9.7	13.6	12.2
Molise	14.8	25.3	25.6
Campania	14.7	19.5	16.2
Puglia	12.8	17.8	16.2
Basilicata	18.0	27.8	25.0
Calabria	5.9	18.7	14.1
Sicilia	11.6	15.9	14.2
Sardegna	17.4	21.4	21.5
Italy	10.2	14.3	13.2

Source: INEA 1995a

The table shows the high degree of vulnerability of certain Regions to the
withdrawal of such support. In particular, subsidies in the Valle d'Aosta
amounted to about 30 per cent of value added, in contrast with Liguria where
the corresponding figure was only 5.2 per cent. The South and Centre of the
country appear to be more vulnerable than the North, on the whole.

9.4   Loss of competitiveness

9.4.1 Loss of EU protection
In this context, EU 'protection' will be understood both as the barriers erected
against imports from non-EU countries and as EU help in placing exports on
non-EU markets.

Italy is, in fact, a net importer of agro-food products. These accounted for 15 per cent of total imports in 1994 and 7.1 per cent of total exports. About two thirds, both of exports and of imports, however, involve countries of the EU. Changes here will be affected by the extent to which EU preference is maintained, as well as by possible future enlargements of the Union to countries with the capacity to trade in the same type of products.

A further 9 per cent of imports come from non-EU developed countries, whilst this group absorbed 19.3 per cent of exports in 1994. The USA (7 per cent) and Switzerland (5 per cent) accounted for the largest shares of exports to this group of countries.

A large proportion of Italian exports, however, are of products which have hitherto experienced a rather low level of protection, whether from tariffs, from variable import levies or from export restitutions. Fruit and vegetables, fresh, dried and processed, accounted for 29.5 per cent of agro-food exports in 1994; wine represented a further 12.1 per cent. Tariff reductions foreseen in the Agreement by the EU for fresh fruit are of about 2 per cent, bringing the total rate from about 9 per cent to about 7 per cent with slight variations according to the specific product (OECD, 1995b). Restitutions will be reduced by the agreed 32 per cent by the year 2000, probably involving such important products for Italy as tomatoes, table grapes, peaches, nectarines and apples (Table 9.3). Nevertheless, these products are exported mainly within the EU and therefore are not subject to export restitutions at present.

Table 9.3   Some of the main items in agro-food exports, 1994 (billion lire)

	Value	% agro-food exports
Wine	2695.7	12.4
Confectionery	1638.8	7.5
Pasta	1197.6	5.5
Preserved Fruit & Veg.	1080.3	5.0
Cheese	1042.8	4.8
Preserved Tomato	1040.9	4.8
Dessert grapes	833.0	3.8
Olive oil	682.3	3.1
Peaches and nectarines	663.0	3.0
Rice	634.8	2.9
Preserved meat	612.2	2.8
Liqueurs	527.1	2.4

Source: Calculated on data from INEA, 1995d and INEA, 1996d

As with other forms of agricultural support, the lowering of rates of external protection will have a greater impact in some areas of the country than in others. As shown in Table 9.4, agro-food exports are heavily concentrated in a few Regions: in fact six out of twenty Regions accounted for almost 70 per cent of total agro-food exports in 1994. In all these six regions, exports accounted for more than one third of the total value of agro-food production, but the proportion was particularly high in Piemonte (71.5 per cent) Emilia Romagna (47.8 per cent) and Campania (45 per cent). Thus any loss in competitiveness will be particularly strongly felt in these Regions.

Table 9.4   Agro-food exports – principal exporting Regions, 1994

	% all ag-food exports	% ag-food exports/ total agr. production	% ag-food exports/ total export
Emilia Romagna	16.6	47.8	10.5
Piemonte	15.1	71.5	8.1
Lombardia	14.5	37.8	3.4
Veneto	10.8	36.2	5.5
Campania	5.7	45.0	23.6
Toscana	4.6	40.0	3.9
Total, 6 regions	67.3	n.a	n.a
Total Italy, 20 regions	100	n.a	7.0

Source: Calculated on data from INEA (1995b), and INEA, 1995c

9.4.2 Unsuitable productive and commercial structures

The latest Agricultural Census figures (1990) show that there are 3 023 344 farms in Italy, of which more than one million have a total land area of less than one hectare. The average utilized agricultural area per farm is about 5 hectares and typically, this is divided into several fragmented plots. Censuses, conducted at ten year intervals, show only a very weak movement to enlargement and consolidation of farms. Since 1970, the number of farms has fallen by about 600 000, equivalent to 16 per cent (Table 9.5).

On the basis of these statistics, then, it would appear that farm structures are very unsuitable for the introduction of cost effective and technically sophisticated agricultural practices.

On the contrary, structural change in the food retailing system has been going on apace. Starting from a narrow base at the beginning of the 1980s, the modern food retailing sector has, since then, experienced an impressive rate of growth. Between 1982 and 1993, the number of supermarkets increased by a factor of 2.4, and at the same time the average size of store increased (Table 9.6). During the 1990s, hard discount stores have appeared and by end 1993 there were 325, mostly in the North of the country; by end 1995, there were 2210 (INEA 1996b).

Table 9.5   Number of farms and total area by size of total farm area (area in ha)

Class of total farm area	1970		1982		1990	
	No. farms	Total area	No. farms	Total area	No. farms	Total area
Without land	5591	0	10 176	0	16 061	0
Less than						
1 ha	991 662	481 722	1 040 957	506 210	1 061 711	525 577
1–2	590 942	814 640	641 127	884 246	700 767	982 229
2–3	335 995	798 958	372 621	885 335	430 977	1 032 849
3–5	373 850	1 411 820	419 911	1 584 646	496 626	1 887 743
5–10	354 401	2 436 234	397 823	2 731 129	482 985	3 326 590
10–20	201 321	2 747 371	217 137	2 958 790	250 255	3 398 671
20–30	65 242	1 561 974	66 464	1 588 085	68 291	1 632 316
30–50	49 743	1 870 238	48 549	1 818 718	46 950	1 763 864
50–100	32 722	2 217 719	31 735	2 154 812	30 013	2 046 616
>100	21 875	8 361 678	22 670	8 519 524	22 662	8 468 192
Total	3 023 344	22 702 355	3 269 170	23 631 495	3 607 298	25 064 643

Source: ISTAT, Censimento dell'Agricoltura, 1990; INEA, (1993)

Table 9.6   The development of supermarkets between 1982 and 1995

Years	Number	Area (m^2)	Employees (n.)
1982	1521	1 184 372	31 324
1983	1599	1 246 257	33 008
1984	1784	1 403 091	36 147
1985	1959	1 652 374	40 668
1986	2198	1 748 630	45 439
1987	2391	1 931 799	50 325
1988	2570	2 048 096	53 422
1989	2818	2 276 395	59 010
1990	3176	2 610 995	64 687
1991	3399	2 865 887	70 531
1992	3465	2 889 409	69 803
1993	3696	3 132 273	76 096
1994	3906	3 378 683	80 271
1995	4198	3 616 636	83 209

Source: Ministero dell'Industria, del Commercio e dell'Artigianato, 1996

As compared with other countries, the proportion of food sales passing through the modern retailing sector is still relatively limited: latest estimates put it at 40 per cent, but this compares with a figure of less than 20 per cent at the beginning of the 1990s (Table 9.7).

Table 9.7   Household purchase of food by type of retail outlet, 1994 (%)

	Super/Hypermkt	Discount	Traditional	Other	Total
Pasta	62.5	16.8	11.2	9.5	100
Wine	60.9	15.4	17.9	5.8	100
Milk	56.2	10.9	21	11.9	100
Cheese	54.6	8.2	28	9.2	100
Processed meats	51.7	7.3	33.6	7.4	100
Olive oil[a]	46.1	9.0	3.7	41.1	100
Meat	43.6	2.3	48.6	5.5	100
Fruit	40.5	4.7	34	20.8	100
Vegetables	37.7	4.8	34.4	23.1	100

Note: [a]   Including non packaged oil and produce consumed by farm family
Source: ISMEA/Nielsen 1995

Meanwhile, the number of traditional retail outlets has decreased significantly, by 19 per cent between 1982 and 1993.

It is well known that the modern food retailing sector imposes stringent conditions on its suppliers both of fresh and processed produce. As in the primary sector, the Italian food processing industry is numerically dominated by small firms, although their weight, in terms of proportion of sales, varies considerably from one sector to another. Small firms find difficulty in fulfilling the quantity requirements of modern retailing and fear to be overtaken by foreign firms, especially in view of the fact that foreign-owned food retailing chains are making rapid headway in the Italian market: apart from their presence in supermarkets, it was estimated that 25 per cent of hard discount stores were foreign owned in 1993.[1] Clearly, the multinational character of the retailing enterprises facilitates a wider choice of national origins for produce.

9.5   Countervailing arguments

The gloomy picture illustrated above, with the aid of official statistics is, however, subject to modification in the light of evidence available at 'grass roots' level but which is rather more difficult to discipline into a tabular form.

---

1   The percentage dropped to an estimated 13 per cent by end 1994, but the proportion of turnover absorbed amounted to 20 per cent, the foreign-owned stores being above average in size (INEA, 1995e)

Beginning with the constraints to income levels and to technical and cost efficiency apparently imposed by the small average size of farms, it can be argued, on the one hand, that farms are effectively larger than the statistics show and, on the other, that certain types of farming yield a high value of production on relatively small areas of land.

The apparently small size of farm has some impelling institutional reasons for existing. Firstly the system of taxation presently in force induces farming families to divide property between different family members in order to minimize the tax burden, even though the management of the family property may be unified. Secondly, prolonged immobility in the land market together with bitter experience (for land owners) accumulated in the past as regards conditions for renting land discourage formal enlargement of farm size. Nevertheless, a variety of informal arrangements have evolved which have enabled farmers to enlarge the area on which they actually operate.

The small farm, on the other hand, is not necessarily a low revenue farm. In certain parts of the country, the growing period can extend over almost the whole year, and especially in the case of vegetable cultivation, the successive crops yield a high return per hectare.

Turning now to the problems posed by changes in the structure of the retailing system: these can best be met by the Italian agro-food sector by exploiting its characteristics of flexibility and its capacity to produce high quality products.

As regards the high quality of products, one might ask whether this will continue to be an important element in demand with the further spread of modern retailing. On the positive side, however, it can justifiably be claimed that the home market continues to privilege quality, whereas exports of Italian agro-food products tend to be mainly of high quality, high price products, the demand for which may be relatively insensitive to the type of price competition that is likely to be activated by reductions in trade barriers.

Finally, considering the fears of operators with respect to the reduction of price and income support, the possibility exists that the conditions created by the Uruguay Round Agreement may lead to a rise in world price levels, to the advantage also of Italian producers.

But, one may ask, is all this enough?

9.6   Environmental aspects

As is well known, the Agreement permits public financing, amongst other things, for environmental programmes. These should relate to 'fulfilment of specific conditions including production methods or inputs, and shall compensate only for increased costs of compliance' (OECD, 1995a).

Environmental policy in Italy is framed, of course, within EU policy and includes many initiatives of which, in the present context, those relating to the measures accompanying the MacSharry reform (agro-environmental measures and forestry measures) seem particularly relevant.

As regards forestry measures, implementation of Reg. 2080/92 has been slow and by the end of 1996, authorization had been given for afforestation of only 45 000 hectares of formerly arable land, as compared with a forecast of 132 000 hectares (INEA 1997b).

As regards agro-environmental measures (Reg. 2078/92), regional plans submitted potentially involve 11 per cent of the total agricultural area utilized and 3 per cent of the national stock of adult bovine equivalents. Again, interest has varied from Region to Region, involving a maximum of 63 per cent of area in Veneto, with more than 20 per cent in other northern Regions such as Lombardia, Bolzano, Valle d'Aosta, Piemonte, but less than 2 per cent in the southern regions of Calabria and Molise.[2]

The take-up, however, has initially been slow. Difficulties in aligning each of the 21 Regional zonal plans with the requirements of the EU Commission led to delays in implementation: only one plan had been approved by the end of 1993 and by the end of 1994 approval was still pending for 3 Regions. By the end of 1996, however, applications had been approved affecting more than 75 000 beneficiaries and an area equivalent to 6.9 per cent of the cultivated area (INEA 1997a) (Table 9.8).

Despite the fact that the use of chemicals in Italy is relatively limited as compared with that in other EU countries, the greater part (70 per cent) of the resources in the plans are destined to measures designed to reduce the negative impact of agriculture on the environment as opposed to those for rewarding farmers for positive externalities related to the care of natural space and protection of the territory. As part of these measures, an area of 16 000 ha is foreseen for initiation or continuation of organic farming, but this is a rather limited area as compared with the 63 000 ha already engaged in organic farming, and the further 29 000 ha under conversion. In addition to organic farming, the practice of low impact farming is becoming increasingly widespread and is believed to involve about 10–15 per cent by value of tree crop production, including at least 20 per cent of the peaches and pears produced in Emilia Romagna, a notable proportion of which are destined to the export market (INEA, 1995g and Sansavini, 1995).

Altogether, after a hesitant start, organic and low impact methods of farming are becoming more widespread, and although this may be partly in view of financial aid, it is certainly also due to an increasing public awareness of the potential benefits of the systems which is, moreover, reflected in the purchasing requirements of modern retailing and of the processing industry. The motivation

2   The multiple factors contributing to regional differences in the causes of negative environmental externalities from agriculture and the efficacy of measures to remedy them are amply analysed in Povellato (1996)

Table 9.8   Area and livestock units foreseen in zonal plans and those actually engaged in 1994 as compared with total utilized agricultural area and livestock units

	Plan area (ha)	% of U.A.A.	Area 1994 (ha)	Livestock units plan	% of tot. livestock units	Livestock units 1994
Piemonte	299 913	26.8	0	15 490	1.9	0
Valle d'Aosta	25 157	26.0	8746	1500	5.0	251
Lombardia	218 556	19.8	0	65 654	4.8	0
Prov. Bolzano	76 849	28.2	39 891	973	0.8	0
Prov. Trento	94 456	63.0	16 504	1141	2.4	1041
Veneto	103 600	11.8	9202	8050	1.1	854
Friuli	30 860	12.0	478	2700	2.3	0
Liguria	6495	7.0	185	1400	6.0	520
Emilia Romagna	162 080	13.2	3623	30 400	3.9	4678
Toscana	41 807	4.5	0	9384	4.2	0
Umbria	20 737	5.2	4907	1453	1.3	47
Marche	90 055	16.4	1936	0	0	0
Lazio	76 250	9.1	4170	12 000	3.0	0
Abruzzo	47 330	9.1	0	0	0	0
Molise	3713	1.5	1448	0	0	0
Campania	64 969	9.8	0	42 166	12.0	0
Puglia	53 355	3.7	0	10 909	5.3	0
Basilicata	49 128	7.9	0	5517	4.2	0
Calabria	7580	1.1	0	0	0	0
Sicilia	70 298	4.4	4213	10 000	2.0	0
Sardegna	62 638	4.6	2430	600	0.1	0
Italy	**1 605 826**	**10.7**	**97 733**	**219 337**	**3.1**	**7391**
North	1 017 966	19.6	78 629	127 308	3.2	7344
Centre	228 849	8.5	11 013	22 837	2.6	47
South incl. islands	359 011	5.0	8091	69 192	3.1	0

Source: INEA, 1995

seems to have little to do with a new form of protectionism, but rather with the need to maintain a high and reliable quality of product on both home and export markets.

9.7   Forebodings

A logical consequence of liberalization of international trade is the increase in the number of companies operating across national boundaries. From there, the second step may well be a diversification of the nationality of ownership of companies. On the other hand, the skills and financial resources needed for facing the risks of operating internationally may well prove beyond the means of small or medium-sized enterprises. Thus, as is happening particularly in the processing sector of the Italian agro-food sector, the environment becomes particularly favourable for large multinational corporations. Nestlé, Unilever, Philip Morris and Del Monte have all expanded their interests in Italy in recent times, and the list could continue. At times, they have taken over solid family firms; in other cases, they have seized the opportunities offered (usually second hand) by the privatization of state-owned industries (INEA, 1994a; INEA, 1995d; INEA, 1996a).

It is not intended here to resuscitate the embittered debate of the 1970s on the merits and demerits of multinationals. Instead, it seems opportune to pose some questions first, as to their role in favouring competition, the prime objective of the Uruguay Round negotiations, and secondly, as to the possible repercussions on the level of employment, the major problem at present facing the European Union as a whole.

The substantial human and financial resources at the disposition of multinational giants permits them to undertake promotional campaigns which would be beyond the means of smaller companies; the complexity of accounting practices may make it impossible to verify whether or not such campaigns are compatible with anti-trust or anti-dumping regulations. Meanwhile, their internal logic may dictate a notable mobility in the location of production towards areas of 'least cost', opening up the prospect that they may initially, by vigorous competition, replace small or medium industries in a specific location, but subsequently move on, leaving no permanent replacement in terms of the job opportunities previously offered by the small and medium-sized enterprises (SMEs) (Loseby, 1997).

9.8   Conclusions

Altogether, it appears that the direct effects of the Uruguay Round on the Italian agro-food sector may be less adverse than at first sight was feared.

As regards farm incomes, there had already been considerable adjustments to diversify sources of farm household incomes on non-commercially viable farms in the period before the Agreement; moreover, there will be opportunities for expanding activities on those farms which are commercially viable as, with the ageing farm population, the number of farmers declines for demographic reasons; at the same time, there may be some hopes for removing that element of the rigidity in land markets associated with farm income support.

As regards the effects on competitive conditions, these too may not be overwhelming, even if the decline in the degree of protection leads to competition from lower priced competitors, because much produce competes on quality rather than on strictly price considerations. Nevertheless, some sectors and some areas could be extremely vulnerable. As regards processed products, as has been pointed out (OECD, 1995a) the improved procedure for the settlement of disputes foreseen in the Agreement may be an advantage since these products have 'often in the past, been the subject of retaliatory actions in the context of disputes which originated in a primary product sector', an observation highly relevant to the case of Italian agro-food exports to the USA which have on several occasions been subject to embargo following disputes between the USA and the EU as a whole.

The direct effects on the environment may be expected to be slight, but positive. It is unlikely that environmental programmes will be used as a replacement for farm income support to any large extent, though marginal benefits may prove important in certain areas. On the whole, unfortunate past experience as regards the capacity to administer such programmes together with difficulties in public finance lead to this negative judgement.

Finally, it is likely that in Italy, as elsewhere, the reduction in public support to agriculture may have a beneficial effect in removing incentives for aid-seeking distortive activities.

Looking now at the indirect effects of the Agreement on the agro-food sector, one important consideration concerns its likely impact on the structure of the agro-food industry. Will the dismantling of public aid to agriculture and to the agro-food industry lead to a replacement of the bottleneck imposed on markets by public intervention by private forms of market concentration? (OECD, 1996). Will the internationalization of markets, intended by the Uruguay Round, favour large-scale industry at the expense of small and medium enterprises? If so, at what cost, if any, in terms of restriction of competition and of job availability? Although the encouragement of SMEs is considered a fundamental component of EU policy to combat unemployment, little is known about the comparative merits of this type of firm as regards stability in terms of employment, as regards innovative capacity, as regards capacity for affronting changing market demand. That which is known for the Italian agro-food sector is largely positive (Loseby, 1996, Nicholls and Sargeant, 1996).

In conclusion, therefore, difficulties are foreseen for the Italian agro-food sector in affronting the effects of the Uruguay Round, but these are not insurmountable. It appears very necessary, however, that changes in competitive conditions brought about by the Uruguay Round in the name of trade liberalization be accompanied by adequate measures to ensure a competent anti-trust policy.

Bibliography
Anania, G. and F. De Filippis (eds) (1996), *L'accordo GATT in agricoltura e l'Unione Europea*, Milan: Franco Angeli.
Barbero, G. (1982), 'Quante sono le aziende agricole italiane?', *Rivista di Economia Agraria*, No. 2.
Berni, P. and D. Begalli (1996), *I prodotti agroalimentari di qualità: organizzazione del sistema delle imprese*, Bologna: Il Mulino.
Colombo, G. (1995), *Italy and the European Agricultural Policy after the conclusion of the Uruguay Round*, Academy Series, New York: Italian Academy for Advanced Studies, Columbia University.
Colombo, G. and E. Bassanelli (1995), *Quale futuro per l'agricoltura italiana?* Bologna: Il Mulino.

Confederazione Nazionale Coltivatori Diretti (1994), 'GATT 1994: una sfida per gli anni duemila', Rome.

Corazza, G. (1993), 'Trattativa GATT e futuri assetti dell'agricoltura mondiale', *Rivista di Politica Agraria*, No. 2.

De Castro, P. and R. Deserti (1995), 'Imprese multinazionali, strategie di mercato e nuovi scenari del sistema agro-alimentare italiano', *Rivista di Politica Agraria*, No. 2.

Di Sandro, G. (1994), 'Quante sono le aziende agrarie: tremilioni o tre-quattro centomila?' *Rivista di Polica Agraria*, No. 6.

Finuola, R. (1995), La spesa pubblica in agricoltura, Roma: INEA.

INEA (1993), *Italian Agriculture*, an abridged version of the *Annuario dell'agricoltura italiana*, annual publication, Bologna: IL Mulino.

INEA (1994a), 'L'industria alimentare', in *Annuario dell'agricoltura italiana, 1993*, Bologna: Il Mulino.

INEA (1994b), 'Quantificazione della politica agraria', in *Annuario dell'agricoltura italiana, 1993*, Bologna: Il Mulino.

INEA (1995a), 'La produzione e il valore aggiunto dell'agricoltura', in *Annuario dell'agricoltura italiana, 1994*, Bologna: Il Mulino.

INEA (1995b), 'Il mercato dei prodotti agroalimentari', in *Annuario dell'agricoltura italiana, 1994*, Bologna: Il Mulino.

INEA (1995c), 'Dati statistici per regioni 1993–94', in *Annuario dell'agricoltura italiana, 1994*, Bologna: Il Mulino.

INEA (1995d), 'L'industria alimentare', in *Annuario dell'agricoltura italiana*, 1994, Bologna: Il Mulino.

INEA (1995e), 'La distribuzione dei prodotti agro-alimentari', in *Annuario dell'agricoltura italiana, 1994*, Bologna: Il Mulino.

INEA (1995f), 'La spesa pubblica in agricoltura', in *Annuario dell'agricoltura italiana, 1994*, Bologna: Il Mulino.

INEA (1995g), 'L'agricoltura e l'ambiente', in *Annuario dell'agricoltura italiana, 1994*, Bologna: Il Mulino.

INEA (1995h), *Italian Agriculture*, an abridged version of the Annuario dell'agricoltura italiana, annual publication, Bologna: Il Mulino.

INEA (1996a), 'L'industria alimentare', in *Annuario dell'agricoltura italiana, 1995*, Bologna: Il Mulino.

INEA (1996b), 'La distribuzione dei prodotti agro-alimentari', *in Annuario dell'agricoltura italiana, 1995*, Bologna: Il Mulino.

INEA (1996d), 'Il commercio con l'estero dei prodotti agroalimentari,' rapporto 1995, Rome.

INEA (1997a), 'L'agricoltura e l'ambiente', in *Annuario dell'agricoltura italiana, 1996*, Bologna: Il Mulino.

INEA (1997b), 'Le produzioni forestali' in *Annuario dell'agricoltura italiana, 1996*, Bologna: Il Mulino.

Loseby, M. (1996), 'Survival strategies for small and medium-sized enterprises in the Italian food industry' in K. Mattas, E. Papanagiotu and K. Galanopoulos (eds), *Agro-food small and medium enterprises in a large integrated economy*, Wissenschaftsverlag Vauk, Kiel KG.

Loseby, M. (1997), 'Quality certification for traditional products: a comparison between ISO and EU systems', *Proceedings of the 52nd Seminar of the European Association of Agricultural Economists*, Parma, June (forthcoming).

Mastrostefano, M. and M. Rinaldi (1995), 'La SME come gruppo alimentare pubblico: un brillante futuro dietro le spalle', *Rivista di Politica Agraria*, No. 4.

Ministero dell'industria, del commercio e dell'artigianato (1996), Caratteri strutturali del sistema distributivo in Italia al 1 gennaio 1996, Rome.

Nicholls, J. and M. Sargeant (1996), *Marketing in Europe*, Aldershot, UK: Avebury.

OECD (1995a), *The Uruguay Round, a preliminary evaluation of the impacts of the Agreement on Agriculture in the OECD countries*, Paris: OECD.

OECD (1995b), *Impact of the Uruguay Round Agreement on trade and markets for fresh fruit and vegetables*, AGR/CA/APM/FV(95)1.

OECD (1996), *Competition Policy and the Agro-food Sector*, OCDE/GD (96) 81, Paris.

Povellato, A. (1996), 'Italy' in M. Whitby (ed.), *The European environment and CAP reform: policies and prospects for conservation*, Wallingford, UK: CAB International.

Sansavini,S. (1995) 'Dalla produzione integrata alla "qualità totale" della frutta' in *Rivista di Frutticoltura*, No. 3.

Sembenelli, A. and G. Vitali (1996), 'Acquisitions, agreements and innovation in the Italian food industry', in G. Galizzi and L. Venturini, *Economics of innovation: the case of food industry*, Heidelberg: Physica-Verlag.

Venzi, L. (1988), 'The evolution of the agrarian structure in Italy', in *The Dynamics of Agrarian Structures in Europe*, Rome: FAO.

10 The Common Agricultural Policy and the environment: conceptual framework and empirical evidence in the Spanish agriculture[1]

Consuelo Varela-Ortega

10.1 Introduction

10.1.1 General overlook of the CAP and the environment

The agricultural sector in the EU has been confronted recently with the need to reduce surplus production, lower the level of protection within the context of the international agreements and preserve the natural environment. As a consequence new patterns of soil use, choice of technologies, input utilization and crops have been emerging in the different regions of the EU as a response to the new policy programmes. Several questions arise around this issue: what is and will be the response of the farmers to the policy programmes in the diverse EU regions; what type of technological changes will be introduced; what kind of crops will the farmers grow and at what level of intensity in the use of factors of production; which of these factors will be complemented or substituted; and what will be the level of risk that the farmers will be able to bear. Ultimately what will be the consequences of all these decisions on the farmers' income and on the environment. In order to ensure harmony between agricultural production and the protection of the environment the following issues may be underlined. These are namely, the choice of adequate policy programmes, the social biases in the definition and delivery of public goods and services, the institutional framework of property rights and the role of governments in promoting regional and rural development interventions. As a recent preoccupation in the EU, the issue of managing harmony between agricultural and environmental policies is high on the political agendas. The challenge will be to explore, through comparative regional analysis, alternative ways of promoting this harmony.

Along these lines, the reform of the Common Agricultural Policy (CAP) has been an attempt to integrate environmental issues within the main body of

---

1 Part of this chapter is based on the research project: *Analysis of the socio-economic impacts of agricultural reform in certain European regions: competitiveness and environmental protection*, EU Commission – DGVI (contract No. 8001-CT91-0306-4706A), Brussels. (Flichman *et al.*, 1995a, 1995b, Varela-Ortega *et al.*, 1995)

agricultural programmes. The reform advocates a more 'environmentally sustainable form of agricultural production and food quality' and foresees 'a dual role to the farmers as food producers and as stewards of the environment and the countryside' (CEC, 1992). The accompanying measures of the CAP reform related to environmental programmes encourage farmers to adopt or maintain farming practices compatible with the protection of the environment and the maintenance of natural landscapes. However, the effects of the CAP on the environment are various and may differ widely across the EU regions as a consequence of varied ecological factors, farm structures and farmers' behaviour, as well as the institutional framework of property rights structure (Brouwer and van Berkum, 1966; Whitby, 1995; Sumpsi and Varela-Ortega, 1995; Rayment, 1995). Moreover, the environmental effects of these policies are the result of the interrelation of EU policies and the national and regional policy programmes in an increasingly decentralized approach, in which most agri-environmental programmes and measures are to be implemented at a regional level (Buckwell, 1996; CEC, 1995).

10.1.2 The CAP and the environment in Spain

The rapid process of agricultural modernization that took place in the Spanish agricultural sector during the last decades resulted in an increasing intensification of the better farming areas and in a steadily growing abandonment of the less productive marginal zones (Sumpsi and Varela-Ortega, 1995; Baldock *et al.* 1996). This development trend, characterized by an intensification–abandonment dual process, was further aggravated by Spain's entry into the EC as a response to higher income expectations derived from the application of the EC agricultural programmes (Sumpsi and Varela-Ortega 1995; Valladares 1993; Baldock and Beaufoy, 1993; Edgell, 1993). However, the early application of the CAP reform programmes contributed to induce a certain degree of farm extensification following consecutive years of long-term drought. But this trend reverted with the income increase that resulted from higher surface-based payments in the subsequent years of the implementation of the new policy. In fact, irrigation conversions continued to expand and the dual characteristic of Spanish agriculture is still apparent.

These dichotomized farming systems are distributed unevenly across the Spanish territory: dryland areas of low agricultural productivity and high risk of abandonment cover 12 million ha as opposed to the intensive agriculture areas of high polluting potential (namely nitrate pollution) which extend over 3.5 million ha of irrigated surface (1.2 million ha of which are located along the Mediterranean coastline) (Sumpsi *et al.*, 1996). However, among the farming intensification processes irrigation conversions account for the highest levels of adverse effects on the environment (Pérez Ibarra, 1994). More than half of Spain's farming land corresponds to arid or semi-arid regions and therefore agricultural productivity has relied largely on extensive irrigation conversions.

As a result of this trend, irrigated agriculture consumes up to 80 per cent of all water resources in Spain but constitutes a key sub-sector of Spanish agriculture representing a mere 15 per cent of all agricultural land but 60 per cent of the total agricultural production and 80 per cent of all farm exports.[2] However, irrigation policies which have historically stimulated the expansion of water resources, have been strongly debated in recent years, following environmental, economic and budget controversies. Supply and delivery of water resources lagging well behind the demand for water, aggravated in turn by a long-term trend of severe drought periods, result in growing water scarcity problems that determine to a large extent cropping patterns and technologies in agricultural production and therefore interact with the application of agricultural policy programmes.

10.1.3 Policy programmes, the environment and water resources: The objective of this chapter

In this context, it is the aim of this chapter to analyse the interrelated economic and environmental effect of the application of different agricultural policy programmes and the role that a key natural resource, such as water, plays in this relationship in irrigated agriculture. In particular this chapter will investigate the reaction of farmers to different policy scenarios, what changes they will make in their cropping patterns and technological packages and the environmental impacts will be of the production packages chosen by the farmers. Finally we will inquire to what extent availability of water resources will determine the implementation of the policy programmes (such as the CAP reform) and the environmental impacts resulting from their application. We will try to answer all these questions with the aim of bringing some insights into policy analysis and of providing a reference for seeking harmony between agricultural and environmental policies at regional level. This chapter builds partly on prior work by the author (Varela-Ortega *et al.* 1995; Flichman *et al.*, 1995 a,b) in a revised and updated analytical perspective.

10.2   Agricultural policy and environmental quality: A regional case study in Spain

10.2.1 The relevance of regional analysis. The zone of study

The importance of a disaggregated analysis to the evaluation of the environmental impacts of the CAP reform is often emphasized. The relationship between agricultural policies and environmental policies are highly spatial-specific (Just and Antle, 1990; Brouwer and van Berkum, 1996; Sumpsi and Varela-Ortega

---

2   Calculations based on: Ministerio de Agricultura, Pesca y Alimentación (1996): *Anuario de Estadística Agraria*. MAPA, Madrid, and Ministerio de Agricultura, Pesca y Alimentación (1996): *Plan Nacional de Regadíos*. MAPA, Madrid.

1995; Flichman *et al.*, 1995a among others) and this regional specificity will probably be enhanced within the new trend of future reforms (Buckwell, 1996; CEC, 1995). We are therefore interested in the regional impacts of policy programmes, and to undertake this analysis we are going to use as a case study the irrigated agriculture of a fertile zone in Andalucia, Southern Spain, covering part of the provinces of Seville and Cordoba in the valley of the Guadalquivir (Varela-Ortega *et al.*, 1995). This zone is characterized by large-scale, highly capitalized entrepreneurial and commercial agriculture, remarkable productivity potential, crop variety and large farms. In fact the agroclimatic conditions of this area provide a considerable comparative advantage in the production of an ample variety of traditional crops (such as wheat, sunflower, maize, cotton and sugar beet) as well as fruits and vegetables. However, the amply irrigated agriculture of these zones relies heavily on the access to water resources (dependent in turn on rainfall fluctuations) and determines largely the selection of crops and technological packages. This situation, together with the new CAP and the environmental policy programmes that are presently being implemented, is in turn determining the adoption of new technologies in production and the patterns of land use which will have major economic and environmental consequences.

The zone of study includes a basically homogenous farming area which extends over almost half million ha where 92 per cent of the total land is farming land as compared to 64 per cent in the region of Andalucia and 61 per cent at national level. Land structure in the zone of study is considerably more homogenous than in the overall region of Andalucia and bigger farms represent a larger share than the regional or national average. Crop distribution in the zone of study features one of the characteristic irrigated agriculture cropping patterns of the region. Main products are wheat, corn, sunflower and cotton which account for more than 60 per cent of all arable land and are under the regulation of the CAP programmes, thus being the focus of our analysis. Close to 60 per cent of the farming land is irrigated in our zone of study which includes more than 80 per cent of the total number of farms, so that irrigated agriculture is the most prominent feature. With respect to labour characteristics, family labour is scarce in the area of study and off-farm employment is high among land owners. Most of the farm labour is thus hired-in and permanent (technical and/or management) and seasonal workers perform distinct labour activities on the farm. This latter type of labour contracting has been a distinctive feature of Andalusian agriculture and the zone of study follows a similar pattern even more predominantly in the widely irrigated large farms.

The representative farms   To represent the zone of study two statistically based types of Representative Farms (RF) have been selected. Some of the technical parameters have been obtained from a survey conducted in the zone of study (for example machinery and labour requirements, Varela-Ortega, 1994). The land distribution by farm size in the zone of study tells us that two important size groups emerge from the current distribution of land: the group defined by farms between 20 to 100 ha and the one with farms over 100 ha, representing 25 per cent and 53 per cent of the whole area in the zone of study. The production system defined by the RFs reproduces the actual farm distribution in the zone of study determined by physical parameters (surface, soil and rainfall distribution), farm management parameters (crop types, techniques, rotation possibilities, water demand and machinery requirements), production costs, labour parameters (type of contracting, management and supervision requirements and seasonal constraints) and financial parameters. A detailed description of the RFs is shown in Table 10.1 (Varela-Ortega *et al.*, 1995).

10.2.2 The methodological framework

The methodology used is based on the joint analysis of the agronomic and the economic characteristics of the agricultural production systems of the region studied. For that purpose we have integrated an Agronomic Model (AM) with a Mathematical Programming Model (MPM) (Flichman *et al.*, 1995b) that allows us to predict with reasonable accuracy the possible impacts on the farmers' economy and on the environment of different policy programmes. Farmers respond to policy changes by choosing different technological production packages and it is therefore necessary to obtain a detailed description of all possible techniques (i.e. a complete set of production possibilities). In general, empirical information on production technologies is based on data from field experiment station and is limited to actual combinations of production factors. Potentially feasible combinations when relative prices change are therefore not available. An attempt to fill this information gap is to use an agronomic model which provides the engineering production functions that simulate production outcomes of any type of technical combination. The agronomic model (AM) we use is the plant growth simulation model EPIC[3] which generates reliable information on crop yields for any given combination of factors (for example, fertilizers, irrigation water, tillage equipment, crop varieties, rotations, weather and soil conditions). The information generated by the AM is then integrated into the MPM providing part of the technical coefficients such as crop yields and water use as well as pollution indicators (nitrate loss including leaching, sub-surface flow and run-off). Therefore this modelling enables the economic and environmental effects of different policy programmes to be analysed, measuring the policy-induced response in terms of farm income and cropping patterns and associating the techniques selected in the optimization process with crop yields and potential pollution levels.

---

3 EPIC: Erosion Productivity Impact Calculator. USDA Agricultural Research Service and Texas A&M University. Williams *et al.* (1984)

Table 10.1 Description of the representative farms

	Rep. Farm 1	Rep. Farm 2	Observations
Physical parameters			
Surface (ha)	60	200	
Irrigated %	100	100	
% Good soil	60	40	
% Medium soil	40	60	
Rainfall (mm/year)	548	512	
Farm management parameters			
No. of crops	4	4	
Possible techniques	3	3	
Most water demanding crop	Corn: 7760 m^3/ha		
Least water demanding crop	Durum wheat: 0		Extensive techn.
Machinery constraints	No		
Own harvesters	No		
Highest net margin	Cotton		
Lowest net margin	Sunflower		Without subsidies
Rotation constraints	No sunflower after sunf.		
Limit to d.wheat (ha)	20	60	
Costs of production (pta./ha)			
1 hour of tractor use	2000		For MB plough
Harvester rental	5000–9000		For wht.,sflw,corn
Cotton harvesting	18 000		In pta./ton
Per ha fixed costs	20 000		
Labour management			
No. of perm. workers	1	3	
Supervision parameter	0.1		See model
Permanent lab. costs	pta. 2 million/year. worker		
Lowest monthly limit of perm. lab hours	104 hours in March and May		
Highest monthly limit of perm. lab hours	160 hours in July		
Per hour season wage	1000 pta/hour		
Financial parameters			
Short-term int. rate (paid)	0.11		
Short-term int.rate (received)	0.05		
Overdraft int. rate	0.3		
Long-term int. rate (paid)	0.1		
Long-term int.rate (received)	0.08		
Minimum income	150 000		Pta/month
Max. short-term debt	1.5	6	In pta million
Initial long-term debt	6	20	In pta million
Initial saves	3	8	In pta million

Exchange rate: 125 pta/US$ (1996)

The model   The MPM is a recursive farm model of constrained optimization in which the farmer maximizes his net farm revenue. Optimization is annual and the results of each year affect the following year in the five year simulation period, such as yields associated to certain crop rotations, investment and financial flows. Risk is treated in the model considering different 'states of nature' (Freund, 1956); (Tauer, 1983), defined by climatic conditions, prices and subsidy expectations (Flichman *et al.* 1995a). The climatic conditions are built using a long series climatic database (25 years) and its effects on crop yields. Price and subsidy expectations are built according to the farmers' response on price and subsidy variations from a survey conducted in the zone of study (Sumpsi and Varela-Ortega 1994).

The *objective function* is:

$$\text{MAX } U(X_t, Y_t) = E[\text{NETINCOME}(X_t, Y_t)] - \varphi \cdot \lambda(X_t, Y_t) \quad (10.1)$$

Where U(.) is the utility level, X_t is the set of production activities in period t, (defined by a combination of crop type, soil quality, production technique, previous crop grown and policy regulation). Y_t is the set of financial variables, (monthly cash-flow, interests, investment level); E[.] is the expected value operator; φ is the risk-aversion coefficient; $\lambda(X_t, Y_t)$ is the sum of negative deviations, shown in equation (10.4), from the net income denoted by $E[\text{NETINCOME}(X_t, Y_t)]$ as expressed in equation (10.2) below and P_t is the price vector in period t.

$$\text{NETINCOME}(X_t, Y_t) = \text{REVENUE}(X_t; P_t) + \text{SUBSIDY}(X_t) \quad (10.2)$$
$$- \text{VARCOST}(X_t) - \text{FINANCOST}(Y_t, Y_{t-1}) - \text{FIXEDCOSTS}$$

where $\text{REVENUE}(X_t; P_t)$ are the crop revenues that result from combining yields obtained in the AM (EPIC results) with crop surface and crop prices, $\text{SUBSIDY}(X_t)$ is the sum of all subsidies under the CAP-reform programmes, $\text{VARCOST}(X_t)$ represents the sum of all variable costs and $\text{FINANCOST}(Y_t, Y_{t-1})$ the net financial costs dependent on financial decisions in years t and $t-1$.

The *constraints* are (omitting some other technical, financial and policy constraints):

(i) Risk constraints   Represent the negative deviations of real net income from its expected value for a given combination of uncertain outcomes, such as subsidies, yields and prices, denoted respectively by parameters *e,q,n* , as expressed in equation (10.3).

$$\text{NETINCOME}(X_t, Y_t; e, q, n) + \text{DEV}(e, q, n) \geq E[\text{NETINCOME}(X_t, Y_t)] \quad (10.3)$$

The sum of all possible negative deviations of actual income from expected income are expressed in equation (10.4) (for 30 potential combinations of unsure outcomes of subsidies, yields and prices) and appear in the objective function to define the farmers risk tolerance level.

$$\Sigma_e \, \Sigma_t \, \Sigma_n \, \text{DEV}(e, q, n) \leq \lambda(X_t, Y_t)*30 \quad (10.4)$$

(ii) Crop rotation constraints   Express the recursivity of the model and represent crop rotation limitations and effects, so that all land available is under the set-aside requirements of the CAP reform and all land allocated to a given crop farmed after another crop cannot exceed the total land allocated to the latter in the previous year, such that Σ (ALL CROPS$_t$, after wheat) $\leq \Sigma$ (wheat$_{t-1}$).

$$\Sigma \, X_t \leq \Sigma \, X_{t-1} - \text{SETASIDE}(X_t) \quad (10.5)$$

(iii) Labour constraints   Account for the difference between the two types of labour contracting, a predominant feature of the zone of study. Equation (10.6) expresses the amount of labour services used for specific farming activities where seasonal labour is the usual form of contracting (for example, irrigation, harvesting, weeding). Permanent labour in the farm, expressed in equation (10.7), is allocated to such activities as seeding and ploughing and also to the supervision of hired seasonal workers. Based on an ample survey conducted in the zone of study, the coefficient α indicates the allocation of permanent labour to the supervision of seasonal labour. Supervision of seasonal labour is a major task in the commercial agricultural farms of southern Spain and largely determines management decisions and crop choice (Varela-Ortega, 1994). It can be considered as a transaction cost derived from the need to ensure labour productivity (de Janvry *et al.*, 1989, Eswaran and Kotwal 1986) and from the presence of asymmetric information and shirking behaviour that characterize the labour market conditions (Binswanger and Rosenszweig 1986).

$$\Sigma(X_t*\text{SEASLAB}(X_t)) \leq \text{SEASON}(t) \quad (10.6)$$

$$\Sigma(X_t*\text{LABOR}(X_t)) + \alpha*\text{SEASON}(t) \leq \text{FARMLAB} \quad (10.7)$$

(iv) Water availability constraints   Expresses water availability to the farmers as a vector of six components which represent the amount of water resources available for each of the simulated years (WAT(t)). It takes different values to simulate the farmers' response to different water scenarios. The amount of water

needed for a given crop is expressed by WATER(X_t). In fact, more than half of the irrigated farms in the area suffer recurrent water shortages, and water potential demand frequently exceeds the volume of water actually delivered to the farms.

$$\Sigma(X_t * \text{WATER}(X_t)) \leq \text{WAT}(t) * \text{SURFACE} \qquad (10.8)$$

Environmental impacts are measured by the pollution indicators obtained in the Agronomic Model defined by total nitrate loss in the farm. EPIC calculates total nitrate loss in each cropping activity (defined as the combined outcome of a given crop type, soil quality, production technique, rotation effect and policy requirements) associated with the model's optimal solutions. The pollution parameters are presented as associated parameters to the production activities and therefore the potential pollution impacts derived from each MPM result can be evaluated.

10.3 Results and discussion

Simulation results are shown in Tables 10.2, 10.3 and 10.4 for the six simulated years (1990/91 to 1995/96) summarizing the most important results of the model: farm income, crop and production technique selection, water consumption and nitrate pollution. Simulated scenarios include different policy programmes, farm structure, water availability and risk tolerance. Not all possible combinations are included in the tables but these are complemented with Figures 10.1–10.7. Two policy scenarios have been simulated, one represented by a price-based structure (pre-CAP reform) and another featuring a price–subsidy structure (CAP reform). Therefore, the last three simulation years show the difference between the results of the former policy (continuing price trends) and the CAP reform (prices and subsidies) (scenarios 4 and 2 respectively). Two risk aversion coefficients have been considered to simulate risk neutral farmers and risk averse farmers in each of the policy scenarios.

Two scenarios for water availability have been simulated to analyse how the quantity of water affects the farmers' decisions in the two policy contexts. In particular, which are the crops that farmers will grow, what techniques will they use, what levels of farm income will be attained and what will be the induced environmental impact. The irrigation water shortages that occurred in 1992/93 were simulated and the model replicates with reasonable accuracy crop patterns actually present in the area during that particular year, confirming land-use trends in the region.

As different years in the simulation horizon represent various water availability levels, Tables 10.2 and 10.3 include the two different water resource situations for the same year 1995/96 to allow for policy comparison under water abundance and under drought conditions. Two types of farm have also been considered to

Table 10.2 Simulated results for farm 1 (PHI = 0, water scenario = 1, policy scenario = 2)

Season		90/91	91/92	92/93	93/94	94/95	95/96	95/96* (W2)
Surface (ha)		60	60	60	60	60	60	60
Allocated surface (%)	D. wheat	22.5	27.6	33.3	18.3	22.1		33.3
	Corn	62.3	49.1		10.1	43.5	65.6	28.5
	Cotton	15.2	23.3	15.6	18.7	22.8	22.8	22.5
	Sunflower			38.4	40.7			4.0
	Fallow			12.7	12.2	11.6	11.6	11.6
Techniques (%)	T1 (int.)	100.0	100.0	34.3	81.7	100.0	100.0	34.2
	T2 (ext.)			65.7	18.3			65.8
Nitrate loss (kg/ha.year)		129.0	113.3	52.8	77.3	111.6	136.7	77.5
Income ('000 pts)		5592.4	6317.7	6497.6	7790.6	8005.5	8315.2	7649.2
Income (index: 1991=100)		100.0	113.0	116.2	139.3	143.2	148.7	136.8
Production ('000 pta)		18 583.1	18 942.5	9423.5	11 108.6	14 630.7	16 010.1	1261.0
Subsidy payments ('000 pta)				6263.2	6998.8	4583.9	4323.1	4797.8
Water use (m³/ha)		6502	6000	2340	3870	5400	6781	3870
Water availability (m³/ha)		6850	6000	2340	3870	5400	6930	3870
Water dual value (pta/m³)			7.9	13.7	6.7	1		15.1
Dual value for land	Soil 1	134.7	93.9	135.4	152.0	156.9	162.9	89.7
('000 pta/ha)	Soil 2	170.5	124.1	135.4	166.8	189.4	196.2	90.3
	Average	149.0	105.9	135.4	157.9	169.9	176.2	90.0

Notes
* Simulated results for year 1995/96 in Water Scenario 2 (W2) (water shortage)
F1 – small farm
PHI 0 – risk neutral farmers
PHI 1 – risk averse farmers
W1 – humid year
W2 – dry year
P2 – policy scenario with CAP reform
P4 – policy scenario without CAP reform

Table 10.3 Simulated results for farm 1 (PHI = 0, water scenario = 1, policy scenario = 4)

Season		90/91	91/92	92/93	93/94	94/95	95/96	95/96* (W2)
Surface (ha)		60	60	60	60	60	60	60
Allocated surface (%)	D. wheat	22.5	27.6	76.8	58.7	37.2	12.2	54.7
	Corn	62.3	49.1		18.1	39.5	64.4	22.1
	Cotton	15.2	23.3	23.2	23.3	23.3	23.4	23.3
	Sunflower							
	Fallow							
Techniques (%)	T1 (int.)	100.0	100.0	46.5	82.7	100.0	97.2	60.0
	T2 (ext.)			53.5	17.3		2.8	40.0
Nitrate loss (kg/ha.year)		129.0	113.3	56.8	112.0	126.8	141.8	83.5
Income ('000 pta)		5592.4	6317.7	3431.0	4384.5	5410.2	6155.7	4547.1
Income (index: 1991 = 100)		100.0	113.0	61.4	78.4	96.7	110.1	81.3
Production ('000 pta)		18 583.1	18 942.5	13 098.3	15 219.6	17 276.0	18 975.2	15 004.1
Subsidy payments ('000 pta)								
Water use (m³/ha)		6502	6000	2340	3870	5400	6930	3870
Water availability (m³/ha)		6850	6000	2340	3870	5400	6930	3870
Water dual value (pta/m³)			7.9	21.6	7.5	6.5	5.8	12.7
Dual value for land ('000 pta/ha)	Soil 1	132.5	91.8	66.0	45.6	81.5	78.3	64.8
	Soil 2	170.5	124.1	54.1	47.9	113.2	114.8	64.6
	Average	147.7	104.7	61.2	46.5	94.2	92.9	64.7

Notes
* Simulated results for year 1995/96 in Water Scenario 2 (W2) (water shortage)
F1 – small farm   PHI 0 – risk neutral farmers
PHI 1 – risk averse farmers   W1 – humid year
                              P2 – policy scenario with CAP reform
W2 – dry year
P4 – policy scenario without CAP reform

Table 10.4 Simulated results for farm 1 (PHI = 1, water scenario = 1, policy scenario = 2)

	Season	90/91	91/92	92/93	93/94	94/95	95/96
Surface (ha)		60	60	60	60	60	60
Allocated surface (%)	D. wheat	19.2	18.2	33.3	31.4	19.0	9.3
	Corn	57.1	44.3		18.2	47.8	57.3
	Cotton		21.8	17.4	21.0	21.5	21.7
	Sunflower	23.7	15.7	36.9	17.6		
	Fallow			12.4	11.9	11.8	11.8
Techniques (%)	T1 (int.)	100.0	100.0	29.8	75.3	81.0	90.8
	T2 (ext.)			70.2	24.8	19.0	9.3
Nitrate loss (kg/ha.year)		120.1	94.0	41.4	81.8	115.8	116.6
Income ('000 pts)		5221.9	5983.5	6581.6	7469.4	7534.9	7830.9
Income (index: 1991=100)		100.0	114.6	126.0	143.0	144.3	150.0
Production ('000 pta)		16 310.1	18 660.0	9794.8	12 541.3	14 362.3	15 187.2
Subsidy payments ('000 pta)				6092.1	5405.1	4619.1	4495.6
Water use (m³/ha)		6113	6000	2340	3870	5400	6113
Water availability (m³/ha)		6850	6000	2340	3870	5400	6930
Water dual value (pta/m³)			4	12.3	6.6	1.7	
Dual value for land	Soil 1	114.6	91.9	98.3	119.3	127.7	134.5
('000 pta/ha)	Soil 2	150.6	124.2	98.4	126.1	151.1	163.4
	Average	129.0	104.8	98.3	122.0	137.0	146.1

Notes
* Simulated results for year 1995/96 in Water Scenario 2 (W2) (water shortage)
F1 – small farm   PHI 0 – risk neutral farmers
PHI 1 – risk averse farmers   W1 – humid year
W2 – dry year   P2 – policy scenario with CAP reform
P4 – policy scenario without CAP reform

196

account for structural effects of the policy programmes. Pollution indicators are also shown in Tables 10.2–10.4 as total nitrate loss for all the possible combinations of the selected simulation scenarios. Figures 1–7 summarize the results and show some of the combined effects of the simulated scenarios.

10.3.1 Trade-off between farm income and environmental quality? The role of water for irrigation

In Figures 10.1 and 10.2 we can observe the evolution of income in the two policy scenarios (CAP reform denoted by P2 and no CAP reform denoted by P4), for the two types of farms (F1 for the small farm and F2 for the large) in two different situations of irrigation water availability (W1 for water abundance and W2 for water shortage) and for the same level of risk tolerance (risk averse farmers).

Income comparisons of the two policy scenarios show certain instability during the first years of the CAP reform implementation, due to an excessive farming of oilseeds as a response to the special transitory subsidy regime applied in Spain. Income stabilizes after this and shows a clear increase under the CAP reform with respect to the pre-CAP reform scenario for the two types of farm, and shows a certain degree of structural differentiation, larger farms being better off than smaller ones. Income would be expected to decrease if the pre-CAP reform programmes were continued, due to a gradual decrease in prices and no

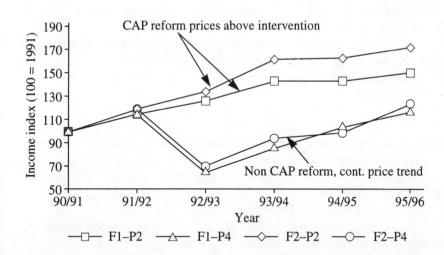

W1 (water scenario, humid year), W2 (water scenario, dry year, F1 (small farm), F2 (large farm), P2 (policy scenario with CAP reform), P4 (policy scenario without CAP reform), PH1 (risk averse farmers)

Figure 10.1   Income trend: W1, 2 farms, scenarios P2 and P4, PHI = 1

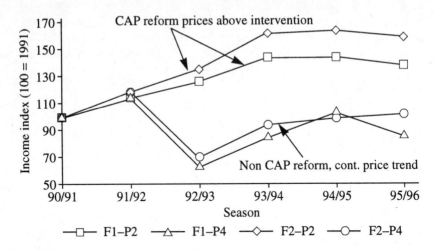

W1 (water scenario, humid year), W2 (water scenario, dry year), F1 (small farm), F2 (large farm), P2 (policy scenario with CAP reform), P4 (policy scenario without CAP reform), PH1 (risk averse farmers)

Figure 10.2   Income trend: W2, 2 farms, scenarios P2 and P4, PHI = 1

implementation of direct income compensation payments except for the oilseed subsidy programmes.

Availability of water resources makes a large impact on farm income levels. In fact, when a drought is simulated (as happened in reality in 1992/93) income declines sharply, especially in the no-CAP reform scenario, the price-subsidy structure of the CAP reform acting as a shelter for the production decrease in the dry year. In a water shortage scenario (Figure 10.2) income declines in both policy options, reversing the upward income trend. Although larger farms have clear advantages under both policy scenarios this is reinforced when water shortages are present as small farms have less capacity for profitable extensification practices (i.e. for moving towards less intensive techniques and crops consuming less water). Differences in water availability emphasize the economies of scale of technical extensification.

Figures 10.3 and 10.4 depict the combination of two production techniques, intensive (Technique 1) and extensive (Technique 2). In general nitrate pollution will be lower under the CAP reform but the extent of this reduction depends on the quantity of water resources available to the farmer. More intensive techniques will still tend to appear when water is abundant (especially in the case of risk neutral farmers) but extensification increases more sharply – therby reducing the nitrate loss – when water shortages are present.

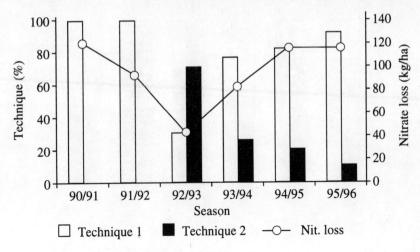

Note: Technique 1: intensive technique, Technique 2: extensive technique

Figure 10.3   Techniques and nitrate pollution: humid year, CAP reform scenario

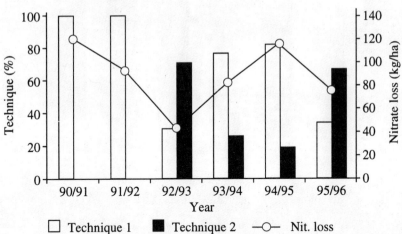

Note: Technique 1: intensive technique, Technique 2: extensive technique

Figure 10.4   Techniques and nitrate pollution: dry year, CAP reform scenario

Overall we can expect farmers to choose more diversified cropping patterns and to use less intensive techniques when the CAP reform is being implemented (Figures 10.5 and 10.6) but to respond closely to subsidy fluctuations. In fact the choice of techniques will be in general a result of crop choice so that we will see farmers moving from more intensive water consuming crops (corn and cotton)

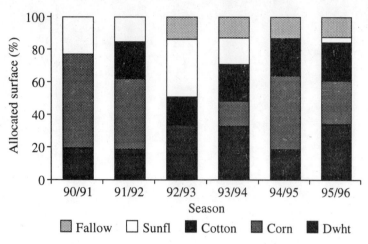

Figure 10.5   Cropping pattern: CAP reform scenario

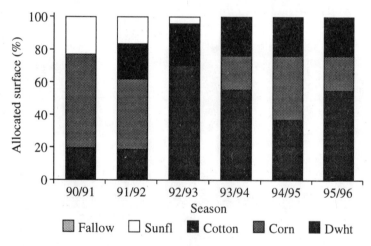

Figure 10.6   Cropping pattern: non-CAP reform scenario

to less intensive, low water demanding crops (wheat and sunflower) when water shortages are expected under the same policy scenario (Figures 10.5 and 10.7). However, the structure of prices and subsidies introduced in the CAP reform keeps the farmers from suffering a sharp decline in income. When a dry year is simulated (for 1995/96), we can observe that in the CAP reform scenario farmers lose a mere 8 per cent of their income because the productivity decline is compensated for by an increase of almost 10 per cent in subsidy payments. On the other hand, when CAP reform programmes are not applied, farmers lose

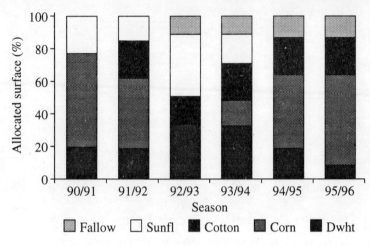

Figure 10.7   Cropping pattern: CAP reform scenario, humid year

more than 26 per cent of their income in drought periods as the decline in farm production is not compensated for with direct payments. Farmers respond to water shortages by changing their cropping pattern, and crop variations are more drastic in the CAP reform as the price-subsidy structure allows for a more flexible crop choice. Under the CAP reform, when water is not abundant, farmers choose to grow a higher proportion of crops that demand less water (more than one third of the total surface is allocated to wheat that was virtually non-existent in the humid year, and corn is sharply reduced from 66 per cent to 28 per cent). This situation of income maintenance under the CAP reform shelter has been confirmed by 1997's economic results in the region where, in spite of four consecutive years of severe drought and the subsequent output reduction, agricultural income rose in the area according to official figures of the Spanish Ministry of Agriculture.[4]

The comparison of two different levels of risk tolerance is depicted in Figure 10.8. We can observe that risk averse farmers attain higher income levels in both policy scenarios than the risk neutral farmers. However, the CAP reform reduces clearly the effects of the different risk attitudes, so that income levels attained by risk neutral farmers are practically the same as the income level obtained by the more cautious farmers. These equalized differences are in accordance with the fact that the CAP reform is viewed by farmers as a protective environment in which management decisions play a less important role in farm income results. Moreover, risk averse farmers will tend to use more

4   Ministerio de Agricultura, Pesca y Alimentación (1997): *Anuario de Estadística Agraria*, MAPA, Madrid.

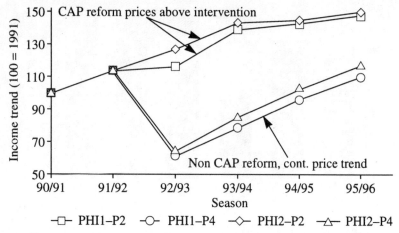

Figure 10.8   Income trend: Farm 1, W1 (risk aversion comparisons)

extensive techniques than risk neutral farmers and in turn these will produce higher levels of pollution than their risk averse counterparts.

10.4   Conclusions

In general we can conclude that the new policy programmes of the CAP reform will tend to shift agricultural production to less intensive systems. This will in turn cut down nitrate emissions and reduce environmental impact. This situation will be clearly dependent also on the quantity of water resources for irrigation but in general water will be allocated to crops consuming less water in the CAP reform scenario for all levels of risk tolerance. However, this response may appear rather ambiguous when water is not a limiting factor and more risk tolerant farmers will choose to intensify their productive systems even in the new policy programmes. Crops grown will tend to be less risky and the crop pattern will show a preference for subsidized crops as a response to the increasing relative importance of the subsidy with respect to the product price. This trend follows slightly different responses depending on the different attitudes of farmers towards cropping decisions. Riskier crops (i.e. high yield variation following climatic variability, water hazards and high supply-response price fluctuations) are substantially reduced among risk averse farmers (for example, cautious farmers cultivate 70 per cent less cotton than the more risk tolerant farmers), following the standard pattern found in the literature (Feder, 1980, Roumasset, 1976).

One of the most significant differences that we can observe between the two simulated scenarios are related to farm income. The advantage of the reform scenario is clear for all farm types and risk levels, but it becomes more apparent when water shortages occur. Farmers benefit from the structure of prices and subsidies introduced by the CAP reform by being able to sustain their income levels, counterbalancing the sharp output decline that occurs in drought periods. During the first years of the CAP reform implementation, the reduction of prices counter-weighted by the compensation payments, produced a reaction among farmers who were inclined to consider the new policy as a more protective environment. Subsidies were considered as a sure event and yield variations had less effect on farm income than in the previous policy context. As a consequence, managerial decisions played a less determinant role in the farmer's production outcomes and income levels thus cancelling out the differences between traditional cautious farmers and risk tolerant farmers. Lower risk premiums are perceived in the new policy context and the cost of buying security, measured as the expected income loss, is lower in the CAP reform scenario than in the previous policy. Buying security for a farmer is 50 per cent less expensive in the new CAP reform scenario than before as he would have to sacrifice around 5 per cent of his income instead of 10 per cent under the old policy. However, a subsidy guided agriculture is foreseen in this region under the new policy scenario but with a key role to be played by the water resources irrigation.

10.4.1 Farmers' response to water saving policies. A key element in the interaction of agricultural policy and the environment

In fact we can conclude from our results that in this zone the access to water resources largely determines agricultural production – cropping patterns and techniques – and therefore the response of the farmers to the new policy programmes. This in turn affects the impact on the environment. Before the CAP reform programmes were established this zone featured a more 'production oriented' agriculture. Risk averse farmers would cultivate less risky and lower water demanding crops so that they would value their water resources less (willing to pay a lower 'price' – shadow price – for extra water volumes) than the risk neutral farmers who will grow more water demanding and more productive crops. However, when the CAP reform programmes were implemented a more 'subsidy oriented' agriculture was established and the difference in the willingness to pay for extra units of water became less apparent between cautious and risky farmers. However, when real water shortages occur the 'price' of water increases substantially among risk tolerant farmers.

Irrigation water saving policies are then considered essential for the interrelation of the CAP reform programmes and the environmental impacts in specific areas of highly water dependent agricultural production. Meeting goals of such policies is a difficult requirement that needs careful considerations. The environmental impacts of policy programmes, as we have just discussed, have a marked geographical dimension so that the regional and local differences of the environmental impacts of these policy programmes have to be carefully studied. Water saving policies, at national and regional level, can have distinct local effects in terms of the farmer's water demand response (Varela-Ortega *et al.*, 1998) and these can play a decisive role in the application of agricultural policy programmes and their related environmental effects.

Indeed, in several countries that have to face long-lasting periods of water shortage a key instrument that has been analysed to increase water savings is the establishment of water pricing schemes (Cummings and Nercissiantz, 1992; Rosegrant *et al.*, 1995, Wilchens, 1991; OECD, 1987) and the regional dimension of such policies has been also stressed as related to cropping patterns and technological choice (Moore *et al.*, 1994; Boggess *et al.*, 1993; Caswell *et al.*, 1990) as well as to pollution emissions (Mapp *et al.*, 1995; Helfand and House, 1996). The effects of the application of different irrigation water saving

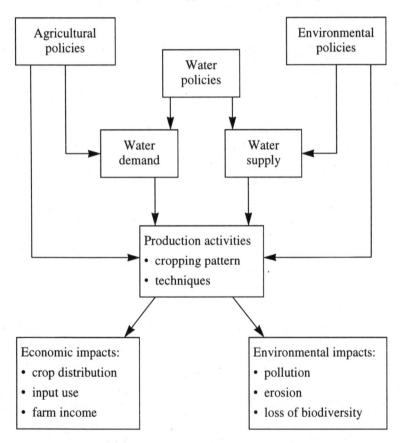

Figure 10.9   Relationships between agricultural, environmental and water policies

policies (i.e. administered water pricing policies) has been studied in two different water districts in our zone of study (Varela-Ortega *et al.*, 1998). The conclusions of this research establishes that there are clear differential effects across irrigation districts. In fact, water pricing policies need to be applied in a discriminatory manner following a clear regional pattern. Moreover, if these policies are not applied in a discriminatory way (that is, without considering the local dimension of the quantity–price responses in the water demand schedule) high water prices may interfere and induce undesirable effects in the application of the CAP programmes, such as reducing the allocation of land to cotton, sugar beet and alfalfa and increasing the land allocated to wheat or sunflower exceeding the permitted area and incurring the related penalties. Figure 10.9 summarizes the interrelationships of agricultural, environmental and water policies.

As a general conclusion for policy analysis we will have to stress the need to integrate agricultural policy, environmental policy and water policy, so as to integrate the role of natural resources – when they constitute a limiting factor for agricultural production – into the interactions of agricultural policy and environmental policy. The CAP reform (and most probably its foreseeable future trends) calls for less intensive agricultural systems and less environmentally damaging farming practices. New policies designed for the management of water resources have therefore to conform with these criteria and be more accurately entwined in this general EU farm policy context in which integration of agricultural and environmental policies is to be foreseen. This research has tried to bring some understanding to the interrelationships of these two policies and call some attention to the role that water resources can play in the policy integration process.

References

Baldock, D. and G. Beaufoy (1993), *Nature Conservation and New Directions in the EC Common Agricultural Policy: the Potential Role of EC Policies in Maintaining Farming and Management Systems of High Nature Value in the Community*, London: Institute for European Environmental Policy.

Baldock, D., G. Beaufoy, F. Brouwer and F. Godeschalk (1996), *Farming at the margins. Abandonment or Redeployment of Agricultural Land in Europe*, London: Institute for European Environmental Policy (IEEP) and The Hague: Agricultural Economics Research Institute (LEI-DLO).

Binswanger, H. and M. Rosenszweig, (1986), 'Behavioural and material determinants of production relations in agriculture', *The Journal of Development Studies*, 22(3), 503–39.

Boggess, W., R. Lacewell and D. Zilberman (1993), 'Economics of water use in agriculture', in: G.A. Carlson, D. Zilberman and J.A. Miranowski (eds), *Agricultural and Environmental Resource Economics*, Oxford: Oxford University Press, pp. 319–92.

Brouwer, F. and S. van Berkum (1996), *CAP and Environment in the European Union*, Wageningen, The Netherlands: LEI-DLO, Wageningen Pers.

Buckwell, A. (1996), 'Transformación de la PAC en una política rural más integrada', *Revista Española de Economía Agraria*, 176–7, 13–37.

Caswell, M., E. Lichtenberg and D. Zilberman (1990), 'The effects of pricing policies on water conservation and drainage', *American Journal of Agricultural Economics*, **72**, pp. 883–90.

Commission of the European Communities (CEC) (1992), Regulation (EEC) 2078/92, Brussels.

Commission of the European Communities (CEC) (1995), Agricultural Strategy paper, Brussels: EU Commission.

Cummings, R.G. and V. Nercissiantz (1992), 'The use of water pricing as a means for enhancing water use efficiency in irrigation: case studies in Mexico and in the United States', *Natural Resources Journal*, **32**, 731–55.

De Janvry, A., E. Sadoulet and M. Fafchamps (1989), 'Agrarian structure, technological innovations and the state', in P. Bardhan (ed.) *The Economic Theory of Agrarian Institutions*, Oxford: Oxford University Press, pp. 356–82.

Egdell, J. (1993), 'Impact of agricultural policy in Spain and its steppe regions. Studies in European agriculture and environment policy', Sandy, UK: RSPB.

Eswaran, M. and A. Kotwal (1986), 'Access to capital and agrarian production organisation', *The Economic Journal*, **96**(382), 482–98.

Feder, G (1980), 'Farm size, risk aversion and the adoption of new technology under uncertainty', *Oxford Economic Papers*, **32**, 263–83.

Flichman, G., A. Garrido and C. Varela-Ortega (1995a), 'Agricultural policy and technological choice: a regional analysis of income variation, soil use and environmental effects under uncertainty and market imperfections', in: L. M. Albisu and C. Romero (eds), *Environmental and Land Use Issues. An Economic Perspective*, Kiel: Wissenschaftsverlag Vauk, pp. 227–37.

Flichman G., P. Webster, C. Varela-Ortega, M. Cabelguenne C. Marques, A. Rossi and J.P. Boussemart (1995b), 'Analysis of the socio-economic impacts of agricultural reform in certain european regions: competitiveness and environmental protection', Report of EU project (contract no. 8001-CT91-0306-4706A), Brussels: EU Commission, DG VI.

Freund, R. (1956), 'The introduction of risk into a programming model', *Econometrica*, 24, 253–63.

Helfand, E. and B. House (1996), 'Regulating nonpoint source pollution under heterogeneous conditions', *American Journal of Agricultural Economics*, **77**(4), 1024–32.

Just, R. and J. Antle (1990), 'Interactions between agricultural and environmental policies: a conceptual framework', *American Economic Review*, **80**(2), 197–202.

Mapp, H., D. Bernardo, S. Sabbbagh and K. Watkins (1995), 'Economic and environmental impacts of limiting nitrogen use to protect water quality. A stochastic regional analysis', *American Journal of Agricultural Economics*. **76**(4), 889–903.

Moore, M.R., N.R. Gollehon and M.B. Carey (1994), 'Multicrop production decisions in Western irrigated agriculture: the role of water price', *American Journal of Agricultural Economics*. **76**(4), 859–74.

Organization for Economic Cooperation and Development (OECD) (1987), *Pricing of water services*. Paris: OECD.

Pérez Ibarra, C. (1994), 'Alteraciones ambientales en las transformaciones en regadío', *El Campo*, 'Agricultura y medio ambiente', **131**, 117–33.

Rayment, M. (1995), *A Review of the 1992 CAP Arable Reforms*, Sandy, UK, RSPB.

Rosegrant, M.W., R.G. Scheleyer and S.N. Yadav (1995), 'Water policy for efficient agricultural diversification: market based approaches', *Food Policy*, **20**(3), 203–23.

Roumasset, J.A. (1976). *Rice and Risk. Decision Making among Low-Income Farmers*, Amsterdam: North Holland Publishing Co.

Sumpsi, J.M. and C. Varela-Ortega (1994), 'El mercado de la tierra y las nuevas tendencias de cambio estructural', *Papeles de Economía Española*, **60**(61), 126–40.

Sumpsi, J. and C. Varela-Ortega (1995), 'The Common Agri-environmental Policy and its applications to Spain', in: L.M. Albisu and C. Romero (eds), *Environmental and Land Use Issues. An Economic Perspective*, Kiel: Wissenschaftsverlag Vauk, pp. 119–33.

Sumpsi, J.M., C. Varela-Ortega and E. Iglesias (1996), 'The CAP and the environment in Spain', mimeograph, national report of the project: F. Brouwer, and S. van Berkum (1996), 'CAP and the Environment: analysis of the effects of the CAP on the environment and an assessment of existing environment conditions in policy' (contract no. B4-3040/94/000963/MAR/B2), Brussels: EU Commission, DG XI.

Tauer, L. (1983), 'Target MOTAD', *American Journal of Agricultural Economics*, **65**(3), 606–10.

Valladares, M.A. (1993), 'Effects of the EC policy implementation on natural Spanish habitats', *The Science of the Total Environment*, **29**, 71–82.

Varela-Ortega, C. (1994), 'Encuestas de Costes de Transacción en las explotaciones del Valle del Guadalquivir', mimeograph, Research Project of the Joint Committee Spain–USA.

Varela-Ortega C., A. Garrido and M. Blanco (1995), 'Analysis of the socioeconomic and environmental impacts of different policies in the Spanish region of Andalucia', mimeograph, regional report of the project: Flichman *et al.*, 'Analysis of the socio-economic impacts of agricultural reform in certain European regions: competitiveness and environmental protection', Report of EU project (contract no. 8001-CT91-0306-4706A), Brussels: EU Commission, DG VI.

Varela-Ortega, C., J.M., Sumpsi, A. Garrido, M. Blanco and E. Iglesias (1998), 'Water pricing policies, public decision making and farmers' response: implications for water policy', *Agricultural Economics* (special issue of the XXIII Conference of the IAAE , Sacramento, CA., USA, 10–16 August 1997), vol. 18.

Whitby, M. (1995), 'Transactions costs and property rights: the omitted variables', in L. M. Albisu and C. Romero (eds), *Environmental and Land Use Issues. An Economic Perspective*, Kiel: Wissenschaftsverlag Vauk, pp. 3–12.

Wilchens, D. (1991), 'Motivating reductions in drain water with block-rate prices for irrigation water, *Water Resources Bulletin*, **27**, 585–92.

Williams, J., C. Jones and P. Dyke (1984), 'EPIC, A Modeling Approach to Determining the Relationship between Erosion and Soil Productivity', *Trans. American Society of Agricultural Engineering*, **27**, 129–44.

11   The productivity of agrochemicals in Greece

Joseph N. Lekakis

11.1   Introduction

Agrochemicals constitute the main production inputs associated with the questions of competitiveness and ecological sustainability in modern agriculture. On the one hand, the use of fertilizers and other chemicals such as pesticides worldwide has had enormous benefits in terms of crop yields and food production, by stimulating plant growth and reducing pest attacks and weed competition. The key attribute of agrochemicals affecting agricultural competitiveness is their productivity (Barkema *et al.*, 1990). On the other hand, however, these same inputs have generated both serious ecosystem disturbances and human health impacts (Conway and Pretty, 1991).

Environmental problems in Greek agriculture appear to be related to production inputs, especially fertilizers, which were heavily subsidized by the government until the late 1980s, and imported pesticides (Lekakis and Kousis, 1994). This is evidenced in the concentrations of substances such as nitrites and nitrates in certain fresh surface water bodies in Greece. According to the country's national report in the Rio Conference, concentrations of these substances in fresh surface waters exceed normal levels throughout the year, seasonally reaching high levels in some rivers and lakes (MOE, 1991). The government attributes high levels of pesticide residues to an excessively high rate of application by farmers within shorter intervals, the careless preparation of the spraying liquid, the washing of spraying equipment, and the careless disposal of used pesticide containers (MOE, 1991).

Summarizing the findings of rich experimental research conducted by Greek natural scientists on the use of fertilizers, a recent report, which was prepared for the European Commission by an *ad hoc* group of the Greek Ministry of Agriculture, concludes that nitrogen uptake levels depend largely on soil characteristics, type of crop, fertilizer chemical composition, as well as time and method of application (MOA, 1992). The report considered nitrogen uptake levels in Greek agriculture to be low, and as such it suspected them to be environmentally offensive. Finally, no specific conclusions were reached concerning other chemicals, including pesticides.

The discussion above suggests that, in Greece, agrochemicals may have been used not only in an environmentally damaging way, but also at an unproductive rate. While the latter remains a plausible hypothesis, no work has attempted to explore and qualify this issue using quantitative analysis to date, even at the sectoral level. Simultaneously, given the recent GATT agreement, the competitiveness of Greek agriculture in the future depends, to a large extent, on how productively agrochemicals will be combined in production. This requires knowledge of past agrochemicals productivities. In addition, the more rational use of these inputs in production, which seems inevitable following the abolition of input subsidies, will ameliorate environmental problems in Greece.

This chapter computes productivity measures for fertilizers and chemicals in crop production in Greece during the period 1971–95. Section 2 briefly reviews the literature on productivity analysis. Section 3 presents the theoretical model. Section 4 develops the empirical model and provides the estimates including productivity indexes for chemicals and fertilizers. Finally, section 5 presents the conclusions of this work.

11.2 Productivity analysis

The two major methods of measuring productivity are the multi-factor indexes and the single-factor or partial indexes (Capalbo, Ball and Denny, 1992; Capalbo *et al*, 1991; Capalbo and Antle, 1988; Ball, 1985; Caves *et al.*, 1982; Christensen and Jorgenson 1969). The multi-factor productivity indexes are given as the ratio of output to an aggregate index of production inputs. The partial productivity measures relate output to a single input, usually, labour or land (Denny and Fuss, 1983; Ragner *et al.* 1986; Thirtle and Bottomley, 1992). As a general rule, multi-factor productivity indexes are better measures of change in the overall production efficiency. According to Fabricant (1959), 'The broader the coverage of the resources, the better the productivity measure. The best measure is the one that compares output with the combined use of all resources.' The single-factor indexes tend to assign an overriding significance to the average product of a single factor as the indicator of productivity, concerning the entire process.

Single factor measures have been proposed by Christensen *et al.* (1980) and have been further developed by Adelaja (1992) who employed them to study the productivity of materials in the US food manufacturing sector during the period 1964–84. These measures are not to be interpreted as indicators of the overall efficiency of production, but only as indicators of the efficient utilization of the individual inputs in question. The single factor measures used in the present chapter are not simple average productivity statistics but composite measures, the derivation of which takes into account both the rate of technical change in the sector as a whole, and the changes in the utilization of fertilizers and chemicals relative to other production inputs.[1]

---

1   A number of economic studies on the efficiency in the use of single inputs such as pesticides, which are relevant to the theme of this chapter, exist for the US agricultural sector (Lichtenberg and Zilberman, 1986; Carrasco-Tauber and Moffitt, 1992; Chambers and Lichtenberg, 1994). Those studies, however, focus on the specification of agricultural production functions in the presence of pesticides rather than on calculating single factor productivity measures.

11.3   The theoretical model

Technology of crop production in Greece is assumed to be represented by a twice continuously differentiable function F,

$$Y(t) = F(X_K(t), X_L(t), X_N(t), X_F(t), X_C(t), t), \tag{11.1}$$

where X_K is capital, X_L is labour, X_N is land, XF is fertilizers, X_H is chemicals and t is time standing for disembodied technological change. It is also assumed that F is well behaved, that is increasing and quasi-concave in $X_j, j = K, L, N, F, H$ and that it exhibits constant returns to scale.[2]

Let $w_j, j = K, L, N, F, H$ be the prices of capital, labour, land, fertilizers and chemicals, respectively. Since F is well behaved, there exists a cost function, C, which is dual to F such that

$$C(w(t); Y(t), t) = \min_X w'(t) X(t), \tag{11.2}$$

where w and X are 5×1 vectors of input prices and quantities, respectively. C is increasing, concave and linear homogeneous in prices. Also, given the assumption of constant returns to scale, relation (11.2) may be written as

$$C(w(t); Y(t), t) = C^u(w(t); t) Y(t), \tag{11.3}$$

where C^u is the unit cost function representing the minimum average and marginal cost of producing Y.

Total Factor Productivity (TFP) is the average product of all production inputs, that is,

$$TFP(t) = \frac{Y(t)}{M(t)}, \tag{11.4}$$

where $M(t)$ is an aggregate input index. Differentiating (11.4) logarithmically with respect to time yields the rate of TFP growth as

$$T\dot{F}P(t) = \dot{Y}(t) - \dot{M}(t) \tag{11.5}$$

where the dot stands for logarithmic derivative. To make (11.5) operational a form for the time rate of change in $M(t)$ must be specified. A standard approach

2   Constant returns to scale impose restrictions on the production technology. They are, however, commonly used in productivity analysis (Ball, 1985; Thirtle and Bottomley, 1992; Adelaja, 1992).

is to specify it as the weighted average of the time rates of change of individual inputs, weights being cost shares (Chambers, 1989). For the problem at hand,

$$\dot{M}(t) = \sum_j S_j(t)\dot{X}(t)_j, \quad j = K, L, N, F, H, \tag{11.6}$$

with $S_j(t) = w_j(t)X_j(t)/C(t)$ being the share of the jth input in C. Combining (11.5) and (11.6) yields

$$T\dot{F}P(t) = \dot{Y}(t) - \sum_j S(t)_j \dot{X}(t)_j. \tag{11.7}$$

Relation (11.7) applies exactly only to data generated continuously. For discrete economic data, the rate of TFP growth can be approximated by the Tornqvist-Theil Divisia Index as

$$\log\left(\frac{TFP_t}{TFP_{t-1}}\right) = \log\left(\frac{Y_t}{Y_{t-1}}\right) - \sum_j \frac{1}{2}\left(S_{j,t} + S_{j,t-1}\right)\log\left(\frac{X_{j,t}}{X_{j,t-1}}\right). \tag{11.8}$$

Christensen *et al.* (1980) define productivity growth rate of an individual input i as

$$FP_{i,t} = \log\left(\frac{Y_t}{Y_{t-1}}\right) - \log\left(\frac{X_{i,t}}{X_{i,t-1}}\right). \tag{11.9}$$

Combining (11.8) and (11.9) and taking into account that $\sum_j S_j = 1$, gives

$$FP_{i,t} = \log\left(\frac{TFP_t}{TFP_{t-1}}\right) + \sum_j S_{j,t}\left[\log\left(\frac{X_{j,t}}{X_{j,t-1}}\right) - \log\left(\frac{X_{i,t}}{X_{i,t-1}}\right)\right], \quad i, j = K, L, N, F, H. \tag{11.10}$$

Empirical implementation of (11.10) requires cost shares and quantities for all inputs as well as an estimate for the rate of total factor productivity growth.

The latter can be obtained from the cost function since, under constant returns to scale, it is the case that

$$-T\dot{F}P = \Theta(t) = \frac{\dfrac{\partial C}{\partial t}}{C} = \frac{\dfrac{\partial C^u}{\partial t}}{C^u}, \qquad (11.11)$$

where Θ is the rate of cost diminution (Chambers, 1989). Substituting (11.11) into (11.10) yields

$$FP_{i,t} = -\Theta_t + \sum_j S_{j,t}\left[\log\left(\frac{X_{j,t}}{X_{j,t-1}}\right) - \log\left(\frac{X_{i,t}}{X_{i,t-1}}\right)\right]. \qquad (11.12)$$

Relation (11.11) suggests that productivity growth of the individual input i can be obtained as the sum of the rate of TFP growth (or equivalently the negative of the rate of cost diminution) and a weighted average of the changes in input i relative to changes in the remaining inputs, weights being cost shares.

11.4   The empirical model and the estimation results
The unit cost function C^u is specified as transcendental logarithmic (Diewert, 1976),

$$C^u = a_0 + \sum_j a_j \ln w_j + \frac{1}{2}\sum_j\sum_i a_{ji} \ln w_j \ln w_i + \sum_j b_{jt}\ln w_j + g_1 t + \frac{g_2}{2}t^2.$$

$$\qquad (11.13)$$

Linear homogeneity of the unit cost function in prices and symmetry require

$$\sum_j a_j = 1, \quad \sum_j\sum_j a_{ji} = 0, \quad \sum_j b_j = 0, \quad a_{ji} = a_{ij}. \qquad (11.14)$$

Differentiating (11.13) with respect to input prices gives the factor share equations,

$$S_j = a_j + \sum_i a_{ji} \ln w_i + b_j t, \quad j,i = K,L,N,F,H. \qquad (11.15)$$

Differentiation of (11.13) with respect to t gives the rate of cost diminution as

$$\Theta = g_1 + g_2 t + \sum_j b_j \ln w_j. \tag{11.16}$$

The unit cost equation (11.13) and four out of five cost-share equations (the chemicals cost-share equation has been dropped) is estimated as a simultaneous system by the iterative Zellner estimation procedure which yields estimates asymptotically equivalent to maximum likelihood (Kmenta and Gilbert, 1968)[3]

Table 11.1 presents coefficient estimates for the translog unit cost function as well as estimates of the Allen partial elasticities of substitution. The model fits the data quite well. The coefficients of determination range from 0.66 to 0.96. To be an adequate representation of the underlying technology the estimated unit cost function must be monotonically increasing and concave in inputs. Here, monotonicity is satisfied everywhere but concavity is broken for four observations. However, as noted by Wales (1977), such a minor violation does not necessarily undermine the assumption of cost minimization.

As shown by Binswanger (1974), the Allen partial elasticity of substitution between inputs i and j is

$$\sigma_{ij} = \frac{a_{ij}}{S_i S_j} + 1, \quad \text{for } i \neq j$$

while the ith input's own Allen partial elasticity of substitution is

$$\sigma_{ii} = \frac{\left(a_{ii} + S_i(1 - S_i)\right)}{S_i^2}.$$

On the basis of the Allen partial elasticities of substitution, capital is complement to all other inputs but land. Labour is complement to all other inputs but chemicals. Land is complement to all other inputs but capital. Fertilizer is complement to all other inputs but chemicals while chemicals is substitute to labour and fertilizers and complement to land and capital. The own-price elasticities are obtained by multiplying the own elasticities of substitution with their respective cost shares. The own-price elasticity of capital is –0.17, the own-price elasticity of labour is –0.15, the own-price elasticity of land is –0.25, the

---

3   Parameter estimates from the Zellner procedure may not be invariant to the equation dropped if significant autocorrelation exists. To address this issue each equation of the system was initially estimated separately and Box–Jenkins tests were made for the order of autocorrelation.

Table 11.1   Coefficient estimates and Allen elasticities of substitution

Parameter	Estimate	t-stat.	Parameter	Estimate	t-stat.
a_F	−1.77	−6.52[*]	b_K	0.0037	2.32[*]
a_{FF}	0.03	13.9[*]	a_L	9.49	11.97[*]
a_{FK}	−0.02	−8.65[*]	a_{LL}	0.17	−10.39[*]
a_{FN}	−0.003	−0.84	b_L	−0.0045	−11.35[*]
a_{FL}	−0.02	−4.95[*]	g_1	−0.39	−0.67
b_F	0.0009	6.81[*]	g_2	0.0019	0.66
a_N	−2.6	−4.03 [*]	a_0	388.6	0.66
a_{KN}	−0.003	−0.41	a_{FH}	0.018	
a_{NN}	0.13	8.49[*]	a_{NH}	−0.021	
a_{LN}	−0.11	−6.93[*]	a_{LH}	0.004	
b_N	0.0014	4.11[*]	a_{KH}	−0.009	
a_K	−0.59	−1.89[**]	a_{HH}	0.0085	
a_{KK}	0.09	11.01[*]	a_H	−4.15	
a_{LK}	−0.05	−7.92[*]	b_C	0.017	

$R^2(F)=0.90$, $R^2(N)=0.66$, $R^2(K)=0.83$, $R^2(L)=0.81$, $R^2(C^u)=0.96$

σ_{FF} −7.41	σ_{FL} −0.25	σ_{FK} −3.11	σ_{FL} −0.68	σ_{FH} 17.2
σ_{NN} −0.94	σ_{NK} −0.1	σ_{NL} −0.721	σ_{NH} −4.62	
σ_{KK} −1.27	σ_{KL} −0.81	σ_{KH} −4.07		
σ_{LL} −0.25	σ_{LH} 0.37			
σ_{HH} −23.1				

Notes:
1. Single and double asterisks denote significance at 5 and 10 per cent respectively.
2. The coefficients for which no t-statistic is presented are calculated from the symmetry and the homogeneity restrictions.
3. The Allen partial elasticities of substitution have been evaluated at mean values of the data.

own-price elasticities for fertilizers and chemicals are −0.37 and −0.29, respectively.

The rate of cost diminution is obtained by differentiation of the unit cost function (11.13) with respect to t. The annual average percentage rate of cost diminution per period is shown in Table 11.2.

Input-specific measures of productivity growth are derived from relation (11.12). Table 11.3 presents productivity indexes for fertilizers and chemicals, while Table 11.4 presents a summary of the rates of productivity growth for those inputs.

Table 11.2   Rate of cost diminution

Period	Value
1971–82	–0.24
1983–95	–0.13
1971–95	–0.18

Table 11.3   Productivity indexes for fertilizers and chemicals (%)

Year	Fertilizers	Chemicals
1971	100.0	100.0
1972	92.2	95.6
1973	86.3	92.4
1974	77.6	84.8
1975	78.1	89.8
1976	69.8	87.2
1977	63.8	82.4
1978	62.5	84.5
1979	58.3	75.3
1980	58.6	77.8
1981	77.5	85.2
1982	54.6	71.7
1983	48.7	60.4
1984	48.7	68.3
1985	48.1	59.6
1986	48.1	63.5
1987	44.7	59.6
1988	46.1	44.0
1989	46.1	33.9
1990	40.4	30.2
1991	41.4	27.8
1992	47.2	23.5
1993	49.6	22.6
1994	50.1	22.4
1995	47.9	22.1

The productivity level of fertilizers in 1995 is less than half that in 1971. The productivity level of chemicals in 1995 is just above one fifth of the level in 1971. These results correspond to how the use of these inputs has evolved in the period

Table 11.4   Annual average rates of productivity growth (%)

Period	Fertilizers	Chemicals
1971–82	–5.02	–2.7
1983–95	–1.01	–9.04
1971–95	–2.9	–6.03

under investigation, relative to the changes in crop output. Specifically, during 1971–95, crop output increased at an average annual rate of 1.56 per cent, while fertilizer use increased at 2.42 per cent and chemical use at 5.9 per cent. In the sub-period 1971–82 the average annual rates of growth were 3.1, 5.1 and 2.9 for output, fertilisers and chemicals respectively. This appears to explain why the fall in productivity of fertilizers was much faster than it was for chemicals during that period. In the sub-period 1983–95 the average annual rates of growth were 0.28, –0.09, and 7.9 per cent for crop supply, fertilizers and chemical use respectively. This appears to explain the dramatic decrease in chemical productivity in that sub-period and the slowing down (even reversal in the latest years) in the downward trend of fertilizer productivity. Figure 11.1 displays the natural logarithms of crop production, fertilizers use, and chemical use in constant (1970) million drachmas.

Relation (11.13) suggests that an implicit representation of input-specific indexes of productivity growth is

$$FP_i = FP_i(w), \tag{11.17}$$

where w is the vector of input prices. Several explicit specifications will allow estimation of short-run and long-run impacts of the determining factors v on FP_i. Although an Almon specification would be desirable, a Koyck function of the following form,

$$PF_{i,t} = d_0 + \sum_j d_j w_j + hFP_{i,t-1}, \tag{11.18}$$

is used here because of limited data. In this expression, d_j is the short-run effect of a change in the determining factor on the productivity of input I, while $d_j/(1-h)$ is the long-run effect. Table 11.5 presents parameter estimates of Koyck Distributed Lag Functions for fertilizers and chemicals.

For the Koyck function of fertilizers four coefficients are statistically significant at 5 per cent level or less, namely, the intercept, and those

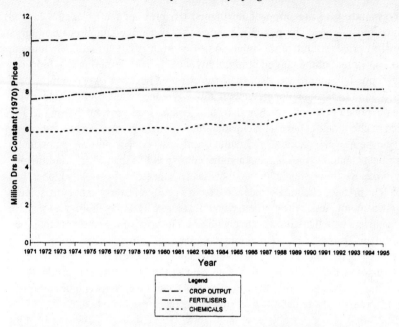

Figure 11.1   Natural logarithms of crop output, fertilizers and chemicals in Greek agriculture

Table 11.5   Parameter estimates of Koyck functions

Variable	Fertilizers		Chemicals	
	Estimate	t-stat	Estimate	t-stat
d_0	0.16	3.20^*	0.69	3.27^*
d_1	0.003	0.42	0.016	0.91
d_2	0.02	3.47^*	0.03	2.61^*
d_3	−0.016	$−2.25^*$	0.004	0.34
d_4	0.016	1.67	−0.03	−1.51
d_5	−0.03	−0.93	−0.01	−1.56
h	0.72	12.8^*	0.21	1.1
	$R^2 = 0.97$		$R^2 = 0.98$	

Notes:
The coefficients d_1 to d_5 correspond to the prices of chemicals, fertilizers, land, capital and labour, respectively.
Single asterisks denote significance at 5 per cent level.

corresponding to the price of fertilizers, the price of land, and the lagged productivity level. The positive sign of the own-price suggests that higher fertilizer prices stimulate short- and long-run productivity growth in that input. The coefficient of the lagged productivity level is 0.72, implying that long-run effects are 4.3 times higher than short-run effects. The prices of two complement inputs, land and labour, appear to work towards reducing fertilizers' productivity. But the price of capital, which is also complement, works towards raising it. The price of chemicals appears to have no influence on the productivity of fertilizers.

For the Koyck function of chemicals only two coefficients are statistically significant, namely, the intercept and that corresponding to the price of fertilizers. Nevertheless, the *t*-statistics of two more coefficients are substantially higher than one. The price of chemicals appears to have a positive, although not statistically significant, impact on the productivity of that input. The same holds for the price of fertilizers which is substitute to chemicals. The price of the complement input, capital and the price of the substitute, labour, appear to work towards reducing productivity of chemicals. The price of land, however, appears to have no influence on the productivity of that input. Finally, the lagged productivity level has no influence on the current productivity level, implying that there is no difference between short- and long-run effects for chemicals.

11.5 Conclusions

Within the limitations of the employed model, despite the fact that technical change has been positive, the productivity both of fertilizers and chemicals during the period 1971–1995 has been found to decrease with time. This appears to be explained by the individual growth rates of output, fertilizers, and chemicals during that period. Fertilizer productivity slightly reverses its trend in the early 1990s. This may be attributed to the fertilizer price increase following the abolition of input subsidies which was announced in the late 1980s and came into effect in 1992.

The productivity of chemicals decreases throughout the studied period and this may stem from the fact that demand for chemicals has become less sensitive to price change, as farmers have become dependent on them.

These findings support the hypothesis that in Greece agrochemicals have been used at an environmentally damaging and unproductive rate. While this is true for the entire agricultural sector, it by no means implies that productivity growth at the regional or specific crop production level has followed the same trend. Therefore, to assist in policy analysis, additional research at that level is certainly warranted.

Finally, although no definitive conclusions on Greek agricultural competitiveness can be drawn from the results of the model on technical change, this change has been rather small.

Acknowledgements   Many thanks to Dr. Panos Fousekis and Ms Aspasia Papakonstandinou for their invaluable assistance while preparing this chapter, and to Professors John M. Antle and Susan Capalbo for pointing out errors and obscure points in an earlier draft. The usual disclaimers apply.

Data appendix

The prices and quantities of crop production, fertilizers and chemicals come from the National Accounts of Greece. The prices of capital, labour and land come from the National Statistical Service of Greece. Labour and capital quantities, however, are available for the total agricultural sector and not for crop and livestock production, separately. In order to derive capital and labour series for crop production the assumption has been made that the use of labour and capital in this sub-sector can be given by the share of crop production in total agricultural output.

References

Adelaja, A. (1992), 'Material productivity in food manufacturing', *Americam Journal of Agricultural Economics*, **74**, 177–85.

Ball, V. (1985), 'Output, input, and productivity measurement', *American Journal of Agricultural Economics*, **67**, 475–86.

Barkema, A., M. Drabenstott and L. Tweeten (1990), 'The Competitiveness of US Agriculture in the 1990s', in K. Allen (ed.), *Agricultural Policies in a New Decade*, Resources for the Future and National Planning Association, Washington, DC.

Binswanger, H. (1974), 'A Cost Function Approach to Measurement of Factor Demand and Elasticities of Substitution', *American Journal of Agricultural Economics*, **56**, 377–86.

Capalbo, S., V. Ball and M. Denny (1992), 'International comparisons of agricultural productivity: development and usefulness', *American Journal of Agricultural Economics*, **74**, 1292–7.

Capalbo, S., M. Denny, A. Hoque and C. Overton (1991) 'Methodologies for comparisons of agricultural output, input, and productivity: a review and synthesis', USDA, ERS, Agriculture and Trade Analysis Division.

Capalbo S. and J. Antle (eds) (1988), *Agricultural Productivity: Measurement and Explanation*, Washington, DC: Resources for the Future.

Carrasco-Tauber, C. and L. Moffitt (1992), 'Damage control econometrics: functional specification and pesticide productivity', *American Journal of Agricultural Economics*, **74**,158–62.

Caves, D., L. Christensen and W. Diewert (1982), 'Multilateral Comparisons of Output, Input, and Productivity Using Superlative Index Numbers', *Economic Journal*, **92**,73–86.

Chambers, R. (1989), *Applied Production Analysis: A Dual Approach*, London: Cambridge University Press.

Chambers, R. and E. Lichtenberg (1994), 'Simple Econometrics of Pesticide Productivity', *American Journal of Agricultural Economics*, **76**, 411–17.

Christensen, L. and D. Jorgenson (1969), 'The Measurement of U.S Real Capital Input', *Review of Income and Wealth*, **5**, 292–320.

Christensen, L., D. Cummings and D. Jorgenson (1980), 'Economic growth, 1947–73: an international comparison', in J. Kendric and B. Vaccara (eds), *New Developments in Productivity Analysis*, Chicago: NBER.

Conway, G. R. and J.N. Pretty (1991), *Unwelcome harvest: Agriculture and pollution*, London: Earthscan.

Denny, M. and M. Fuss (1983), 'Intertemporal changes in the level of regional labor productivity in Canadian manufacturing,' in A. Dogramaci (ed.), *Developments in Econometric Analysis and Productivity*, Boston: Kluwer Academic Publishers.

Diewert, W. (1976), 'Exact and Superlative Index Numbers', *Journal of Econometrics*, **4**, 116–45.

Fabricant, S. (1959) 'Basic Facts of Productivity Growth', NBER, Occasional Paper No. 63.

Kmenta, J. and R. Gilbert (1968), 'Small sample properties of alternative estimators of seemingly unrelated regressions', *Journal of the American Statistical Association*, **63**, 1180–200.

Lekakis, J. N. and M. Kousis (1994), 'Agriculture and the environment in Greece', *Progress in Rural Policy and Planning*, **4**, 177–207.

Lichtenberg, E. and D. Zilberman (1986), 'The econometrics of damage control: why specification matters', *American Journal of Agricultural Economics*, **68**, 261–73.

MOA (Ministry of Agriculture) (1992), 'Agriculture and the state of the environment in Greece', internal report, Athens, July (in Greek).

MOE (Ministry of Environment) (1991), 'National report of Greece', prepared for the UN Conference on Environment and Development, Brazil, June 1992.

Ragner, A., J. Whittaker and K. Ingersent (1986), 'Productivity growth in agriculture revisited: a measurement framework and some empirical results', *Journal of Agricultural Economics*, **37**, 127–50.

Thirtle, C. and P. Bottomley (1992), 'Total factor productivity in the UK agriculture, 1967–90', *Journal of Agricultural Economics*, **43**, 381–99.

Wales T. (1977), 'On the flexibility of flexible functional forms: an empirical approach', *Journal of Econometrics*, **5**, 183–93.

PART IV

12 Agriculture and the environment in transition: a case study of Estonia

Tim T. Phipps and Paavo Eliste

Agriculture is fundamentally linked with the environment. The negative environmental links have been well documented: sediment, agricultural fertilizers, and pesticides can severely damage aquatic ecosystems and pollute ground and surface water. Cultivated cropland can damage or supplant wildlife habitat. Agricultural expansion has been the primary reason for draining wetlands in the US and Europe. The positive environmental linkages of agriculture are also present in both the US and Europe: agriculture provides open space in an increasingly urbanized and congested world, can provide pleasing landscapes such as the vineyards in France, Germany, and Italy, stone fences in Great Britain, and dairy farms in Switzerland. In countries that would otherwise be dominated by forest, for example, Sweden and Estonia, agriculture can provide the kind of border habitat preferred by deer and certain avian species.

These positive and negative effects are externalities. The business structure of farming, with the operator generally residing on the farm, insures that some account will be taken of these externalities in management decisions. After all, the farmer's family usually obtains its drinking water from a source near the farm and experiences the positive and negative aesthetic impacts of farming more directly than the surrounding community. In general, however, a free market will lead to oversupply of the negative externalities and an undersupply of the positive externalities without some form of policy intervention or institutional arrangement.

The issue of agriculture and the environment is much larger than the relatively simple problem of dealing with the market failures that exist in a free market. The situation is greatly complicated by agricultural price and income support and supply control policies that push the market failures sometimes in the right direction but usually in the wrong direction. Free trade is generally held to worsen the environmental externalities of agriculture though there is little empirical evidence one way or the other. The trade picture is also constantly changing, with new GATT agreements, US and EU agricultural policy reforms, and potential expansion of the European Union. Finally, there are the Central and Eastern European (CEE) economies in transition. The potential effects of transition to a market economy on the environmental impacts of agriculture and on future European and world trade patterns are very significant.

Our plan is first to give a brief overview of the effects of market distorting agricultural income and price supports on the environment. We will spend more time on the effects of transition on agriculture and the environment. Then we will briefly address some issues involving trade and the environment. Finally, we will examine one economy in transition and one environmental issue in some detail: Estonia and the issue of wetland preservation.

12.1   Agricultural policy and the environment

Following Antle and Just (1991), it is useful to distinguish the impacts agricultural price and income support policies have on the intensive and extensive margins. Effects on the intensive margin alter the derived demand for variable inputs including labour, fertilizers and pesticides. Intensive margin effects influence the per-hectare rates of application of inputs and are therefore directly related to the amount of input that migrates from the farm to the environment. Extensive margin effects result from changes in the level of profits or rent generated per hectare. A change in land rent will alter the amount of land in production and therefore influence the level of conversion of non-agricultural land including wetlands and other fragile lands to crop production. Most agricultural income and price support policies will affect both margins. In the following we assume that all farmers are profit maximizers and price takers in the input and output markets. We will also assume we are dealing with a small open economy. This is a reasonable assumption for a country such as Estonia. It is not a reasonable assumption for Central and Eastern Europe plus the Commonwealth of Independent States (CIS) taken as a whole.

12.1.1 Price support policies

There are a number of policies that raise the effective output prices received by farmers, including the price support programmes in the US and the variable levy of the Common Agricultural Policy (CAP) in the EU. Other programmes that increase the prices received by farmers include subsidized exports, import restrictions, and supply-control programmes such as set-asides. A price support policy will affect both the intensive and extensive margins. For a normal input, a rise in the output price, *ceteris paribus*, will increase the total demand for the input and the per-hectare use of the input. If the input is a polluting input, such as fertilizers or pesticides, a price-support policy will lead to increased environmental damage. As shown by Antle and Just, the environmental damages of the policy will depend on the joint distribution of input use, production, policy induced price effects, and environmental characteristics.

An output price increase will also shift the extensive margin outward by increasing the returns to land. If land is heterogeneous, the increase in land rents will result in land of lower productivity being brought into agricultural production. Often this land of lower productivity is steeply sloped, has thin topsoil, or contains wetlands. Farming steeply sloped land results in increased loss of topsoil and runoff of pesticides, fertilizers and sediment. The conversion of wetlands results in loss of the environmental services generated by the wetland including loss of wildlife habitat. On the positive side, higher agricultural rents will tend to keep in agriculture land that has a high opportunity cost in farming (due to urban encroachment or other development pressures), thus contributing open space and scenic amenities.

12.1.2 Income support policies

Both the US and the EU are increasingly replacing price supports with direct income supports due to the growing expense and trade distortions of price supports. In the US these policies included the target price/deficiency payment programme which has been replaced (with the passage of the Federal Agricultural Improvement and Reform Act in 1996) with the flexibility payment programme. In the EU such payments are called CAP reform payments or area payments, a policy that came out of the MacSharry reform that is designed to compensate farmers for reduced price supports (Folmer *et al.* 1995).

There can be a significant difference between the environmental impacts of price support programmes and income support programmes, depending on how the payments are calculated. The negative environmental impacts of price supports arise because the supports raise the incentive price upon which farmers base their production decisions. The target price/deficiency payment programme made a direct payment to the farmer equal to:

$$(P_T - P_M) \text{ Base Yield,}$$

where P_T is the policy-determined target price, P_M is the market price (which generally will be greater than or equal to the policy-determined support price) and the base yield is based on past yields and cultivated acreage. Base yields were frozen at their 1986 levels in the 1985 Farm Bill.

Because base yields were frozen in 1986, farmers' production decisions could not affect their deficiency payments. Therefore their incentive or marginal price was the market price. The new flexibility payment programme in the US, which replaced the deficiency payment programme, is similar in that payments are based on past, not current, production levels. The CAP reform payments are also similar in their effect because they are based on the area farmed rather than on yield.

While income support payments do not affect the intensive margin in theory, they may affect the extensive margin depending upon eligibility requirements. If the farmer must continue to operate the farm in order to receive the payments, the payments may serve to keep in production marginal land that otherwise would leave farming. Whether this is good or bad from the standpoint of society depends on whether on net the farm produces negative or positive externalities.

12.1.3 Supply control policies

Price and income support policies are often paired with supply control policies in an attempt to reduce budget pressures and reduce surplus production. In the US, both short-term and long-term acreage retirement programmes have been used. Farmers are generally required to remove a percentage of their base acreage from production for one year in order to qualify for price support loans and deficiency payments. This percentage is set annually by the Secretary of Agriculture. The US also pays farmers to take land out of production. Since 1985, paid land diversions have generally been for conservation and environmental purposes, for example, the Conservation Reserve Programme and the Wetlands Reserve Programme.

The European Union introduced paid set-asides in the 1980s. Under the MacSharry reform, large farmers (those who produce over 92 metric tons of grain equivalents) are required to set aside 15 per cent of their basic area in order to receive CAP reform payments.

Supply control policies operate at both the intensive and extensive margins. The effect of set-aside policies on per-hectare variable input use depends on whether the inputs are net substitutes or complements with land. Farmers will tend to increase application rates of substitute inputs per hectare and reduce application rates of complementary inputs. To the extent that fertilizers and pesticides are net substitutes for land (which is an empirical issue), set-asides will lead to higher rates of application of these inputs on the land that remains in production. Whether this leads to an overall increase or decrease in input use depends on elasticities of substitution among inputs and is again an empirical issue.

The influence of supply control on the extensive margin depends on how the set-asides affect farmer costs of production and the incentive prices received by farmers. Requiring a set-aside (as distinct from a voluntary set-aside) raises a farmer's average cost of production because of the fixed costs (and possibly variable maintenance costs) of the idle land. If the set-aside has no impact on the incentive price received by farmers, the set-aside will tend to reduce land rents and shift the extensive margin in because of the increase in average costs. If the set-aside raises the incentive price received by farmers by reducing market supply, the effect on land rent and the extensive margin will depend on whether the increase in revenues offsets the increase in costs.

In any case, the effects of set-asides on either margin are likely to be small unless the required set-aside is set higher than has been the case in the past. This is because farmers are good managers and will take their least productive land out of production first and will also learn to adjust their optimal farm size to accommodate the required set-aside.

The environmental impacts of set-asides also depend greatly on whether the time period is one year or longer and what is done with the idled land. Long-term set-asides are much more valuable for wildlife habitat than annual set-asides, for example.

12.2 Transition, agriculture, and the environment

The period of transition to a market economy, as experienced in Central and Eastern Europe and the former Soviet Union, brings about many economic changes that affect agriculture and consequently, the environment. Like the agricultural policies discussed above, transition factors can affect agriculture by altering the incentive prices received by farmers or the costs of inputs. There are also several other factors that are unique to the transition process. The factors we will discuss are lack of secure property rights and free transfer of land; suboptimal farm size and fragmentation of land parcels; incomplete capital markets and credit rationing; and uncertainty about future agricultural policies, trade relations, markets and prices. There are many other important transition factors that are not discussed here. These include human capital, transactions and relocation costs, former cooperative workers with a low opportunity cost of their labour, outmoded and non-competitive processing sectors, lack of market infrastructure, lack of housing for displaced farm workers in urban areas, and lack of a well-developed agricultural extension service.

12.2.1 Land Market Issues

One of the most fundamental elements of the transition process is land reform. This is particularly true for agricultural land, given the relative importance of the agricultural sectors in most transition economies.[1] While some transition countries, such as Poland, had a large number of privately owned farms, that was not the case for most countries of the former USSR. In most cases large state and cooperative farms controlled agricultural land. One of the primary problems of transition in agriculture is the transfer of ownership of land and existing businesses from the state to private owners and the creation of a well functioning land market. The actual process of privatization of agricultural land varies from country to country. It has ranged from rapid and complete distribution of the state and cooperative farms to private ownership (Albania, Romania, and Latvia) to systems in which most of the cooperatives were left intact with

---

1   As noted by Csaki, prior to the transition period agriculture contributed 15 per cent of the national income and provided 20 per cent of the jobs in Central and Eastern Europe plus the Commonwealth of Independent States. That same region has 8 per cent of the world's population and almost 20 per cent of the world's arable land.

ownership of the assets distributed to the members (Ukraine and Russia) (Csaki, 1995).

The most common approach to land reform in Central and Eastern Europe has been to try and restore title to the land to prior owners (restitution). Again, the actual approach varies from country to country. Some countries require that the former owners cultivate the land in order to claim it; others, such as Hungary, issued vouchers to former land owners that can be redeemed for land or other state assets (see Csaki for individual country details).

From an economic efficiency standpoint, the means of distributing the land to private ownership is less important than the ability of the new owners to freely transfer title to the land. Free transferability speeds the process of getting the land into the hands of the most capable farm managers and the process of adjustment to a more efficient farm size. Unfortunately, many transition countries place limits on land transferability and land use, such as limits on farm or household plot size, requirements that the land stay in agricultural use, limits on foreign ownership, and limits on lease terms and rent.

Transition in the agricultural land markets has a number of effects that are relevant to this paper. The first is the issue of optimal farm size. In the typical case, a country is moving from having large and inefficient state-owned and collective farms to having small private units. Here again Latvia is a good example of this trend with the average size of newly created private farms around 20 ha (The World Bank, 1996). While the small units are known for their relatively high productivity, they are in most cases smaller than optimal or equilibrium size. There is also the problem of fragmentation as an operator tries to make up an efficient operating unit from the available land for sale or rent.

During transition, as firms experience economies of size, they will also experience increases in profitability (from reduced average cost of production and given the assumption that output prices do not fall with the increased production). This will raise rents to the relatively fixed factor (land), shifting out the extensive margin and bringing more land into cultivation. As land price is determined at the margin, this will also raise the price of land.

The lack of a clear title, free transferability, and well-functioning lease/rental markets for land create a number of economic problems. In addition to slowing the process of transition to operating units of an efficient size, these problems increase the transaction costs of buying and selling land and of size adjustment. These costs have a negative impact on a farmer's bid price for additional land. Such transaction costs reduce the use of land rental as a means of adjusting the size of the farm, and lower the price of farmland.

The environmental consequences of this shift again depend on whether the land produces net negative or net positive externalities. Since by definition land at the extensive margin is land of marginal productivity, it is more likely that the land will be a wetland or land that is ecologically fragile. The more rapid the process of transformation in the land market, then, the more pressure will be placed on wetlands and other fragile lands of ecological importance.

Land market transition may also affect the intensive margin, depending on the form of the production functions. If the production functions are non-homothetic, changes in size may lead to shifts in the variable input mix. If the West is any guide, this shift will be towards greater mechanization and greater use of chemical inputs, with obvious environmental consequences.

12.2.2 Incomplete capital markets
One of the major problems affecting the development of the transition economies is the lack of well-developed capital markets. Efficient capital and land rental markets are needed to ease the transfer of operation of farmland to the best farm operators and to encourage operators to operate units of an efficient size. Part of the problem is in developing the institutions needed to support a capital market. There is also a 'chicken and egg' problem. In order to have access to credit, a farm operator needs equity in assets that can be pledged as collateral. Unfortunately, in most transition economies people do not have the wealth needed to access credit. Even individuals that own land because of restitution have difficulty pledging the land as collateral, because of problems with obtaining clear title to the land and limitations on transfer of title.

12.2.3 Market uncertainty
The period prior to transition was one of low but stable output prices, available and often subsidized inputs, and ready output markets. The transition period in most countries has brought a rapid rise in the relative price of inputs, limited availability of capital equipment and agricultural chemicals, and uncertain output markets.

The rise in input prices relative to output prices clearly reduces profits and returns to land. Taken alone, this would shift in the extensive margin, resulting in less land being cultivated and reducing land prices. The rise in variable input prices relative to land prices would also affect the intensive margin, resulting in reduced per-hectare use of variable inputs such as agricultural chemicals. This would make agricultural production less intensive and probably reduce the amount of land in agriculture, depending on the opportunity cost of operator labour and the land.

Increased uncertainty about future input and output prices reduces the incentives to enter or stay in farming. As noted by Csaki, the primary reason people in the transition economies are reluctant to enter or stay in farming is 'the fact that in Central and Eastern Europe today private farming is too risky and promises relatively modest income compared to the risks' (p. 34). Since the price a land buyer would be willing to pay equals the present discounted value of the future rental stream, anything that makes that rental stream lower or more risky will tend to lower the bid price for land.

The increased market uncertainty may be beneficial to the environment as it induces farmers to diversify their crops. The latter would improve the soil properties and reduce erosion.

12.3   Trade and the environment

The agricultural production capacity and export potential of many Central and Eastern European countries is high. One indicator of this is the rapidity with which they have achieved grain self-sufficiency following the fall in production in the early stages of the transition (USDA). In most analyses, the CEE countries are expected to have even greater output potential in livestock production. The effects of this expanding productive and export capacity on the transition economies and the environment depend on a number of factors.

While the transition economies have the agricultural resources to support production for export, export markets are currently very limited due to trade barriers and the partial loss of markets in the former Soviet Union. Future expansion will depend on continuation of the market access agreements between CEE countries and the EU, the rate of economic growth in the CIS, continued CAP reforms, and the next stage of agricultural trade reforms under GATT. Any policy move that gives CEE countries favourable access to EU markets will increase the prices received by farmers in CEE. The current GATT agreement, while modest in its impact on agricultural trade, should lead to increased world market prices of most traded commodities due to restrictions on export subsidies and market access requirements (OECD 1995). All of these policies will have the same environmental consequences as an increase in price support. It is ironic that trade and internal agricultural policy reforms that are designed to reduce farmers' incentive prices in the US, EU and Japan, will have the opposite effect on incentive prices received by farmers in the CEE.

12.4   Summary

For the CEE countries, a number of forces are pushing in the same direction. If the transition process continues to move in a private enterprise, free market direction, improvements in capital and land markets, economies of size, improvements in the processing sector and market infrastructure will all serve to increase the efficiency of CEE agriculture and reduce average costs of production. The GATT, CEE market access agreements, and other trade reforms should serve to raise world market prices and the prices received by CEE farmers.

The culmination of these forces will affect the intensive and extensive margins. At the intensive margin, application per hectare of variable inputs, including agricultural chemicals, would be expected to increase. This will lead, in the absence of environmental controls or incentives to the contrary, to increased water pollution and other environmental and health impacts of agricultural chemical use. The increased profitability and reduced riskiness of farming will tend to shift out the extensive margin, raising land rents, land prices, and the amount of land in cultivation. The environmental consequences of this shift depend on the environmental characteristics of the land brought into production.

We turn next to an analysis of one of the CEE countries in transition: Estonia.

12.5   Case study of Estonia

We have chosen to highlight Estonia for a number of reasons. First, Estonia has been relatively radical in moving towards a free market economy from a centrally planned system. Second, it still contains a high percentage of wetland resources in spite of three decades of agricultural pressures. While the process of transition has significantly reduced the agricultural pressures on wetlands, another ecological crisis is emerging in Estonia, as semi-natural wetlands are disappearing at an alarming rate due to the decline of traditional agricultural activities needed to maintain these marginal lands.

We begin this section with a review of major macroeconomic policies and reforms in Estonia during the economic transition period. Given the dynamics of transition processes we avoid getting into specific details of various reform policies. Instead we focus our attention to the effect of macroeconomic policy liberalization on environmental resources such as wetlands. The last section of the chapter focuses on the policies that will reduce the asymmetries in the incidence of environmental costs and benefits.

12.5.1 Current policy framework

Since 1992 the Estonian economy has undergone radical structural adjustment. The guiding principles of policy reforms have been trade liberalization and a balanced budget. As with other transition economies the restructuring has not been painless. Several sectors, including agriculture, have experienced dramatic contractions. Furthermore, the declining real incomes and erosion of a number of previous social guarantees have caused tension between many social groups.

Radical reform policies, however, seem to have paid off as the Estonian economy shows clear signs of recovery. Within a few years of independence Estonia managed to reduce its dependence from the Former Soviet Union (FSU) and reorient its economy towards more stable Western markets. However, in spite of the general success of transition policies, restructuring of agriculture has lagged behind the rest of the economy. The break off from the Soviet Union and the collapse of the managed inter-republic trade seriously hurt agriculture as the sector was not able to deal with huge over capacity and technological inefficiency. The addition of radical price and trade liberalization policies further contributed to difficulties in the sector. Finally, the inability to solve complex institutional problems such as farm restructuring and land reform has suppressed the formation of an optimal scale of farm operation. As a result the gross agricultural output fell 53 per cent during the period of 1986 to 1995 (Table 12.1).

Table 12.1   Gross Agricultural Output (GAO) index, 1986–96 (1986 = 100)

GAO	1987	1988	1989	1990	1991	1992	1993	1994	1995
Total	97.4	93.8	100.9	87.7	84.2	68.4	63.1	57.0	52.9
Crops	88.8	74.4	96.6	72.6	77.7	66.1	73.3	63.1	56.7
Livestock	101.4	102.7	102.8	94.6	85.1	67.2	53.9	50.2	47.9

Source: The World Bank (1997)

The current macroeconomic framework in Estonia can be characterized as having virtually no policy-induced price distortions. The role of the government has been mainly to insure a favourable macroeconomic environment by encouraging competitive markets with minimal barriers to entry, maintaining a stable currency, and reducing inflationary pressures. In trade policy there are almost no tariff and non-tariff barriers for most imports and exports including agricultural products.

While free trade and the commitment to a balanced budget have been the main characteristics of reform policies in Estonia they have not been without political opposition. The pressure has been especially strong from farm groups who have intensively lobbied for managed agricultural trade and price support policies. Although a number of farm support programmes have been passed in the Parliament since 1993, none has been implemented, as it has been not been possible to finance the required level of support, given the tight budget.

The success of macroeconomic stabilization policies is inherently contingent upon prevailing institutional constraints. In agriculture, two important reform policies – farm restructuring and land reform – will determine the future efficiency of farm operations. The goal of farm restructuring, which started in 1992, is to reorganize agricultural production from large-scale collective and state farms to viable private farms. The objective of the reform was to return private property, which was nationalized during the collectivization period, to the previous owners or their descendants. The remaining assets of the state and collective farms were transferred to workers in the form of shares. Restructuring created three types of farm: legal production units, privately owned family farms, and subsidiary plots (Table 12.2). The first category is large-scale farms composed of the remnants of state and collective farms. Ownership of these

Table 12.2   Contribution of various farming categories to agricultural production in 1995

	Total production (%)	Use of cultivated land (%)
Farm enterprises	51	48
Family farms	17	29
Household plots	32	23

Source: The World Bank (1997)

enterprises is transferred to previous employees by distributing shares or assets. Many of these enterprises have not been able to adjust to changed market conditions and now face serious financial difficulties or bankruptcy, imposing an additional burden on the economy. It is interesting to compare the continuing high efficiency of the household plots relative to the other organizational structures.

Although the first land reform laws were passed in 1991 progress has been modest because of numerous financial, technical, and legal impediments. However, the major cause of the slow pace is the desire to restitute the land to previous owners. There is a huge pool of eligible owners as about two-thirds of Estonians consider themselves legal heirs of former owners (European Commission, 1995). Furthermore, the pre-emptive rights of current users of the land along with the complexity of compensating previous owners or substituting other land plots have further complicated the restitution process.

The slow progress of land reform has limited the access of farmers to financial markets, as commercial banks are reluctant to provide credit due to lack of collateral or unclear property rights. Hence, most of the agricultural credit has been channelled to farmers through special credit lines financed from the state budget. The interest rate has been subsidized to below the market rate.

12.5.2 Macroeconomic liberalization and the environment
Many economic reforms initiated to promote efficient resource allocation are also environmentally beneficial (see Gandhi, 1996 for an extensive review). As discussed in the sections above, eliminating price support programmes and liberalization of foreign trade may have positive impacts on the environment. Combining environmental goals with the goals of macroeconomic stabilization is especially relevant to transition economies given the limited resources available for satisfying competing social needs.

Commercial agricultural activities cause a number of environmental disturbances such as contaminating ground- and surface waters due to nutrient runoff, pesticide pollution, or erosion and destruction of fertile soil layers.

Recently the alarming rate of degradation of wetlands due to agricultural and urban development pressures has gained prominence in the national environmental strategies of many industrial countries. The potentially irreversible nature of conversion of wetlands further emphasizes the need to address the issue.

In spite of extensive drainage activities during the Soviet period, wetlands in Estonia still host an outstanding biodiversity in the Baltic Sea Region. Currently, various types of wetlands constitute roughly one third of the total area of Estonia. Approximately one fifth of these are semi-natural wetlands (WWF-Denmark, 1994). The combined effects of transition and elimination of price supports have reduced environmental pressures along the extensive margin as about thirty per cent of the arable land was left uncultivated in 1996 (World Bank, 1997). Now, the process of transition has created an opportunity to preserve the remaining ecologically valuable wetlands before future development pressures again raise the opportunity costs of preservation.

In recent years the importance of Estonian wetlands has been highlighted and local initiatives have been launched with international support to maintain their ecological value (WWF-Denmark, 1994). This has become extremely important in the on-going process of land reform, as new landowners are understandably more interested in increasing the market value of their lands than maintaining the social benefits of wetlands.

Wetlands generate multifunctional environmental services that provide numerous private and social benefits at a variety of scales. From an ecosystem perspective, the total economic benefits of environmental services from wetlands can be divided into primary and secondary benefits (Gren *et al.*, 1994). The primary benefits of the wetlands reflect the ecosystem's self-organizing capacity, i.e., functions that maintain its ability to return to a steady state equilibrium after external shocks. Secondary benefits represent the wetlands life-support services such as flood protection, acting as a trap for nutrients, promoting groundwater recharge, and serving as habitat for wildlife. All of these diverse benefits are dependent on the existence of the wetland ecosystem (see also Folke, 1991).

We will classify secondary benefits produced by wetlands in Estonia by their geographical extent. We will thus differentiate among the flows of environmental services at the local (i.e. country level), regional (i.e. the Baltic Sea drainage basin), and global levels. Table 12.3 summarizes some of the secondary benefits produced by coastal wetlands in Estonia by their geographical extent.

Eliminating policy distortions at the sector level yield economic gains and environmental benefits. However, the residual imperfections of the policy may sometimes give rise to environmental harm if serious market failures exist. The latter is especially the case when agricultural activities produce positive externalities as a by-product of farm operations. Open space, wildlife habitat, or countryside amenities are all well-known benefits produced by traditional agricultural practices. In Estonia, for example, some valuable semi-natural

Table 12.3   Benefits of Estonian wetlands by their geographical extent

Local benefits	Baltic Sea regional benefits	Global benefits
		1. Biodiversity
	1. Nutrient trap of agricultural runoff to Baltic Sea	
1. Flood protection		
2. Groundwater recharge	2. Nursery for fish	
3. Nursery for fish	3. Biodiversity	
4. Nutrient trap of agricultural runoff to ground- and surface waters		
5. Extractive uses/peat mining		
6. Recreation		
7. Biodiversity		

ecosystems, such as coastal and wooded meadows and flood plains, have been formed through the centuries of interaction between hydrological conditions and traditional agricultural activities such as grazing, mowing, and reed harvesting. These semi-natural wetlands form internationally important resting and foraging areas along the East-Atlantic migratory corridor where migratory birds stop to feed and rest *en route* before continuing the flight to the breeding areas in the Arctic. They are also important in terms of cultural and natural heritage values as they form an important feature in the traditional Estonian coastal landscape.

Liberalization of agricultural markets during the recent years has curtailed agricultural activities on economically marginal lands.[2] As managed ecosystems, coastal meadows and flood plains require continuous human intervention in order to maintain their unique habitats. There is a threat that long-term underutilization of these environmentally sensitive lands may cause serious degradation of biodiversity. Without continuous grazing of coastal meadows and mowing of flood plains and wooded meadows, wetlands become overgrown with undesirable tree and shrub species that are less suitable for migrating birds. Gradual loss of coastal wetlands in Estonia may have only incremental consequences to the global diversity of migratory bird populations. Yet ultimately these gradual losses may pass threshold levels beyond which loss of the resource may become irreversible.

---

2   We assume here that economically marginal lands correspond with ecologically marginal lands, which seems to be the case in Estonia. However, as shown by Heimlich (1989), the two may not be always the same. For example, land idled to meet set-aside requirements may not be subject to high rates of soil erosion, although it is marginal in economic terms since profit maximizing farmers retire the least productive land first.

As semi-natural wetlands provide non-market public goods, private markets fail to allocate them at socially optimal levels. The policy objective is thus to induce agricultural producers to consider the social benefits their activities generate. In essence, efficient environmental policy should seek to provide a set of incentives that induce profit-maximizing producers to satisfy these conditions.

The first attempt in Estonia to induce private farmers to internalize the positive externalities of their activities occurred in the Matsalu State Nature Reserve (MSNR) in Estonia. The MSNR was created in 1957 to protect one of the largest and ecologically most valuable semi-natural wetland complexes in the Baltic Sea Region. Due to its strategic location along the East-Atlantic Flyway, the reserve was designated a wetland of international importance under the Ramsar Convention in 1976. More than 2 million birds migrate through the wetlands' open landscapes and waters of the reserve annually. In addition to rich bird life, the wetlands in the MSNR also have great botanical value. This is especially true of the wooded meadows which support some of the richest plant communities in Europe (HELCOM, 1995).

To maintain optimal levels of management activities, the MSNR's administration has entered into contracts with local landowners and agricultural producers to graze coastal meadows and mow flood plains and wooded meadows. The contracts are designed to provide the minimum compensation/subsidy per hectare necessary to maintain adequate levels of traditional agricultural activities. Since the funding from the state budget has been tight it is not clear whether similar schemes will also be applied to numerous other coastal wetlands in western Estonia which are not yet under protection.

As shown by Olson and Zeckhauser (1970), optimal levels of public goods will be produced at the least cost when more efficient technologies are used. As most of the remaining large-scale production units in Estonia are struggling both with management and technological inefficiencies, there seems to be a good potential to achieve simultaneous multi-goal environmental and regional development objectives by integrating traditional small-scale family farming more extensively with current and future environmental programmes.

12.6   Policy implications

The policy problem of maintaining the economic and ecological values of Estonia's wetlands is complex because agriculture plays both a positive and a negative role in their preservation. For some wetlands, such as coastal meadows and flood plains, limited agricultural activities in their traditional form are necessary to preserve their value for waterfowl habitat. For natural wetlands, such as mires and bogs, the demand for agricultural land directly competes with the very existence of the wetlands.

The process of transition in Estonia's agricultural sector should then also have both positive and negative effects on wetlands. In the positive case, as transition increases the profitability and reduces the riskiness of agriculture, agricultural activity would be expected to recover in places like the semi-natural wetlands. This is particularly true for the activities that are ecologically important such as grazing and the derived demand for cattle fodder. As the economy of Estonia improves and the trade barriers in east and west are reduced, the demand for livestock and livestock products should rise. It will be necessary to limit the intensity of agricultural activities in such areas, but the process of transition is at least consistent with preserving the ecological values of the wetlands.

Policy problems may be more severe in areas where the agricultural development that will result from transition is inconsistent with maintaining the value of wetlands. As the transition progresses, increased demand for farmland will increase conversion pressures on wetlands and increase political pressures on the Estonian government to maintain and perhaps improve the drainage systems.

Wetlands in Estonia provide benefits to the citizens of Estonia as described above. Even so, the current state of the economy in Estonia does not bode well for wetland retention for two reasons. First, even if the government of Estonia wished to preserve more wetlands, they do not currently have the budget to do so. The government is currently having trouble maintaining its existing conservation system. Second, current low income and wealth levels in Estonia are likely to reduce people's preferences for the environmental benefits generated by wetlands relative to the marketable products that could be produced if the wetlands were converted to farm or forest land. As a result, Estonians' willingness to pay for wetlands retention is doubtless lower today than it will be in the future as the economy improves.

There is thus a potential problem of irreversibility in the absence of policies to protect wetlands. As shown by Fisher *et al.*, (1972) if: (1) the demand for the environmental services produced by an undeveloped ecosystem will rise in the future relative to the demand for marketable goods that would be produced from its development; and, (2) such development is irreversible; then, (3) it may be optimal for society to limit current development. For Estonia, limiting development would entail both passively allowing some of the existing drainage systems to decline, and active protection of other valuable existing wetlands.

The wetlands of Estonia also generate benefits that transcend the boundaries of the country, by filtering the water that enters the Baltic Sea and by providing support and habitat for migratory waterfowl. As such, these wetlands produce a transboundary positive externality. There is a large and growing literature on trade, trade policies, and transboundary negative externalities (see, for example, Baumol and Oates, 1988) that would apply in reverse to this case.

The most economically efficient policy would involve taxing conversion of wetlands at the loss in marginal value of environmental services and providing subsidies equal to the marginal value of environmental services provided to farms in areas which require continuous human intervention in order to maintain its ecological value. Although the former is politically infeasible, targeting the latter by the spatial scope of the problem may yield simultaneous benefits for environmental improvement and regional development. Other policies could involve purchase of development or conversion rights from the owners of the wetlands or land exchange policies for owners of wetlands.

Second best (trade) policies could be granting preferable trade status with concerned developed countries in exchange for a certain level of wetlands protection. The latter seems to be equitable at a global level as biodiversity will be preserved, but would have the perverse effect of increasing pressures to develop wetlands on land that was not placed under protection because of the effects of increased output prices on the extensive margin of production.

Whatever policy approach is taken, the longer the wait the greater the cost. Because of the effects of transition, the opportunity costs of preserving wetlands or of allowing drained land to revert to wetlands is currently low. As the transition progresses, as land markets and capital markets become more efficient, as world trade in agricultural products becomes less restricted, that opportunity cost will rise along with the price of farmland. Accumulating larger wetland resources under state or other protection now does not mean that they can not be reallocated to developed uses if warranted in the future. As demand for drained lands increases, some of the protected wetland areas could be sold at a price that reflects their true social value or with restrictive easements that limit their use. This might help ensure the sustainable use of these valuable environmental resources.

References

Antle, J.M. and R.E. Just (1991), 'Effects of commodity program structure on resource use and the environment', in R.E. Just and N. Bockstael, (eds), *Commodity and Resource Policies in Agricultural Systems*, Berlin: Springer Verlag.

Baumol, W. and W. Oates (1988), *The Theory of Environmental Policy*, Cambridge: Cambridge University Press

Csaki, C. (1995), 'Presidential address: where is agriculture heading in Central and Eastern Europe? Emerging markets and the new role for the Government', in G.H. Peters and D.D. Headley (eds), *Agricultural Competitiveness: Market Forces and Policy Choice*, proceedings of the 22nd International Conference of Agricultural Economists, Brookfield, Vermont: Dartmouth Publishers.

European Commission (1995), *Agricultural Situation and Prospects in the Central and Eastern European Countries. Estonia*, Directorate General for Agriculture, Working Document.

Fisher, A.C. , J. Krutilla and C.J. Cicchetti 1972. 'The economics of environmental preservation', *American Economic Review*, **62**, September, 605–19.

Folke, (C. 1991), 'The Societal Value of Wetland Life Support', in C. Folke and T. Kalberberg (eds), *Linking the Natural Environment and the Economy: Essays from the Eco-Eco Group*, Dordrecht: Kluwer Academic Publishers.

Folmer, C., M.A. Keyzer, M.D. Merbis, H.J.J. Stolwijk and P.J.J. Veenendaal (1995), *The Common Agricultural Policy beyond the MacSharry Reform*, Amsterdam: North-Holland, 347pp.

Gandhi, V.P. (ed.) (1996), *Macroeconomics and the Environment*, Washington, DC: International Monetary Fund.

Gren, I-M, C. Folke, K. Turner and I. Bateman (1994), 'Primary and secondary values of wetland ecosystems', *Environmental and Resource Economics*, **4**, 55–74.

Heimlich, R. (1989), 'Productivity of Highly Erodible Cropland', *Journal of Agricultural Economics Research*, **41**(3).

HELCOM (1995), *Protection of the Coastal Wetland Area Matsalu Catchment Area*, Estonian–Swedish joint project, Tallinn, Stockholm.

Olson, M. and R. Zeckhauser (1970), 'The Efficient Production of External Economies', *American Economic Review*, LX (June), pp. 512–17.

Organization for Economic Cooperation and Development (OECD) 1995, *The Uruguay Round. A Preliminary Evaluation of the Impacts of the Agreement on Agriculture in the OECD Countries*, Paris: OECD.

World Bank (1997), *Estonia. Agricultural and Forestry Policy Update*, Washington, DC: Natural Resource Management Division, Country Department IV, Europe and Central Asia Region.

World Bank (1996), *Latvia. Agricultural Policy Update*, Washington, DC: Natural Resource Management Division, Country Department IV, Europe and Central Asia Region.

WWF-Denmark (1994), *Project WETSTONIA. Conservation and Management of Estonian Wetlands*, Project Progress Report, Project No. 9E.0048.07.

13 European agriculture and the CAP: retrospect and prospect[1]

George P. Zanias

13.1 The CAP: past and present

Traditionally, the CAP has been based on a price policy. This is mainly due to historical reasons since the original six member states had similar policies and, in this way, a minimum disruption in the policy environment at that time was achieved. The adoption of alternative policy instruments would have different consequences for the consumers and the taxpayers. Thus, the application of, say, a deficiency payment system would involve a much larger burden for the small (at that time) EC budget. Transferring the large part of the cost of agricultural support to the consumers was considerably easier at that time because when the CAP was set up, the post-war food shortages and high food prices were still alive in the minds of the consumers. Furthermore, the administrative apparatus for the implementation of support measures involving direct payments to producers was lacking in many places while the farm population was much larger, and therefore the administrative cost of direct payments was considerably higher.

The achievement of high degrees of self-sufficiency, the appearance of considerable surpluses, and the slow structural change attained by the early 1970s led to the beginning of introducing socio-structural directives to supplement the price policy. The 1980s have been marked with attempts to modify the traditional price mechanism of the CAP. The fast increasing agricultural budget and, from the mid-1980s, the pressure from trade partners are the main forces behind these attempts. The common denominator in all these attempts was the control of production and hence of the budget burden of the CAP.

Co-responsibility levies (that is, producer taxes on milk and cereals), guarantee thresholds (on a range of products including cereals and certain fruits) and marketing quotas (sugar and milk) are the main instruments used during the 1980s to restrict surplus production. Some complementary measures like consumer subsidies and marketing campaigns were also used. The limited success of all these measures to control production and budget expenditure led to the adoption of the most radical reform of the CAP so far in 1992.

---

1 This chapter is based on research financed by the General Secretariat for Research and Technology and coordinated by the Research Centre of the Athens University of Economics and Business.

The 1992 reform package aimed at giving a greater play to the market forces and limiting the open-ended nature of support along with other lower key objectives, such as the partial satisfaction of environmental concerns and of the interests of the consumers. Greater play of the market forces meant lowering the support prices for a number of sectors. Because the resulting impact on farming income would be politically unacceptable some form of compensation was provided.

At the heart of the reform lie the cereals as well as the oilseeds and protein crops which are interdependent in the production decisions of the farmers. Thus, a significant price cut of 29 per cent from its 1991/92 buying-in price of cereals was adopted and phased in over a period of three years starting from 1993/94. Farmers were compensated for these price cuts by a per hectare compensation which was calculated as the product of the price cut and the historical per hectare yield in each region.

This change in the support system moved part of the burden of supporting farmers from the consumers to the taxpayers and the support became open ended only at the considerably lower cereal price which moved close to the world prices. The compensatory amounts are based on historical performance and therefore remain fixed nominally for the duration of the current reform package. As a result of this nominal fixity, the compensation will become lower in real terms over time. Probably the most important consequence of this change is that the direct link that existed between price support and output is now significantly limited.

The partial shift of the support burden from the consumers to the taxpayers would add significant pressure to the budget while production of cereals would tend to be 'frozen' at its relatively high levels at the beginning of the 1990s, with obvious consequences for the budget through the provision of high export refunds. To avoid such undesirable consequences, production was decided to be controlled via a set-aside scheme. At the beginning, this scheme was rotational and required that the large producers (producing more than 92 tonnes of cereals) leave idle (or use it for non-food purposes or for the production of peas for human consumption) 15 per cent of their base area. Small producers would receive the compensation without setting aside land.

The introduction of the set-aside scheme aimed at reducing the volume of production by a smaller percentage because of the slippage effect which may be due to a number of factors such as: ineffective monitoring of the scheme, using more variable inputs on the land used, increasing land productivity when remaining idle once every six years. Later, the option of a permanent set-aside (18 per cent of base area) was also provided while the set-aside percentages have varied considerably since then. Thus, the 15 per cent was reduced to 12 per cent for the second year of application and to 10 per cent for the third year. These changes followed relatively favourable changes in world market conditions while they probably signified the willingness, at that time, of the Commission to use the set-aside percentage as a production controlling mechanism.

The reforms introduced in some other sectors are less radical, but the respective markets are also going to be affected by the reform of the cereals sector. Thus, for the oilseeds and pulses the per hectare payments and set-aside scheme will be applied as for cereals. The livestock and dairy sectors are going to benefit from the reduction in the price of cereals which can justify price cuts for these sectors to maintain profit margins. Thus, the intervention price for beef was cut by 15 per cent from 1993/94, while intervention purchases were limited to 350 000 tonnes. Furthermore, for beef, an extra extensification premium was provided for low stocking densities but the beef and suckler cow premiums were restricted by their number in 1991 and by a producer quota respectively. Quotas are also set for the payments of the ewe premiums in the case of sheep production. Finally, the quota regime already applied to the milk sector is maintained with the quota reduced by 2 per cent. In addition to this, a 5 per cent cut in the intervention price for butter was also implemented.

The reform of the CAP was also aiming to provide more environmentally friendly policy measures which would ease the environmental pressure exerted by the high support prices of the traditional CAP through the intensification of production. Thus, both price decreases and linking the compensatory amounts to historical yields discouraged production-intensive practices. The introduction of the rotational set-aside scheme also has favourable environmental consequences as it avoids setting aside the least fertile land. The accompanying measures of the 1992 reform package were designed to provide a more direct positive impact on the environment. These measures have generally been well received by the farmers but the practice of continuing to provide high support prices discouraged many farmers from committing themselves to more extensive practices or from dedicating land to environmental purposes.

13.2 The CAP in the medium term

During 1996, the implementation of the 1992 reform of the CAP was completed and in addition was extended to other products not included in the initial package. However, the recent reform package is not destined to 'live' for as long as the traditional CAP. Proposals for a new reform already exist. However, before dealing with the new proposals and the long-term prospects of the CAP we first turn to predicting its operation in the medium term.

In the medium term, the future of the CAP depends mainly on:

1. The results of the recent reform;
2. The implementation of the GATT Agreement on Agriculture.

When the 1992 reform of the CAP was adopted, it was considered by many as the minimum that could be done to deal with the pressures for reform and with the problems of EU agriculture. Thus, it came as a surprise to many that:

1. the large stocks were drastically reduced for all products;
2. expenditure under FEOGA (the European Agricultural Guidance and Guarantee Fund) was kept under control despite fears for the opposite;
3. agricultural incomes increased in all member states and especially the incomes associated with the reformed sectors.

The successful evolution of the above indicators is partly due to domestic and partly to external factors. Internally, the reformed CAP increased the domestic demand for cereals as a result of the lower institutional, and hence producer, prices. In addition, the set-aside scheme contributed to a reduction in production which, combined with the increases in demand, led to a reduction in existing stocks. Finally, the compensation of cereal producers by means of direct subsidies strengthened incomes from farming.

On the external front, a number of favourable developments, relating mainly to the key cereal sector, were realized. The most important development was the large increase in the world wheat prices which virtually made redundant the EU export subsidies. These price increases in the international markets have been the result of a number of developments: the lower stocks in the USA, the continuous reduction in the production of the former Soviet Union, the bad harvest of 1994 in Australia and the strong increase in demand in South-East Asia (mainly by China). As a result of these developments, international stocks reached their lowest level since 1973.

Assisted by international developments, it seems that the reformed CAP is coping well with the obligations that arise from the implementation of the GATT Agreement on Agriculture. In fact, even when the agreement was concluded it was clear that the reformed CAP would have problems only to meet the volume constraint of the export subsidy provision. The development of international prices reduced the need for export subsidization and the volume constraint will probably be met during the implementation period.

Therefore, the last reform package seems to be capable of dealing with the forthcoming developments till the end of the present millennium. Any problems arising can be dealt with by the policy measures currently available.

13.3   The long term CAP determinants
As the end of the century approaches, it will become increasingly difficult for the reformed CAP to cope with the increases in productivity which will lead to higher production levels that need be exported, as domestic demand is rising very slowly. The relatively favourable prospects for the international markets

predicted for the near future do not seem sufficient to avoid the building up of new surpluses and the constraints set by the GATT will become binding. At this point it will be realized that whereas the reformed CAP was a domestic affair, in the sense that it could be changed if domestic priorities dictated such a change, the ceiling introduced by the GATT on the use of the production and trade distorting forms of agricultural support is of a permanent nature, and EU policy makers lose permanently a certain degree of control over designing domestic agricultural policies. Thus, it will be difficult to reverse certain changes which have already been introduced unilaterally by the EU.

Under the GATT-specified ceiling of agricultural support, the EU policy makers can pursue domestic objectives by using policy measures which are trade distorting. Any additional support beyond the GATT-specified AMS (Aggregate Measure of Support) has to be given with policy measures which are GATT-friendly. In this sense, the GATT constitutes a blueprint for the future CAP.

The agricultural policy measures which are not trade distorting and therefore not included in the calculation of the AMS are specified in the Agreement on Agriculture. Direct income aids, government service programmes and aids given under the structural measures (Guidance section of FEOGA) figure among the 'Green Box' policies. Thus, the move, under the CAP reform, away from price policies towards direct income aids and the strengthening of the structural measures, acquires a permanent nature with the GATT.

Furthermore, the common element in these policies is that they involve transfers from the taxpayers (budget) rather than from the consumers which accounted for the greater part of the transfers to producers under the traditional CAP. This feature is bound to invoke the budget constraint which already exists in the EU. If further support of the agricultural sector is required in the future or if further switches from price to direct income òr structural support take place, these have to be financed by the EU budget. It should, however, be reminded that a limit on agricultural expenditure exists in the EU since 1984, when it was decided that the growth in agricultural expenditure cannot exceed 74 per cent of the growth in EU GDP. If this constraint cannot be overcome, then other forms of supporting the farming community have to be sought including the possibility of a partial re-nationalization of the CAP.

Although the quantitative and qualitative constraints imposed by the GATT constitute an important determining factor of the CAP, it is the prospective eastward enlargement which invokes a deep discussion on the future of the CAP.

A number of factors make this enlargement (to include the Central and Eastern European Countries (CEECs)) very important for the CAP and EU agriculture. This enlargement involves an increase in the EU population by about 100 million but its GDP by a single digit percentage. Agricultural land will increase by about 50 per cent but the farm population will more than double. It is this last factor which, coupled with the low level of support of agriculture in the CEECs, constitutes the greatest concern for the CAP. It should probably be mentioned here that the entry of the CEECs to the EU also arouses considerable concern for the Structural Funds of the EU (currently absorbing 32 per cent of the budget) since these countries are poor and in need of structural adjustment.

The magnitude of the problems that will be created make it almost certain that the current CAP cannot be in place when the CEECs enter the EU. Two major problems will arise: a budgetary problem and a possible conflict with the commitments under the GATT.

The CEECs produce agricultural products which are very similar to the current EU and they have a very great potential to increase production once the transition period to the market economy is over and the proper incentives are given by the adoption of the CAP. A number of estimates exist[2] for the budgetary cost of applying the current CAP to the CEECs. One of the latest is that by Tangermann and Josling (1994). According to their estimates, the extra cost from the price alignment for the Visegrad countries only amounts to 9 billion ECUs in 1993 prices. If the compensatory amounts are also given to the Visegrad farmers (as is the case with the last European Free Trade Association (EFTA) enlargement), this will cost another 4.3 billion ECUs. Adding the cost of price alignment and compensatory amounts for the case of Bulgaria and Romania also will on aggregate cost the EU approximately an extra 20 million ECUs. The European Commission, in its *Agricultural Strategy Paper* (1995), converges to an estimate of 11 billion ECUs. Comparing these figures to the current cost of the CAP of about 36 million ECUs and taking into account the fact that the budgetary contributions of the CEECs will be relatively small, then an insurmountable problem arises.

Such a high budgetary cost will most probably be politically unacceptable while it will certainly violate the agricultural expenditure guideline. Even if this internal EU affair were to be somehow solved, a conflict with the GATT would almost certainly arise. Assuming that, when the CEECs enter the EU, their GATT commitments (based on their low previous levels of support) will merge with those of the EU, the CAP-21 will violate the commitments on the internal support and the subsidized exports. The only way out of this conflict is the re-negotiation of certain terms of the Agreement on Agriculture but it is far from certain that the GATT partners will accept a higher degree of protection for EU-21 agriculture, at least without some other compensation, especially since the GATT calls for further liberalization of the world agricultural trade which will start being negotiated before the end of the century.

The magnitude of the budgetary and GATT problems will depend on: the size of the difference between the EU and world agricultural prices, the changes in the CEEC agricultural output and the changes in CEEC demand for agricultural

2   See Blackwell *et al.* (1994) for a collection of the existing estimates.

products. As these countries exit from the current transitional period and as growth accelerates, the demand for certain agricultural products will increase. However, given the existing unexploited potential, the growth in the volume of output is expected to be faster, leading to the creation of surpluses which will be added to the existing EU-15 surpluses. None of these factors would, of course, matter if the EU agricultural prices were close to the world prices. In this way the budgetary burden would be very small or non-existing while GATT commitments could easily be met.

Lowering the prices further to a level close to the world prices will solve most of the budgetary and GATT problems but it will create others. Thus, it would be politically unacceptable for EU-15 to lower the farm prices further without further compensation in the spirit of the 1992 reforms. Even without extending these compensations to the CEEC farmers a budgetary problem will arise in EU-15. Extending these compensatory amounts to the CEEC farmers would be prohibitive. A possible way out of this problem is the relaxation of the financial solidarity principle of the CAP to allow for incomes policies for the agricultural sector to be pursued at national level as well. Such a development is in line with the subsidiarity principle and it reduces the magnitude of EU financed support and therefore the cost of absorbing the CEECs. This, however, constitutes a rather radical solution which leads to a partial re-nationalization of the CAP and hence the abolition of the CAP. Furthermore, such national aids could only be given as long as they do not distort competition across borders in the EU.

It must have become clear by now that the long-term prospects of the CAP are very uncertain and that there is no easy solution to the policy problem. The engagement of agriculture into another round of trade liberalization negotiations under the WTO, scheduled to begin in 1999, adds another dimension to the problem. At the same time, the interaction between agriculture and the environment becomes an increasingly important determinant of the different policy options as the concept of public spending for the protection of natural resources and the enhancement of the countryside becomes increasingly accepted. On the demand side, the consumer requirements from agriculture are also changing and moving away from the quantitative ones towards the health and food safety requirements.

13.4   The new Commission proposals and the future shape of the CAP

As early as the end of 1995 the European Commission participated in the debate about the future shape of the CAP with the publication of the *Agricultural Strategy Paper* which outlined three possible solutions to the policy problem. First, was the preservation of the status quo. Such an option as a long term solution suffers from the problems outlined above. Ironically, the advocates of this solution are effectively supporting, in the longer term, the radical reform of the

CAP which will be required to face the intense problems that the long continuation of the present CAP will accumulate.

The radical reform of the CAP constituted the second alternative scenario. This scenario is supported by academics but also by some northern member states, and effectively leads to a re-nationalization of the CAP. It is based on the elimination of price support and quantity restrictions (quotas) and the compensation of the farmers with direct subsidies which will be gradually reduced while at the same time national subsidies will increase. This scenario has basically two weaknesses: the large increase of the cost of the CAP in the interim period of adjustment and the high social and environmental cost especially for the less favoured areas.

The third scenario concentrated on developing the 1992 approach. This scenario lies in between the other two and it stresses the need for an integrated approach to developing the rural areas. This option also constitutes the European Commission's choice, who presented in July 1997, as part of the *Agenda 2000* (1997), its proposals for a new reform of the CAP based on the ideas included in this option.

New policy objectives figure as part of the new CAP proposals. These objectives concentrate on the improvement of agricultural competitiveness, the enhancement of economic diversification in rural areas, the integration of environmental goals and the promotion of economic cohesion within the Union. The last three of these objectives do not belong to the ones included in the Treaty of Rome and show the changing priorities for a future agricultural policy.

The Commission proposes the satisfaction of the above objectives through deepening the 1992 reform. Thus, new proposals are made for the crop sector (cereals, oilseeds and protein crops), the beef sector and the dairy regime. In addition, the Commission also suggests a rural and an agri-environmental policy.

Lowering support prices and compensating the farmers for their income losses via direct payments is proposed for the crop sector. Two notable differences exist compared to the 1992 reform. First, the compensation accounting for the price reductions can be varied if the market prices are sustained at levels higher than the ones currently foreseen. In this way, the Commission wishes to avoid the over-compensation that existed in some cases under the 1992 reform when international prices rose significantly. The second difference has to do with the abolition of the compulsory set aside and therefore the differentiation existing under the 1992 reform between small and large producers. In this way, the Commission wishes to take full advantage of the forecasted favourable developments in international markets as using the set-aside as a supply control mechanism would necessitate raising the set-aside percentage to very high levels.

For the beef sector the Commission also proposes a reduction in support prices and an increase in direct payments. No change in the quota system or its level is suggested for the dairy regime. However, a price reduction is envisaged here also and the introduction of a new direct payment. In this case a warning also exists that the quota level may be cut in the future if a need arises. With regard to the Mediterranean products the Commission will prepare new proposals.

As becomes clear, the Commission proposes a further shift of support from prices to direct payments. This, on its own, is bound to have favourable environmental implications as the 1992 reform had. However, strengthening of the environmental content of the CAP is also proposed via targeted agri-environmental measures which should be reinforced and encouraged through increased budgetary resources. A strengthening is also suggested for the existing accompanying measures which were introduced by the 1992 reform.

It is obvious that the new Commission proposals move the financial burden of the CAP further from the consumers to the taxpayers. This move requires further resources from the budget which, however, are expected to be provided through the increases in the Union's GDP while keeping the percentage of their own resources constant. It also becomes obvious that these proposals facilitate greatly the application of the CAP to the prospective new members from the CEECs since, as explained earlier, the lower prices reduce the financial requirements of the price policy. This could avoid GATT problems arising with the entry of these countries to the Union and it provides room for further commitments to reduce price support under the WTO negotiations. It should, however, be noted that there is no provision for extending the old and new compensatory payments to the new entrants. The Commission believes that, in this way, the risk is avoided of creating income disparities and social distortions in the rural areas of these countries. However, in this way, the risk of a budgetary breakdown is also avoided.

As a conclusion, it must be stressed that the CAP of the future will differ radically from that of the past. Its acceptance among the consumers, environmentalists and trade partners is guaranteed. Present EU farmers, especially the larger ones, will face a reduction in the CAP component of their income while the farmers of the new entrants will never realize subsidy levels like the ones realized by the farmers in the current member states.

References

Backwell, A., J. Haynes, S. Davidova, V. Courboin and A. Kwiecinski (1994), 'Feasibility of an agricultural strategy to prepare the countries of Central and Eastern Europe for EU accession', Report to the Commission of the European Communities.

Commission of the European Communities (1995), *Agricultural Strategy Paper*, CSE(95) 607.

Commission of the European Communities (1997), *Agenda 2000*, Communication of the Commission, DOC 97/6, Strasbourg, July.

Tangermann, S. and T. Josling (1994), 'Pre-accession agricultural policies for Central Europe and the European Union', Report to the Commission of the European Communities.

Index

50/50 crop/fallow system, 39

Abler, D.G., 14, 52, 66, 67
Adelaja, A., 209
aggregate analysis of
  economic–environment tradeoffs,
    44–50
  AEIs to measure effects of policy
    change, 46–7
  implications for aggregate
    environmental impact
    assessments, 49–50
  water quality, 47–9
Aggregate Measure of Support (AMS),
  137, 244
aggregate pollution: elasticity of, 16–18
Agreement on Agriculture, 89, 135, 137
  and CAP, 243, 244, 245
  impact on Italy see Italy
agricultural chemicals see chemicals
agricultural policy, 14
  and environmental quality in Spain,
    187–205
  interactions with environmental
    policy, 105–8, 203–5
agricultural trade model, 3, 13–24
  comparative statics analysis, 18–21
  elasticities of chemical input use, 22–4
  elasticity of aggregate pollution,
    16–18
  theoretical model, 14–16
agriculture: free trade, environment and,
  1–9
agriculture-environment tradeoffs, 3,
  25–51
  aggregate analysis, 44–50
  conceptual framework, 26–33
    deriving tradeoffs, 28–31
    dynamic considerations, 31
    integrated simulation models, 31–3
    static spatial model, 26–8
  dryland agriculture in the US, 38–44

integrated economic–environment–
    health simulation model 33–8
agri-environmental indicators (AEIs),
  45–9
  measuring effects of policy change,
    46–7
  water quality, 47–9
agri-environmental measures, 76, 77,
  158
  effects, 83–6, 87–8
  future of the CAP, 247–8
  impact in Italy, 178–80
agrochemicals see chemicals
agronomic model (AM), 190–96
AIMA (Italian Intervention Board)
  payments, 171–2
Allen elasticities of substitution, 213,
  214
*American Journal of Agricultural
  Economics*, 1
Andean potato-pasture production
  system, 33–8
Andean weevil, 33
Anderson, K., 1, 13, 44, 58, 61, 145
Ansell, D.J., 80
Antle, J.M., 2, 13, 91, 110, 187, 209, 224
  agriculture–environment tradeoffs, 14,
    26, 27, 31, 44
    integrated simulation models, 33,
      34, 38, 41
  environmental Kuznets curve, 64
  pollution tax, 107
arable farming, 243
  future of CAP, 247
  1992 CAP reform, 76, 77–80, 86–7,
    241–2
area payments, 76, 77–80, 87, 89–90,
  225
arm's length pricing, 117–18, 126–7
Armstrong, H.M., 161
Austria, 5, 135–49
  landscape amenities, 146–8

pollution, 145–6
regional transfers and environmental
    effects, 145–8
social costs and benefits of
    agricultural production, 143–8
transfers to producers, 144–5
Austrian Programme for Environment
    and Agriculture (APEA), 147–8
Azzam, A., 129

Baaske, W., 144
Baldock, D., 154, 186
Ball, V., 209
banana sector, 126–7
Barkema, A., 208
barley, 38–9
Batten, L., 160
Baumol, W.J., 63, 237
Bayfield, N.G., 161
Beaufoy, G., 74, 186
beef
    future of CAP, 247–8
    1992 CAP reform, 76, 77, 80–83, 87,
        242
Ben-David, D., 65
beneficiaries pay principle (BPP), 156–8
Berkum, S. van, 74, 186, 187
Bhagwati, J.N., 135, 136
bilateral oligopoly, 118
Binswanger, H., 192, 214
Birdlife International, 85
Birds Directive, 158, 160
Birnie, R.V., 160
Blackhurst, R., 1, 13
Blochliger, H.-J., 157
Boggess, W., 204
Bonnieux, F., 14
Bottomley, P., 209
Bouma, J., 25
Bromley, D., 155, 167
Brouwer, F.M., 74, 186, 187
Brown, G., 156
Buckwell, A., 186, 188
budgetary problem, 245–6
Bureau, J.-C., 138
Burns, J., 116, 117, 120

Cahill, C., 138
Cahill, S., 101
Capalbo, S.M., 26, 33, 34, 209

capital, 214
capital markets: incomplete, 229
carbofuran leaching, 36–8, 47–9
Carpio, F., 35
Caswell, M., 204
Caves, D., 209
Central and Eastern European Countries
    (CEECs), 230
    enlargement of EU, 244–6, 248
    see also transition, economic
cereals, 243
    1992 CAP reform, 76, 77–80, 87,
        241–2
Chambers, R., 211, 212
cheese, 124–6
chemicals, 78, 105
    elasticities of chemical use, 22–4
    pre-reform CAP and excessive use, 90
    productivity of agrochemicals in
        Greece, 6–7, 208–20
    see also fertilizers; pesticides
Christen, P., 138
Christensen, L., 209, 211
Coe, D.T., 65
Cole, D.C., 35
Colombo, G., 171
commercial structures: unsuitable, 175–7
Common Agricultural Policy (CAP), 6,
    7, 89–90, 240–48
    and the environment, 185–6
    future shape of, 246–8
    integration of policies, 85–6
    long-term determinants, 243–6
    in the medium term, 242–3
    1992 reform, 4, 73–88, 110, 157–8,
        225, 226, 240–42
        agri-environmental measures, 76,
            77, 83–6
        beef regime, 76, 77, 80–83, 87, 242
        cereal regime, 76, 77–80, 87, 241–2
        and extensification issue, 103–5
        impact on intensity of land use and
            land allocation decision, 97,
            98–103
        main features of the reform, 75–7
        and Uruguay Round Agreement,
            170–71
    objectives, 74–5
    and overgrazing on Shetland, 167–8
    past and present, 240–42
    and Spanish agriculture, 6, 185–207

common grazing land, 160
comparative statistics
  agricultural trade model with
    pollution, 18–21
  changes in CAP key policy
    instruments, 98–103, 107
compensation payments
  future of CAP, 247–8
  1992 CAP reform, 89–90, 110, 241–2
    arable sector, 76, 77–80, 86
    beef sector, 76, 80–83
    effects on crop producer behaviour,
      100–101
  Shetland moorlands, 162–8
competition: Italy and, 171, 173–7, 181
complementarity among inputs, 93–4
concentration, 115–17
Connor, J.M., 113
conservation plans, 165–6
Conservation Reserve Programme, 226
consumption, 57, 58, 62–3
continuous cropping, 39
Conway, G.R., 208
Copeland, B.R., 67
Corden, W.M., 138
corner solution, 100, 101–102
cost diminution rate, 213, 214, 215
Council Regulation 2078/92, 74, 75,
  83–6
countryside stewardship goods, 144
Cox, G., 154
Crampes, C., 128
credit, 233
Crissman, C.C., 26, 33, 34, 35
crop producer behaviour model, 4,
  89–111
  comparative static results, 97, 98–103
    extensive margin, 98–102
    intensive margin, 98
    input use, output supply and yields,
      102–3
  environmental and agricultural policy
    interactions, 105–8
  implications for policy design, 103–5
  notations and assumptions, 91–4
  optima and land allocation patterns,
    94–7
  optimal taxation policy and land
    quality heterogeneity, 108–9
crop rotation constraints, 192

Cropper, M.L., 28
cropping patterns, 199–201
Csaki, C., 228, 229
Cummings, R.G., 204

Daberkow, S., 14
dairy cows, 82, 83
dairy sector, 83, 242, 247–8
Daly, H.E., 136
data limitations: and policy analysis,
  50–51
De Janvry, A., 192
dead weight loss (DWL), 140–43
decomposition of effects of trade on the
  environment, 3–4, 52–69
  alternative framework, 55–67
    externality effects, 61–3
    policy effects, 63–5
    scale and mix effects, 56–61
    technology effects, 65–7
  critique of existing frameworks, 53–5
  international issues, 67
Del Monte, 181
Denmark, 78, 80
Denny, M., 209
Dickerson, A.P., 120
Diewert, W., 212
differentiated compensation payment
  scheme, 167
diffusion of technologies, 65
direct payments
  future of CAP, 247–8
  1992 CAP reform, 86, 241–2
    arable sector, 76, 77–80, 87
    livestock sector, 76, 80–83, 87
disaggregate analyses, 26, 49, 50
double-marginalization, 128–9
downstream sectors *see* vertically-related
  markets
Drabenstott, M., 128
Drake, L., 144
Dry, F.T., 159
dryland agriculture, 38–44
Dumanski, J., 137
Durno, S., 160
dynamics, 31

early retirement, 76
Ecological Economics, 1
ecological modelling, 34–5, 40, 161–2

economic–environment–health
  simulation models, 31–3
  Andean potato-pasture production
    system, 33–8

economic–environmental tradeoffs
  aggregate analysis, 44–50
  dryland agriculture in the US, 38–44
economic modelling, 33–4, 41, 162–6
Ecuador, 33–8
Edgell, J., 186
effective rate of protection (ERP), 137–8
elasticities of chemical input use, 22–4
elasticity of aggregate pollution, 16–18
employment, 181
environment: free trade, agriculture and,
  1–9
environment-agriculture tradeoffs *see*
  agriculture-environment tradeoffs
environmental capital stock, 58–61, 66
environmental impact assessments,
  49–50
environmental Kuznets curve, 64
environmental policy
  decomposition, 52–3, 56–7, 63–4, 67
  interactions with agricultural policy,
    105–8, 203–5
  Italy, 178–80
Environmentally Sensitive Areas
  scheme, 157, 165–6
Erdtman, G., 160
Erosion Productivity Impact Calculator
  (EPIC) model, 40, 41–4, 190–96
Ervin, D.E., 129
Estonia, 7, 231–8
  current policy framework, 231–3
  macroeconomic liberalization and the
    environment, 233–6
  policy implications, 236–8
Esty, D.C., 136
Eswaran, M., 192
European Commission, 246–8
European Union (EU), 2, 225, 226
  budget constraint, 244
  budgetary problem, 245
  CAP *see* Common Agricultural Policy
  and CEECs, 230, 244–6, 248
  food sector, 114–22
  Italy and loss of EU protection, 173–5
exports, 173–5

extensification issues, 103–5
extensive margin
  agricultural policy and the
    environment, 224–7
  transitional economies, 227–31
  decisions and agriculture-environment
    tradeoffs, 26, 29, 33–4
  impacts of CAP key policy instrument
    changes, 97, 98–102
extensive technology, 94–7, 100, 101–2
externalities, 129
  decomposition framework, 61–3
  measures of protection and, 5, 135–53
    protection coefficients, 137–43
  positive and negative, 139–43, 155–6

Faasen, R., 73
Fabricant, S., 209
factor prices, 66
family farms, 232–3
farm enterprises, 232–3
farm income *see* income
farm restructuring, 232–3
farm size, 175, 176, 178, 228
farm-specific payments, 162–6
Feder, G., 202
fertilizers, 93–4
  agriculture-environment tradeoffs,
    41–4
  Greece, 208
    productivity, 214–18
  see also chemicals; intensive
    technology
Fisher, A.C., 237
flexibility payment programme, 225
flexible cropping, 39, 41–4
Flichman, G., 187, 188, 190, 191
Folke, G., 13, 234
Folmer, C., 225
food retailing sector, 117, 118–20
  Italy, 175–7, 178
food sector, 4–5, 114–29
  and economic activity, 114–15
  foreign-direct investment, 121–2
  impact of Uruguay Round on Italy's
    agro-food sector, 6, 170–84
  linkages between successive stages,
    117–20
  merger activity, 120–21

policy analysis and vertically-related markets, 122–9
structure of food-processing sector, 115–17
foreign-direct investment, 121–2
forestry, 76, 179
four-firm concentration ratios, 115–17
France, 80
Freeman, A.M., 28
Freund, R., 191
Fuss, M., 209

Gabel, H., 67
Gandhi, V.P., 233
Gardner, B.L., 112, 136
General Agreement on Tariffs and Trade (GATT), 1, 13, 230
   problem and enlargement of EU, 245–6, 248
   Uruguay Round *see* Agreement on Agriculture; Uruguay Round
general equilibrium approach, 112
Gerhold, S., 144
Germany, 80
Gibson, H.D., 120
Gilbert, R., 213
Gimingham, C.H., 158
Giulietti, M., 122
Goldin, I., 58, 61
Grant, S.A., 161
Greece: agrochemical productivity, 6–7, 208–20
'Green Box' policies, 244
green cover, 78
Gren, I.-M., 234
Grossman, G.M., 53, 64, 65
groundwater quality
   AEIs, 47–9
   pollution in Austria, 145–6, 150
   pollution in Ecuador, 36–8
Guyomard, H., 89, 90, 101, 138

Habitats Directive, 158
Hackl, F., 144, 148
Hanley, N., 154, 157
Harold, C., 13, 14
Harper, J.K., 93
Harvey, D., 89
Hawke, N., 79
Hayami, Y., 66

headage payments, 76, 77, 80–83, 164–5
health, 28
   economic-environmental–health simulation models, 31–8
   modelling, 35–6
heather moorland *see* moorland conservation
Heckman procedure, 34–5
Heidebrink, G., 64
Helfand, E., 204–5
Helpman, E., 65
Henson, S., 116, 117, 120
herbicides, 78
   see also chemicals; pesticides
Hertel, T.W., 112
Hill Grazing Model, 161
Hill Livestock Compensatory Allowance Scheme, 167–8
Hodge, I., 155, 167
Hoffmaister, A.W., 65
Hofreither, M.F., 135, 143, 144, 146, 150
Hollander, A., 128
House, B., 205
household plots, 232–3
Hrubovcak, J., 53
Hulme, P., 160
Hutson, J.L., 34

imports, 173–4
income
   feared loss of in Italy, 171–3
   per capita, 64
   Spain, 193–5, 202–3
      tradeoff with environmental quality, 197–202
income support policies, 225–6
industrial sectors, 114, 115
industrialization, 128–9
information provision, 85
initialization, 33
input prices, 98–100, 216–18, 229
input taxes, 107–9
inputs, 92–4
   Allen elasticities of substitution, 213, 214
   decisions and agriculture-environment tradeoffs, 26–31, 33–4
   policy changes and impact on, 102–3

integrated simulation models, 31–3
  economic–environment–health model
    for Andean potato-pasture
    production system, 33–8
integration of policies, 85–6, 110, 205
intensive margin
  agricultural policy and the
    environment, 224–7
  transitional economies, 227–31
  changes in key policy instruments of
    the CAP, 97, 98
  decisions and agriculture-environment
    tradeoffs, 26, 29, 34
  impact of environmental policies,
    107–8
intensive technology, 93, 94–7, 100
interior solution, 97, 98–101
International Agricultural Trade
    Research Consortium (IATRC), 1
international debate, 1, 13
intersectoral spillovers, 63
intra seasonal dynamics, 31
irrigation, 186–7, 188–205
  role of water for, 197–202
Italy, 6, 170–84
  countervailing arguments, 177–8
  environmental aspects of URA,
    178–80
  feared effects of Uruguay Round,
    170–71
    loss of competitiveness, 173–7
    loss of EU protection, 173–5
    loss of income, 171–3
    unsuitable productive and
      commercial structures, 175–7
  forebodings, 180–81

Johansen, J., 160
Johnstone, N., 13
Jorgenson, D., 209
Josling, T., 138, 245
Just, R.E., 2, 26, 44, 91, 110, 187, 224
  pollution tax, 107

Kalaitzandonakes, N.G., 138
Kmenta, J., 213
Knudsen, O., 58, 61
Kotwal, A., 192
Kousis, M., 208
Kovaleva, N., 79

Koyck distributed lag functions, 216–18
Krueger, A., 53
Kuch, P., 90

labour, 188, 214
  constraints, 192
lamb prices, 164–5
land, 66, 214
  crop producer behaviour model, 4,
    90–110
    land allocation patterns, 94–7
    optimal taxation and land quality
      heterogeneity issue, 108–9
  overgrazing, 159, 160–68
  reform, 227–9, 233
  use/management decisions and
    agriculture-environment
    tradeoffs, 26–31, 33–4, 39–44
landscape, 144
  amenities and regional transfers,
    146–8
late blight fungus, 33
Latvia, 228
LEACHA simulations model, 34–5
leaching of pesticide, 34–5, 36–8, 47–9
Legg, W., 138
Lekakis, J.N., 208
Leontief production functions, 21
Level I simulation models, 40–44
Lewis, F.J., 160
liberalization
  macroeconomic in Estonia, 233–6
  trade *see* trade liberalization
Lichtenberg, E., 91, 94
linear programming (LP) model, 162–5
linkages between successive stages,
    117–20
livestock sector, 247–8
  1992 CAP reform, 76, 77, 80–83, 87,
    242
  overgrazing in Shetland, 159, 160–68
location of production, 181
Loseby, M., 182
Low, P., 1, 13, 65
low impact farming, 179–80
Lowe, P., 154, 162
Lucas, R.E.B., 64
Lyson, T.A., 137

Macauley Land Use Research Institute
    (MLURI), 161

MacDonald, A., 158
macroeconomic liberalization, 233–6
MacSharry Reform, 2, 225
Madden, P., 14
Mahé, L.-P., 90, 138
Maier, L., 136–7, 141
management decisions, 26–31
    Andean potato-pasture production
        system, 33–4
    dryland agriculture in the US, 38–40
management rules on set-aside, 78–9, 80
Mapp, H., 204
market shares, 116, 117
markets
    incomplete capital markets, 229
    land 227–9
    uncertainty, 229–30
    vertically-related *see* vertically-related
        markets
Masters, W.A., 138
mathematical programming model
    (MPM), 190–96
Matsalu State Nature Reserve (MSNR),
    236
Matthew, E., 158
McCalla, A., 14
McCorriston, S., 122, 124–5, 126
mean minimum payment, 164–5
mechanical tillage, 39–40, 41–4
Mensbrugghe, D. van der, 58, 61
mergers, 120–21
Meynard, J.M., 93
Michalek, J., 163
Milgrom, P., 94
milk quota, 83, 242
minimum standards, 127–8
minimum tillage, 39–40, 41–4
Miranowski, J., 53
mix effects, 56–61
Monopolies and Mergers Commission,
    118, 119
Montana, 38–44
Moore, M., 204
moorland conservation, 5–6, 158–68
    ecological modelling, 161–2
    economic modelling, 162–6
    heather moorland in Shetland, 159–60
Moorland Extensification Scheme, 167
Moschini, G., 89
multi-factor productivity indexes, 209
multinational corporations, 180–81

National Countryside Monitoring
    Scheme (NCMS), 160
National Fund for the Protection of Rural
    Landscapes, 157
Nehrer, D., 137
Nercessiantz, V., 204
Nestlé, 181
net returns, 33–4, 41–4
neuro-behavioural tests, 35–6
new empirical industrial organization
    (NEIO) approach, 113
New Zealand, 145
Nguyen, T., 61
Nicholls, J., 182
nitrate loss, 41–4, 193–5, 196
nitrate pollution, 146, 150, 198–202
Nitrates Directive 1991, 73
no-till systems, 30, 39
nominal protection coefficient (NPC),
    137–8
non-rotational set-aside, 76, 79–80
North America Free Trade Agreement
    (NAFTA), 14, 53
North American Waterfowl Management
    Plan, 157
Northern Plains of the US, 38–44

Oates, W.E., 63, 237
O'Connor, H.E., 138
Olson, M., 236
organic farming, 179–80
Organization for Economic Cooperation
    and Development (OECD), 1, 61
    AEIs, 45–9
    Agreement on Agriculture, 170, 178,
        181–2
    decomposition framework, 3–4, 53–5,
        56, 63
    PPP, 154
    PSE, 138, 145
organizational capacity, 84–5
Osborne, P., 122
Oude Lansink, A., 90, 101
output
    externality effects, 61–3
    Greek agriculture, 216, 217
    impact of policy changes on output
        supply, 102–3
    scale and mix effects, 56–61
    supply control policies, 226–7, 241–2

output-environment tradeoffs, 29, 30, 34,
36–8
output prices, 65–6, 98–100
output taxes, 107–9
overgrazing, 159, 160–68
own-label products, 119–20

Palomo Molano, J., 86
Pardeller, K., 145, 150
Parker, S., 138
Parsisson, D., 154
partial equilibrium approach, 112
Peerlings, J., 90, 101
per capita income, 64
per-farm payments, 162–6
Pérez Ibarra, C., 186
Perroni, C., 61
Perry, M.K., 129
pesticide registration, 52
pesticides, 31, 47–9, 93–4
impacts in the Andean potato-pasture
production system, 33–8
overuse in Greece, 208
see also chemicals; intensive
technology
Pevetz, W., 144
Pezzey, J., 154
Philip Morris, 181
Pick, D., 14, 67
Piorr, H.-P., 137
policy
data needed to support policy analysis,
50–51
effects in decomposition framework,
63–5
integration of policies, 85–6, 110, 205
problem in Estonia, 236–8
problem in the EU, 243–8
using AEIs to measure effects of
policy change, 46–50
vertically-related markets and policy
analysis, 122–9
see also agricultural policy;
environmental policy
polluter pays principle (PPP), 154–5
pollution
aggregate in agricultural trade model,
3, 13–24
comparative statics, 18–21

elasticity of aggregate pollution,
16–18
crop producer behaviour model, 105–9
decomposition framework, 59–61
nonpoint nature of agricultural
pollution, 52–3
regional transfers in Austria and,
145–6, 150
Spain, 193–5, 196, 198–202
pollution emission tax, 107–9
pollution generation function, 105–7,
109
potato-pasture production system, 33–8
preferable trade status, 238
premium payments, 80–81
Pretty, J.N., 208
price support
CAP, 75, 89, 240
1992 reform, 79, 80–83, 89, 104–5,
241–2
policies, 224–5
prices
incidence and banana sector reforms,
126–7
input, 98–100, 216–18, 229
lamb, 164–5
output, 65–6, 98–100
reform and UK cheese sector, 124–6
wheat, 243
privatization of land, 227–8
producer subsidy equivalent (PSE),
137–45, 148–9
product effects, 54–5
production *see* output
production oriented agriculture, 203
production possibilities frontier (PPF),
59–62
production subsidies, 171–3
production technology *see* technology
productive structures: unsuitable, 175–7

productivity: agrochemicals, 6–7,
208–20
empirical model and estimation
results, 212–18
productivity analysis, 209–10
theoretical model, 210–12
profits, 108
protection
Italy and loss of EU protection, 173–5

measures of and externalities, 5,
    135–53
  Austrian agriculture, 143–8
  protection coefficients, 136–43
provider gets principle (PGP), 156–68
  moorland conservation, 158–68
Pruckner, G., 144, 148
public goods, 5–6, 154–69
  moorland conservation, 158–68
  principles for supply of external
      benefits from agriculture, 156–8
Putter, J. de, 84, 85
Puwein, W., 135

quality
  minimum standards, 127–8
  reference point for environmental
      quality, 155

Rader, T., 93
Ragner, A., 209
Rainelli, P., 14, 90
Ramsar Convention, 236
Rao, P.S.C., 28
ratcheting, 67
Ratcliffe, D.A., 158
Rauchenberger, F., 146
Rayment, M., 186
reduced-form process models, 28
reference point of environmental quality,
    155
Reflection Paper of 1991, 75
regional transfer indicators (RTIs),
    144–5, 146, 147–8
regional transfers, 136, 144–8
  and environmental effects, 145–8
regional zonal plans, 179, 180
Regulation (EEC) 2078/92, 74, 75, 83–6
regulatory effects, 54–5
Reichelderfer, K., 14, 90
Reinert, K.A., 145
re-nationalization of the CAP, 247
representative farms, 188–90
research and development (R&D), 65–6
resource base: changes in, 29–30
restitution of land, 228, 233
retailing, food *see* food retailing sector
retirement, early, 76
Reynolds, R., 145

risk
  constraints, 191–2
  tolerance, 196–202
Roberts, J., 94
Robertson, J.S., 159
Ronnen, U., 128
Ropke, I., 1
Rosegrant, M.W., 204
Rosenszweig, M., 192
rotational set-aside, 76, 79–80
Roumasset, J.A., 202
Runge, C.F., 1, 13, 14
Ruttan, V.W., 66

Salinger, M., 120
Sargeant, M., 182
Sansavini, S., 179
Saunders, C., 137
scale effects, 54–5, 56–61
Schwar, P., 135
Schwartz, N.E., 138
Sckokai, P., 89
Scotland, 5–6, 158–68
set-aside, 100, 102, 247
  1992 CAP reform, 76, 77, 241–2
    conditions and provisions, 78–80,
        87
    extensification issue, 104–5
  supply control, 226–7
Seymour, S., 154
Shaffer, G., 118–19
Shannon, C., 94
sheep, 242
  overgrazing in Shetland, 159, 160–68
Sheldon, I.M., 124–5
Shetland Islands, 159–68
Shortle, J.S., 14, 52, 66
Simpson, I., 167
Sinabell, F., 143
single-factor productivity measures,
    209–10
Sites of Special Scientific Interest, 158,
    167
Smets, H., 154
Smith, K.R., 129
social benefits, 63–4, 143–8
social costs, 63–4, 140–43
  Austrian agriculture, 143–8
soil loss, 41–4
soil science, 26

Spain, 6, 85, 185–207
  agricultural policy and environmental
      quality, 187–202
    methodological framework, 190–96
    representative farms, 188–90
    simulation results, 193–5, 196–202
    water for irrigation, 197–202
    zone of study, 187–90
  CAP and the environment, 186–7
  farmers' response to water saving
      policies, 203–5
Spash, C., 154, 167
Srinivasan, T.N., 135
standards: minimum, 127–8
static spatial model of
      agriculture–environment
      interactions, 26–8
  deriving tradeoffs, 28–31
Steenblick, R., 136–7, 141
Steininger, K., 13, 136
stocking rates, 76, 77, 81–3, 163–4
stocks: reduction in, 243
store lamb production, 160
structural effects, 54–5
Structural Funds, 245
Strutt, A., 58, 61, 145
Suarez, F., 85
subsidies
  production subsidies, 171–3
  taxes and, 237–8
subsidy equivalent (SE), 138–43
subsidy oriented agriculture, 203
Sumner, D.A., 89
Sumpsi, J.M., 85, 186, 187–8, 191
supermarkets, 175–6, 177
supply contracts, 126–7
supply control policies, 226–7, 241–2
sustainability, 136–7
Sutton, J., 53, 116
Switzerland, 157

Tangermann, S., 245
target price/deficiency payment
      programme, 225
Tauer, L., 191
taxation, 107–9
  optimal policy, 108–9
  taxes and subsidies for Estonia
      wetlands, 237–8
Taylor, M.S., 67

technology, 22
  agriculture–environment tradeoffs,
      29–30
  effects and decomposition, 54–5, 65–7
  extensive, 94–7, 100, 101–2
  intensity in Spanish agriculture,
      193–5, 198–9
  intensive, 93, 94–7, 100
Thirtle, C., 209
Thompson, D.B., 158
tillage methods, 39–40, 41–4
Tobey, J.A., 145, 154
Topkis, D.M., 94
total factor productivity (TFP), 210–12
Tracy, M., 74
trade: free and agriculture and the
      environment, 1–9
trade liberalization, 53, 64–5
  effect on global pollution, 3, 13–24
    elasticity of aggregate pollution
        with respect to trade
        restrictions, 16–18
    elasticities of chemical input use
        with respect to trade
        restrictions, 22–4
  impact on global economic activity,
      61
  and sustainable development, 136
transferability of land, 228
transition, economic, 7, 223–39
  agriculture and the environment,
      227–30
    incomplete capital markets, 229
    land market issues, 227–9
    market uncertainty, 229–30
  case study of Estonia, 231–6
  policy implications, 236–8
  trade and the environment, 230
Treaty of the European Union, 75
Tsakalotos, E., 120
Tsakok, I., 138
Tudor, G.J., 158

uncertainty: market, 229–30
uniform payment schemes, 162, 166–7
Unilever, 181

United Kingdom (UK), 114, 157, 158
  dominance of retailers in food sector,
      119

management of set-aside land, 78, 80
moorland conservation in Scotland,
    158–68
processed cheese sector, 124–6
United States (US)
    dryland agriculture in the Northern
        Plains, 38–44
    income support, 225
    supply control, 226
Uruguay Round, 9
    Agreement (URA), 53, 61
    Agreement on Agriculture *see*
        Agreement on Agriculture
utilization rates, 161–2

Valladares, M.A., 186
Varela-Ortega, C., 85, 186, 187–8, 190,
    191
    labour supervision, 192
    water saving policies, 204, 205
Vatn, A., 145–6
vertical contracts, 117–19, 126–7
vertical integration, 126–7, 128–9
vertical restraints, 118–19

vertically-related markets, 4–5, 112–31
    European food sector, 114–22
        and economic activity, 114–15
        food processing sector, 115–17
        food retailing sector, 117
        foreign-direct investment, 121–2
        linkages between successive stages,
            117–20
        merger activity, 120–21
    implications for policy analysis, 122–9
        alternative vertical contracts, 126–7
        further issues, 127–9
        model outline, 123–4
        price reform and UK cheese sector,
            124–6
Vincent, S.A., 80
Vogel, S., 135

voluntarism, 158
Vousden, N., 138

Wagenet, R.J., 28, 34
Wales, T., 214
Ward, S., 158
water
    groundwater quality *see* groundwater
        quality
    resources in Spain, 187–205
        availability constraints, 192–6
        farmers' response to water saving
            policies, 203–5
        role of water for irrigation, 197–202
    water pricing schemes, 204–5
Weinschenck, G., 14
Welch, D., 161
Welsh, R., 137
wetlands, 233–8
Wetlands Reserve Programme, 226
wheat, 38–9
    world prices, 243
Whitby, M., 186
Wigle, R., 61
Wilchens, D., 204
Wildlife and Countryside Act, 157, 160,
    167
Williamson, J., 79
willingness to pay (WTP), 147–8
Winters, A.L., 135
World Bank, 1
world prices, 104
World Trade Organization (WTO), 1, 2,
    246, 248
    see also General Agreement on Tariffs
        and Trade

yields, 102–3

Zeckhauser, R., 236
Zilberman, D., 93
zonal plans: regional, 179, 180